NOTHING HOLY ABOUT IT

Nothing Holy about It

THE ZEN OF BEING
JUST WHO YOU ARE

Tim Burkett

EDITED BY WANDA ISLE

SHAMBHALA · Boston & London · 2015

Shambhala Publications, Inc.
Horticultural Hall
300 Massachusetts Avenue
Boston, Massachusetts 02115
www.shambhala.com

9 8 7 6 5 4 3 2 1

First Edition
Printed in the United States of America

♾ This edition is printed on acid-free paper that meets the
American National Standards Institute z39.48 Standard.
♻ This book is printed on 30% postconsumer recycled paper.
For more information please visit www.shambhala.com.
Distributed in the United States by Penguin Random House LLC
and in Canada by Random House of Canada Ltd

Designed by K. E. White

LIBRARY OF CONGRESS CATALOGING-IN-PUBLICATION DATA
Burkett, Tim, author.
Nothing holy about it: the Zen of being just who you are / Tim Burkett;
edited by Wanda Isle.
pages   cm
ISBN 978-1-61180-194-1 (paperback: alk. paper)
1. Zen Buddhism. 2. Burkett, Tim. I. Title.
BQ9265.4.B87 2015
294.3'444—dc23
2014028100

Contents

Foreword by Norman Fischer

In 1970 the sixty-six-year-old Japanese Zen master Shunryu Suzuki, the first Japanese Zen teacher to establish a center in the West, saw the publication of a compilation of his talks given to American students. That book, *Zen Mind, Beginner's Mind*—the first and only book by Suzuki to appear in his lifetime—became the best-selling and best-loved Zen book ever written. Still in print, and still yearly outselling most other Zen books, *Zen Mind, Beginner's Mind* is quoted extensively by Zen and non-Zen people alike, the phrase "beginner's mind" itself having become a contemporary cultural term. The book's straightforward, honest, and deceptively simple words somehow speak eloquently to our current condition.

Now, almost forty-five years later, Tim Burkett, abbot of the Minnesota Zen Meditation Center, and one of Suzuki's earliest American disciples, is publishing his first book on Zen. Like *Zen Mind, Beginner's Mind, Nothing Holy about It* is also the fruit of a lifetime of practice with others. Like Suzuki Roshi, Tim isn't a writer. Both these Zen men spent their lives working with students, doing what they could to help make the practice clear—steadily, locally, quietly, day by day. Neither had interest in nor time for writing, traveling, or public speaking. But in both cases, devoted students, appreciating the beneficial power of their words and wanting to share those words more widely, spent years of painstaking work transcribing, honing, distilling, until finally they produced texts worthy of the sincere and heartfelt teachings of their teachers. So, many years ago Trudy Dixon, and today Wanda Isle, have birthed lovely and helpful texts—so that you can now hold in your hands a text that is more than another book on Zen—it is a life.

Another similarity between *Zen Mind, Beginner's Mind* and this book is that they both manage, somehow, to speak simultaneously to beginners and to experienced Zen students—a trick not easy to accomplish. When I first read *Zen Mind, Beginner's Mind,* the year it came out, I learned many useful things for my then brand-new practice, but at the same time, I could feel depths I was only dimly aware of. Rereading it over the years, I have been amazed by how many Buddhist teachings and philosophies Suzuki Roshi was referencing, in the simplest of ways, easily and gracefully—and with no sacrifice of depth. This is also true of *Nothing Holy about It.* The reader new to Zen will appreciate Tim's effortless ability to explain things about Zen practice that are usually left unexplained or poorly explained—especially psychological teachings that every contemporary student needs to know—and to do this with grandfatherly generosity and understanding (possibly because Tim, as he often mentions in the book, actually is a grandfather). The experienced Zen student will enjoy and learn from Tim's many teaching innovations that are sometimes entirely original and sometimes surprising reformulations of traditional teachings. I myself, in reading the text, was often startled by his useful descriptions of various stages of practice and listings of practice factors that I had never seen before—Tim's unique down-to-earth teachings.

You can tell a teacher by his or her students and by the environment for practice the teacher has fostered. A visit to the Minnesota Zen Meditation Center, on Lake Calhoun in Minneapolis, tells you a lot about who Tim Burkett is. The place is modest and simple (just an old, though very well kept-up, Midwestern house); the students earnest, hardworking, serious. An atmosphere of friendliness and care pervades.

Tim himself is like this, steady, dedicated, ordinary—and full of fun. He loves to tell stories (as you will soon see), and when he does he smiles broadly, his sparkling blue eyes all but disappearing into his head behind bushy eyebrows. And he laughs a lot. My visits to his house have featured long evenings of quiet storytelling, with laughter and a sweet feeling of friendship—evenings that could have gone on forever.

Not that Tim's life has been entirely easygoing. Having had a stormy youth, and two siblings with mental illness, Tim has spent a full career in the mental-health field, work he's done simultaneously with his Zen practice and as an expression of it. For some years he has been CEO of People Incorporated, one of the largest and most successful mental-health nonprofit organizations in Minnesota.

As you read *Nothing Holy about It*, you'll notice three distinct themes. First, Tim's heart and teachings. Second Tim's life, beginning with his Stanford days—a life whose shape, influenced by many years of Zen practice, is now clear. And third, a portrait of Tim's teacher, Shunryu Suzuki Roshi, who was, during the time Tim knew him, not the legendary Zen master he is today but an ordinary Japanese Zen priest, Rev. Suzuki. As a member myself of Suzuki Roshi's lineage, I have heard many stories about our old teacher, but I have never heard these wonderful, simple, and very personal anecdotes of the very earliest days.

Recently a friend told me that when he practiced Zen in Japan he met a powerful Zen master who declared to him that the future of Zen was in the West. "But," the master added, "the West lacks the true spirit of Zen." "What is the true spirit of Zen?" my friend asked. "Modesty," he said.

So enjoy this wonderful, useful, profound yet modest book that expresses the true spirit of Zen. It and its warmhearted author are blessings for the world, and I am honored and very pleased to introduce them to you.

Editor's Introduction

THIS IS A STORY ABOUT HOW a teacher can change someone's life. The teachings, stories, poems, koans, and personal memories that make up this book are life-affirming, inclusive, and universal.

Nothing Holy about It is not a book just for Buddhists. It is for everyone who is on a spiritual path. It is also for the simply curious, as I was forty years ago when I came across a strange little book titled *The Third Eye*. It opened me up to a different way of thinking about myself and the world. Many years later, I encountered a teacher who showed me how to go beyond my new way of thinking to a new way of *being*. That teacher was Tim Burkett. I believe his book will do the same for a new generation of spiritual seekers.

Tim was only twenty years old when he became a student of Shunryu Suzuki Roshi, abbot of the San Francisco Zen Center, the first Zen center on the West Coast. Today Suzuki Roshi is one of the most renowned Zen teachers in the world, but in 1964 he was virtually unknown outside a small circle of dedicated students. Those early years of American Zen were difficult times, often tumultuous and always uncertain. As a part of that core group, Tim remembers the struggle to raise money for the now-famous Tassajara Monastery, the first Zen monastery outside of Asia. He remembers the rising tensions between Suzuki's American students and his Japanese congregation, and Suzuki's tireless effort to be everything to everybody. Tim remembers the roaring applause when Suzuki followed Janis Joplin on the stage of San Francisco's Avalon Ballroom during a fund-raiser. And he remembers Suzuki's compassionate support for his senior student Trudy Dixon during her struggle with cancer, and his tearful "lion's roar" at her funeral. These stories and many more, told from the perspective of a student who is now himself an old master, create the backdrop and a wonderful ambience for this book.

Tim's Buddhist name is Zentetsu, which means "thorough-going Zen." He received it at his ordination in 1978 from his second teacher, Katagiri Roshi. But Tim is much fonder of another name—Ugly Duckling—given to him when he was a young student struggling to find his way. The story goes that during a two-month practice period at Tassajara, Suzuki Roshi declared that Tim had become . . . a beautiful swan. When Tim tells the story, his face lights up at the words "beautiful swan," and he lifts himself off the cushion as if he might float away.

"Then my teacher said, 'Or maybe you are an ugly duckling!'" Tim frowns and drops back down to his cushion. Then immediately his face lights up again as he peers around the room, quacking like a duck: "*Quack-quack! Quack-quack!*"

In his dharma talks, Tim's teaching style is always fresh and unpredictable, fluid and compelling. One moment he may be chiding and reproachful: "Don't try to be a good Buddhist. To hell with that! That's *extra*." The next moment, he offers a gentle whisper: "Just be who you are. Can you do that? *Can you?*"

Tim's dharma talks are interspersed with unexpected peals of laughter and bemused looks. His view that we were all enlightened before we were born continually bubbles up in new and refreshing ways, allowing him to live lightly and laugh frequently at the folly of human beings.

With personal stories and anecdotes, he shows how relevant the teachings are in ordinary, day-to-day situations. His memories of Suzuki Roshi, just being who he was, are delightful. His stories about his family, especially his grandchildren, add a quality of everyday life that people can relate to. He also shares his personal tragedies, tragedies like those we all experience, often feeling isolated as a result. Tim assures us that we are not isolated—that by our very nature isolation is impossible—and that the home we seek is a place we have never left.

Although Tim's teaching style draws on various forms of Buddhist literature, he urges his students not to use this literature merely to feed their minds. "Zen in not learned—it is imbibed." Through poetry, art, parables, and koans, Tim shows us how to cultivate a Zen life in the small things we do, in how we relate to the people, objects, and activities of daily life.

Part 1 is "Commitment to the Unknown." Tim says, "Committing to the unknown means shedding our ego skin and opening up to this vibrant, oceanic life, a symphony of color, form, and sound." The commitment is to live life fully. To flow with the symphony. To ride the oceanic waves without withdrawing or freezing up. A commitment to the unknown demands our courage and our willingness to allow the heart to open—because when the heart opens just a little bit, the commitment blooms on its own. As Tim says, "It arises from the whole body—the heart, mind, and every cell make the commitment."

Part 2 is "Calling in the Shards," the phrase Tim uses to describe the horrible/wonderful entrance into phase two of Zen practice. Here we start to look closely at our rough edges, our personality shards, which arise from fear, desire, prejudice, aversion, and strongly held beliefs. These shards are like body armor we put on for protection against a tumultuous and unpredictable world. But our body armor is just an illusion; we can't truly separate ourselves from the world.

In phase two of our practice, we start to dissolve the body armor. "Our shards isolate us," Tim says. "And they hurt others with their sharp edges. When we see them clearly, in all their iterations, we are free of them. We just have to see them, because seeing is the beginning of freeing."

Part 3, "When Snow Falls, It Falls on Everything," is the heart of the book, taking us to the core of Zen practice. It's about taking our practice into the world and learning to endure life's sorrows while focusing on the cultivation of equanimity, the abiding stillness behind authentic compassion. A Zen life is not a life without pain. When the heart is open, the pain hurts even more. But there's enough space to hold the hurt without closing down. This is the secret to living an awakened life.

In part 3 Tim shares the pain of losing his only brother to suicide. "It wiped me out," he told me during one of our many interviews for this book. He even told me, "I don't want you to write this chapter about my brother. It's too painful for me." But after his brother's death, Tim dedicated his life to creating programs for those with depression and other forms of mental illness. Thousands have been helped through Tim's nonprofit agency, People Incorporated. And yet, thirty years later, feelings of guilt, regret, and grief still reside in Tim's heart. Tragedies mark us indelibly, but they don't have to close us off from life.

Part 4, "Staying on the Track," is about sticking to our commitment. In the beginning, a spiritual path is lonely. It feels isolating. But as our practice matures and our ability to focus increases, we begin to see through our isolating thoughts. One by one, the veils drop away. The world becomes a more vivid and vibrant place. The mind is waking up to something new, something beyond what is perceived by the thinking mind.

Part 5 is "Time Dissolving into Timelessness." That time dissolves into timelessness—moment by moment—is one of the great mysteries of life. But life's mysteries reveal themselves to us constantly. One glimpse can inspire and encourage us forever. This last part of the book is about cultivating the ability to see the world for the first time. Suzuki Roshi likens it to the warm, familiar feeling of a letter from home. "If you want to read a letter from Buddha's world, it is necessary to understand Buddha's world," Suzuki said. But this is an imbibed understanding. It doesn't come in through the front door of the mind. It slips in during quiet moments when the mind is still and open.

Having learned so much from Tim Burkett during my years of study with him, I have been honored by the opportunity to assemble this collection of stories, memories, and teachings on his behalf. I hope that many readers will find in these pages some of the wisdom, joy, insight, enlightenment, and delight that I have experienced as Tim's student.

—WANDA ISLE

PART ONE

Commitment to the Unknown

ONE

Awakening to the Longing

My first Zen teacher was Shunryu Suzuki Roshi. The title *roshi* refers to a highly venerated, elder master; a literal translation is "old teacher." Suzuki himself resisted the title; nobody wants to be called "old." When I knew him, he was just Suzuki Sensei, or just Sensei, meaning teacher. I often refer to him as Suzuki Roshi because, like it or not, he was and remains a highly venerated teacher—but in my own memories and heart, he is still just Sensei.

For him, the simplest things reflected what's truly important. Water, for instance. From the thunderous rush of a waterfall to the reflective, mirror-like surface of a still lake, water has a way of captivating us and drawing us inward. Suzuki once visited California's Yosemite National Park with two of his students from the San Francisco Zen Center. They drove a red Volkswagen Beetle. Watching Suzuki fold his ninety-pound body into the backseat, I remember thinking the car fit him perfectly.

When he returned from Yosemite, which is known for its spectacular waterfalls, Suzuki was on a natural high. Those waterfalls were all he talked about. He even worked them into a dharma talk that was later transcribed and published in his book *Zen Mind, Beginner's Mind*. How he talked about Yosemite's waterfalls gives us a glimpse into his way of thinking about and being in the world.

"When the water moves along as a river," Suzuki said, "there is no problem." But when the river becomes a waterfall, tiny drops of mist and streamlets split off, isolated from their source, each one alive and totally engaged in the activity of life. The life of a tiny droplet falling such a great distance is filled with difficulty. How lonely to be separated from the river. "What a difficult experience for each drop to come down from the top of such a high mountain," Suzuki said.

Suzuki believed in a universal longing, shared by all human beings, to reconnect with our true, interconnected nature. This longing is the heart's inmost request, calling us to a life of quiescence and composure, which is our natural state of being. When it manifests as a sense of isolation and cut-offness, we may feel as if we're missing something. We don't feel whole or fully engaged in our life. Often it seems that life is moving along without us, like a rushing waterfall.

But how do we respond? What is our longing calling us to do? In Zen we respond by learning to experience life directly, so we can feel our own authenticity. There can be no quiescence or composure without authenticity. In Zen meditation, *zazen,* we keep bringing ourselves back to what is happening right now. It's a simple practice but not easy. In Zen, *just* is an important word. Whenever you see it, you are being asked to let go of something. To see the world just as it is, you must relinquish your distorting ideas, views, and concepts. Most of us prefer to limit our experience, to sit in the Chatterbox Café of our mind, where our inner narrator mediates for us. Rather than interacting with the world directly, we interact with our *thoughts* about the world.

Zen is about seeing the nature of this mediator and gradually letting it go. We start by seeing and accepting all the turmoil that comes up from our busy mind without judging or criticizing, since that judgment or criticism is the voice of the mediator pulling us back into the Chatterbox Café. In meditation, we learn to open up to our immediate thoughts, sensations, and emotions and see how we react to them. Each time we're able to open up a little more, without being pulled back into the Chatterbox Café, our capacity for direct engagement with life increases.

Learning to maintain a balance between going within and staying outwardly engaged is an arduous process, but our longing fuels our commitment and keeps bringing us back to our meditation practice. Even if you've been practicing for forty years, the longing is still there, doing its job of keeping the heart soft, open, and responsive, moment by moment, and leading us back to our true interconnected nature.

The great seventeenth-century Japanese poet Basho is arguably the world's most famous haiku poet. His given name was Matsuo Kinsaku. He lived in a small hut beside a banana tree, called a *basho* tree in Japanese, which was a gift from one of his students. Matsuo Kinsaku took the name Basho because he was inspired by the way the small tree stood outside his hut in sun, wind, or rain with its large, soft, fragile leaves open to the world. His poetry and the way he lived his life reflect a wonderful appreciation for openness and vulnerability to whatever life brought. He longed to experience life's depths and nuances, as in this poem:

In Kyoto
Hearing the cuckoo
Longing for Kyoto

Basho didn't seek to rid himself of his longing. He embraced it. It defined, shaped, and brought meaning into his life. Through it, he learned to trust and to simply be who he was, by no one's authority other than his own.

Basho was not an ordained monk. But he wore the robes of a monk and lived the life of a monk. He was ordained by the authenticity of his heart's longing.

Authenticity is its own authority. According to Suzuki Roshi, it's the only true authority. Suzuki said, "Things go the way the mind goes. If you think you're a monk, you're a monk. If you don't think you're a monk, you're not a monk."

The problem comes when we don't want to feel our longing, so we move away from it. When we try to escape our own heart, we close down, and our life becomes one of isolation and loneliness.

Most religions try to explain the root cause of our loneliness. Often it's an attempt to explain it away, to rid us of it. According to some traditions, we are in exile, alienated from God. From this perspective, we have been ripped out of the fabric of the universe.

However, from a Buddhist perspective, our exile is an illusion perpetuated by our conditioning. In Buddhist thought, we can't be ripped out of the fabric of the universe because we *are* the fabric of the universe. But the fabric is not solid; at the very ground of our being, we are pure, pristine awareness. This pristine awareness is called our basic goodness, or buddha nature. Trust in our basic goodness is the source of spiritual freedom. Without it, freedom is not possible.

In the eighth century, Zen Master Sekito wrote a poem titled "The Sandokai," known in English as "The Merging of Sameness and Difference." In this teaching poem, there's a line that reads, "In the light there is darkness, but don't take it as darkness." We tend to believe there is a thing called darkness and a thing called God and that they oppose each other. But opposition, whether it's between individuals or nations, with all the immoral acts that ensue, arises from our failure to recognize our undivided nature—our basic goodness. So we mark life's passing events with the characteristics of darkness or light, good or bad, right or wrong. We see everything in opposition to something else: up or down, left or right, sweet or sour, white or black. Everywhere we look we see this dichotomy or duality rather than wholeness. Where there's dichotomy, there is solidity rather than fluidity. Everything feels fixed and static rather than impermanent and ever changing.

But transformation depends on wholeness, fluidity, and impermanence. Everything is unfolding within everything else. When our heart is open, great sorrow can roll through like a wave rolling through the sea at great depth, causing all sorts of chaos and upheaval. But when the wave has passed, no trace of it remains. Resilience arises naturally from an open heart.

On and off the cushion—that is, in meditation practice and during ordinary daily life—if we can stay open as our mental and emotional turmoils arise and move through us, our capacity to engage life directly increases. When tragedy strikes, it's natural to want to close our heart to protect it. But transformation happens every time we're able to stay open.

"The Sandokai" continues, "In the darkness there is light; but don't take it as light." If we take it as light, we are judging—separating ourselves from it. Within each of us there is something huge that is beyond us—beyond our thinking and judging mind, even beyond our feelings. We can merge with this openness, where there's room for both sorrow and joy to exist simultaneously.

A personal experience of this sphere of reality is called enlightenment, or satori. Often we have these experiences early on in our practice, and they inspire us. But a satori experience is seductive and can be detrimental if inspiration turns to craving. "In the darkness there is light; but don't take it as light." We yearn to experience the light, but our thinking, judging, comparing mind keeps separating us from it, pulling us back into our isolated Chatterbox Café.

But don't worry. Even the Chatterbox Café is thoroughly permeated by light. If it weren't, we would be trapped there. But it's just made of thought. How impenetrable can it be?

THE EXPERIENCE OF BOUNDLESSNESS

To have a so-called enlightenment experience is of course important, but what is more important is to know how to adjust the flame in zazen and in our everyday life.

—SUZUKI ROSHI

When I first met Suzuki Roshi, in 1964, his attitude toward satori was a surprise to me. It came about this way:

At the time, I was a student at Stanford University. I'd read books by Aldous Huxley describing with reverence his LSD-induced altered states. I'd also read about the enlightenment experiences discussed by Alan Watts and D. T. Suzuki. I was naturally drawn to this kind of stuff.

In my abnormal-psychology class, we studied altered states of consciousness. While researching a paper, I came across *The Teachings of the Mystics,* by W. T. Stace. In that book mystics from every corner of the world and every religious tradition described experiences that took them outside time, to a realm beyond physical boundaries, where no separation of any kind existed. It was a deeply calm and peaceful place, and at the same time dynamic and ever changing. I wondered if this could actually be true.

Arthur Koestler's story in *The Teachings of the Mystics* resonated with me the most because he was not a religious man, nor was he seeking a mystical experience; it just happened. He was a political prisoner during the Spanish Civil War, accused of being a spy for the Popular Front. He was held in isolation in a small cell, waiting to be executed by the Falangists. To occupy his mind, he used a wire from his mattress to scratch mathematical formulas on the wall. Standing back and looking at the symbols, it occurred to him that in the language of mathematics, he could say something precise and meaningful about the infinite. He was in this deeply concentrated state when, quite suddenly, he got a glimpse of the boundless nature of things:

> Then I was floating on my back in a river of peace, under bridges of silence. It came from nowhere and flowed nowhere. Then there was no river and no I. The I had ceased to exist.

I read passages from this book over and over, soaking them up. More and more, I was consumed by the possibility of experiencing for myself what these mystics were talking about. School, friends, and everything else became irrelevant.

Finally, spring break came. I took the train to Utah to go skiing. The whole way, I was glued to *The Teachings of the Mystics*. My first evening in Utah, at a friend's house where I was staying, I met a young woman, a classical pianist. Like the rest of us, she was part of the peace movement and the counterculture of the 1960s, searching for a harmonious way of being in the world. She was slim and modestly dressed, with long brown hair, and was on the quiet side. I started talking about the book I was reading, and her reaction surprised me. She was more than just interested—she lit up.

It turned out she'd had a similar experience herself, but she had never read anything about it. We talked for a while, and then as she was leaving, she paused and said, "I think you are *this* close, Tim." Her thumb and forefinger almost touching—*that close.*

I don't even remember her name, but she is still a mystery to me—because moments after she said those words, I began to feel an incredible sense of peace and calmness. It was completely overwhelming. And joyful. My sense of being an isolated and separate entity vanished. My worries, concerns, and anxieties dissolved. Stillness, spaciousness, and fluidity permeated everything. I went outside to lie in the snow, laughing, with tears of relief and great joy that Tim Burkett's worries and concerns had dissolved.

For several days, joy imbued everything I did. Hitchhiking to the ski resort was a delight—so delightful, I didn't even care about getting there. Just being on the road watching cars pass by was wonderful. But so was everything else—skiing, washing dishes, taking out the garbage, or just being alone. It didn't seem to matter what I was doing. The experience of boundlessness, no separation, and the joy that came with it felt more real than anything else in my life.

On the train back to college, the sense of boundlessness began to fade. For a while I was able to summon it back by repeating a phrase from the book: "the peace that passeth understanding." Over and over, I repeated it. It worked for a while. But by the time I got home, the small, familiar ego self was back, along with all its worries and concerns. I longed to see *beyond* the small self again. But even the memory was becoming distant and remote. I tried to cling to it—to get it back—but I couldn't.

Usually, in those days, alcohol was the answer to my travails. But I had seen beyond the small ego self, and I wasn't ready to give in to my old patterns. In *The Teachings of the Mystics* there's a chapter on Zen. So I went to the Stanford library and requested a phone book. Flipping to the Zs, I found two listings that caught my eye: the San Francisco Zen Center and the Zen Bar. Plan A and plan B.

MEETING SUZUKI ROSHI

Plan A, the San Francisco Zen Center, was on Bush Street in an old synagogue. I found a parking space on the street, approached the building, and rang the bell. A small Japanese man opened the door. He introduced himself as Rev. Suzuki. He wore Japanese work clothes: loose black pants and a black, long-sleeved jacket that tied on the side. He wore slippers, and his head was shaved. He was not a young man, but a youthful glint shone through his eyes. He exuded both dignity and friendliness. I liked him immediately.

He invited me in. I followed him upstairs to a tiny office with a desk, a couple of chairs, a couch, and a small window that looked out on Bush Street. Rev. Suzuki spoke with a heavy Japanese accent, but I had no trouble understanding him. I was excited and a little nervous about meeting a Zen master, but at the same time, I felt comfortable and at ease with him. I eagerly told him about my experience in Utah.

I was expecting an endorsement of some kind, an acknowledgment from a Zen master that something big had happened to me. But there was no endorsement, only two short comments. First, in his kind and gentle voice, Suzuki said, "That is good," which seemed like an endorsement of sorts. Then, just as kindly, he added, "But that is not Zen."

Then he stood and invited me into the next room, the *zendo*, or meditation room. It wasn't very big. There were no windows or furniture. Cushions lined the walls, which were bare and gray. It had a nice hardwood floor, a pleasant smell of incense, and an altar with a candle, a statue, and a vase of fresh flowers. The simplicity was appealing and warm.

We sat on cushions and Suzuki told me about the practice of "sitting still and doing nothing," which is how he described zazen. He told me that he and his students meditated every morning and every evening, and he invited me to come back and meditate with them. I said I would. After all, I was twenty years old, and he was a Zen master, so I suppose I was infatuated. But it was more than that. I felt drawn to him. I still do.

As I walked back to my car, I thought, *Yes, I'm going to do this practice.* But I was still puzzled over his comment that my experience was "not Zen." His English wasn't very good. Probably, I decided, he'd just misunderstood my story.

I never resorted to plan B—the Zen Bar. Instead I drove to the Zen center three or four times a week. We meditated on the cushion for thirty minutes, then did a very slow walking meditation around the room for ten minutes, then back to our cushion for the final thirty minutes of sitting meditation.

There were only six to nine regulars who came to the meditations, and the occasional beatnik or hippie wandering in out of curiosity or boredom. The pleasant smell of incense was often mixed with other smells, such as body odors, pot, or the minty smell of patchouli. Once, a young girl joined us wearing a see-through dress with nothing but bare skin under it and bells on her feet that jingled during walking meditation.

As we exited the zendo after the second meditation session, Suzuki bowed to each of us, one by one. I wondered what he thought as he bowed to the seminaked girl with bells on her feet.

The first year or so, I went to Suzuki frequently with concerns about my practice. He listened patiently. Then he would say,

"Just sit, Tim. *Just sit.*" Two small words, but he said them with such confidence. When the heart is ready, we don't need much encouragement. *Just sit* was enough. But if the heart is not ready, if the way hasn't been opened by the heart's longing, no amount of words will suffice.

There are many stories in Buddhism about the necessity of a ready heart. Like this one:

A young boy goes to a Zen master who has a monastery alongside a stream. The boy says to the master, "Please teach me." The master refuses, telling the boy he is not yet sincere.

"What do you mean, I am not sincere? I want to learn!" the boy insists.

But the master says, "Go away."

The boy goes away, but he keeps coming back, again and again. Over and over, the master sends him away. Finally, one day after the boy says he really wants to learn, the master says, "No. You don't." Then he grabs the boy, drags him into the stream, and holds his head underwater. The boy kicks and struggles. Finally, the master releases him.

"Why did you do that?" cried the boy.

"When you want to learn as much as you wanted that breath, come back, and I will teach you."

BEING SUMMONED

And it was at that age . . . Poetry arrived
in search of me. I don't know, I don't know where
it came from, from winter or a river.
I don't know how or when,
no they were not voices, they were not
words, nor silence,
but from a street I was summoned,

from the branches of night,
abruptly from the others,
among violent fires
or returning alone,
there I was without a face
and it touched me.

—PABLO NERUDA, "POETRY"

Those who practice Zen are summoned to this way of life in much the same way Pablo Neruda was called to poetry. We are called to leave the street behind and enter a world of silence. As human beings, we are continually being summoned from the hurly-burly, chaotic life of the street to a calm, inner stillness. Maybe we listen; maybe we don't. It doesn't matter, because it won't go away. It is our true nature calling. As Zen students, we aspire to listen and respond.

Buddhism is relatively new to American culture. Suzuki Roshi had wanted to come to the United States his whole life. He was born in 1904, but it was not until 1959 that he finally made it here. He left behind his wife, Mitsu, his four children, and his temple. With no idea what to expect, he packed a few bags and moved wholeheartedly into an uncertain future. Suzuki always seemed to lean into uncertainty rather than back away from it. It takes a lot of trust to lean into uncertainty—the unknown.

I was lucky to find a teacher I trusted. Without a trusted teacher, a commitment to the unknown may be impossible. We may have a big opening experience, but there has to be trust if we're going to *stay* open.

The Sanskrit word for trust is *shraddha*. It is often translated as "faith," but "faith" comes with a lot of baggage in Western culture because we associate it with faith in God. Buddha defined shraddha as the type of trust birds have in the tree in which they build their nests.

A summons to the unknown comes in many forms. I have a friend who flew from her home in Chicago to a retreat led by Suzuki Sensei at the San Francisco Zen Center. Several days into the retreat, as she was getting up from her cushion, she glanced over at Suzuki. Their eyes met for just an instant. But in that instant she saw within his gaze an indescribable stillness and spaciousness. She was pierced by it.

Her busy mind, full of complaints, judgments, and criticisms since the retreat began, suddenly fell silent. A deep calm descended upon her. She didn't know what it was or where it came from. But she didn't try to figure it out. She trusted it. She opened up to it. And it changed the course of her life.

BASHO'S *POP!*

> *In plum flower scent*
> *pop! The sun appears—*
> *the mountain path.*

—BASHO

There is an ancient saying that practicing Zen is like walking in mist: you don't even know you're getting wet until you're completely soaked. The mountainous regions of Japan are often shrouded in mist, so when I read Basho's poem, I imagine him walking along a misty mountain path, on and on and on, walking aimlessly until he enters a deeply focused and meditative state—"In plum flower scent."

Suddenly—"Pop!" The sun breaks through. The sun represents enlightenment. The heart and mind suddenly open to something new—the thin layers of bark covering the innermost core of the Basho tree fall away, and clear, sweet water gushes forth. And then—"Mountain path," meaning there is something to do, some way of expressing the experience. Basho was a poet, so he wrote a haiku. If he'd been a carpenter, he might have built something with his hands and with a still, joyful, and focused mind.

This is what we all want, right? To experience Basho's *pop!* for ourselves. He is not talking about some faraway moment on a faraway path. He is talking about *this* moment and *this* spot, right here, right now. Look deeply at this moment, and you discover how one moment conditions the next, so we are always on a path. Maybe your path feels dark and confused. Maybe you feel as if you're stumbling along most of the time. But stumbling in the shadows is part of the path, too. "The Sandokai" says, "Light and dark oppose one another like the front and back foot in walking," one step after another without knowing anything at all because the mind is just still and serene.

After I'd been studying with Suzuki for a couple of years, I became very discouraged with my practice. It was midwinter in San Francisco—cold, wet, and foggy. Often the sun didn't come out for days, which added to my low spirits. One morning after zazen, I started back to my room across from the Zen center. I was walking with downcast eyes, staring at the cement sidewalk, when I saw a little green sprout pushing up through a crack. Imagine it—a tiny sprout pushing up through cement in the dead of winter. How much effort it must have taken. Immediately, my mood lifted.

When I got back to my room, I looked through a book of poems for something to remind me of it. I found one and taped it by the Off button on my alarm clock. For the rest of the winter, the little sprout summoned me, over and over, to honor my commitment. When the alarm went off before dawn, I stumbled across the street to sit with my teacher. One tiny little sprout was all the encouragement I needed.

> *The mountain slopes crawl with lumberjacks*
> *axing everything in sight—*
> *Yet crimson flowers*
> *Burn along the stream.*

—CHIN-DOBA

TWO

From Longing
to Aspiration

A N EIGHT-YEAR-OLD GIRL BECAME ILL and was diagnosed with a life-threatening blood disease. She needed a transfusion, but her blood type was rare. A search went out for a donor. With every passing day, the little girl weakened, and still no donor was found.

Then it was discovered that her six-year-old brother shared her rare blood type. The mother, along with their minister and doctor, sat down with the boy. Would he be willing to donate his blood to save his sister's life?

The boy did not answer right away. He wanted time to think about it. After a few days, he went to his mother.

"Yes, I'll do it," he said.

The following day, the doctor brought both children to his clinic and placed them on cots, side by side. First he drew some blood from the boy's arm. Then he crossed to the sister's cot, inserted the needle, and began the transfusion. Almost immediately, the color poured back into her cheeks.

After a moment, the boy motioned for the doctor to come to his bedside. In a whisper, he asked, "Will I start to die right away?"

Can you imagine this? Can you put yourself in the little boy's shoes? He assumed he was being asked to donate *all* of his blood, and therefore his life. To save his sister, this six-year-old was able to move beyond the conditioned limitations and fears of the ego.

We all have this capacity to move beyond our conditioning . . . but unfortunately for us poor human beings, most of us will relate more closely to my next story—a tale about eagles, backyard chickens, and the human predicament.

One afternoon, a chicken farmer happened across an eagle's egg. He put it with his chickens, and soon thereafter, the egg hatched. The young eagle grew up among the backyard chickens, and whatever they did, the eagle mimicked. He thought he was a chicken. Since chickens can fly only a short distance, the eagle, too, learned to fly short distances.

One day the eagle saw a bird flying high above him. He was very impressed. "What is that?" he asked a hen. "That's an eagle, the king of the birds," she told him. "He belongs to the sky. We belong to the earth; we are chickens." And so the eagle lived and died as a chicken, for that is what he thought he was.

Longing without aspiration is not enough to free us from our conditioned reality. A key component of aspiration is imagination, the ability to travel beyond our limited experience and see the path of others as possibly our own.

When we hear a story about a six-year-old boy willing to give his life for his sister, it sparks our imagination. We wonder what it would feel like to experience compassion deep enough to overwhelm our instinct for self-preservation.

I was inspired by Suzuki Sensei. After he became my teacher, I told my father about him. My father was a cautious and conservative man. "Tim, if you're looking for abiding joy, you are going to be disappointed. There is no such thing in this world."

My father was successful in his law practice, but he was anxious all his life. Suzuki had something I didn't see in my father: a certain type of courage. The type that allows us to recognize the negative, trance-like state that we are in; to acknowledge that we are held there by a mind that continually churns out criticisms, complaints, and rationalizations; and to accept that focusing on our shortcomings and problems only perpetuates the trance.

Courage is the second key component of aspiration. Without it, we remain stuck.

But we have the ability to cultivate the courage we need. We can break through the trance of inadequacy and defectiveness through a regular meditation practice. Meditation slows our mind down, creating some space between our thoughts. Only then is there the possibility of seeing through the trance.

When Arthur Koestler, the political prisoner I talked about in chapter 1, broke through his inner trance, he was elated. On the outside, he was still confined and awaiting execution. But on the inside, he was completely free.

CREATING A PURPOSEFUL LIFE

In his book *Man's Search for Meaning*, Viktor Frankl talks about being in a Nazi concentration camp. The only way he survived was by imagining a future that was important to him. When the war was over, he studied those who survived the Holocaust. The one common denominator was that the survivors thought hard about a life afterward and imagined themselves living it.

As human beings, we need to cultivate this ability to imagine a life full of meaning and to trust it.

For nearly two decades, I've had the privilege of leading a non-profit called People Incorporated that helps people with mental illness, many of whom are homeless and living on the streets. Their lives tend to have little meaning. Their sense of purpose revolves around where their next meal will come from, how to stay warm and dry, and whether or not the public library is open so they'll have a place to go.

When we launched the project, we thought that when we brought homeless people inside, the biggest problem would be dealing with their mental illness and chemical dependency. But we found that when people who have been on the street a long time are given a warm, safe place to live and three meals a day, they often become disoriented. At first we were puzzled. This new condition had nothing to do with their mental illness or chemical dependency. The problem, it turned out, was that they had lost their sense of purpose. Often the disorientation becomes so acute that they grab their sleeping bags and leave the shelter. Being cold and hungry is better than being devoid of purpose.

So now, in small but deliberate ways, we encourage them to consider a purpose beyond the next hour. We ask them about their plans for tomorrow. Sometimes they're stumped. Tomorrow? They often muse over the question, as if the idea of "tomorrow" had not occurred to them. But if they seem receptive, we suggest things to consider. In this way, taking small steps, they begin to develop a vision for the future. But it takes a long time for them. When the mind becomes too fragmented, it is difficult, maybe impossible, to see beyond the immediate wants and needs of the ego.

Living a purposeful life transforms the small "I want" into a great "I aspire." It doesn't mean kicking out the small "I want." It means broadening it beyond the needs and desires of a constricted ego. In the beginning, we may have to nurse our aspiration along, moment by moment, because the pull of ego is ever present. It will always be ever present, even if you've been practicing for forty years.

That may sound discouraging, but even though the egocentric pull is always here, the ability to notice it and return to our aspiration is strengthened through practice. At first you may have to talk yourself back into your aspiration, reminding yourself of it, reaffirming your commitment to the unknown. But eventually, you just notice you've moved away, and the response is to move back. As we steep ourselves in Zen practice, it becomes effortless.

But in the beginning there will be times when we feel like giving up. It seems too difficult. It doesn't seem to be working. When we think this way, our aspiration has dried up. We are trying to get something concrete in a world pervaded by ambiguity. When we try to get something for ourselves, we drain away the power of our aspiration. It's important to recognize that aspiration is not about goal setting.

Sure, we need goals. But if we hold them too tightly, they will feed the trance of inadequacy. If we relate aspiration to a to-do list, it gets mixed up with feelings of failure and doubt.

When I'm trying to raise money for people with mental illness, I frequently meet with legislators who seem totally uninterested in supporting my mission. This might be very discouraging and could even tempt me to give up my mission. But if my aspiration is wholehearted, I will leave the meeting with my aspiration intact, because aspiration is not dependent on outcome. From a Buddhist point of view, aspiration is about shifting our orientation.

It's helpful to formalize our aspiration with a vow. A vow is very specific, and we can bring it to mind quickly. In Soto Zen (the school that I'm trained in) we recite vows every day to keep our intention oriented toward our aspiration. We vow to help all beings through our actions and meditation. We vow to see through delusion. We vow to embody the teachings. And we vow to manifest our true nature of interconnectedness.

VIDYA: SEEING THROUGH THE SELF
TO WHO WE REALLY ARE

Vidya is a Sanskrit word that points to the idea of seeing through the ego. It has the same root as the English word *vision*. An English translation for *vidya* is "clear seeing," but a more accurate translation may be "seeing into" or "seeing through," because vidya is about seeing through our delusions about space, time, and a separate, discrete self. In each moment, either we are manifesting our interconnected nature (vidya) or we're ignoring it (*avidya*).

Vidya is not related to optical sight or mental processes. It's a particular kind of insight, with a resonating quality that penetrates our conceptual constructs of time. The thirteenth-century Zen master Eihei Dogen, who is considered the father of Soto Zen, had a profound understanding of the dynamic relationship between the self, space, and time. His term for this relationship is *being-time.*

Vidya, as I understand it and have experienced it, is one aspect of being-time. It sounds remote and complicated, but the potential to experience vidya is innate in all of us. It is an aspect of present-moment awareness. It arises naturally and spontaneously when we are wholeheartedly immersed in *just* this moment. Vidya is the experiential realization of the interpenetrating nature of past, present, and future.

Perhaps it is easier to say what vidya is *not* rather than what it is.

First, vidya is not restricted by linear time, which is an imposed mental construct. Backward-seeing vidya is not mere memory or an ego-driven attempt to relive events of the past.

Instead, when we experience vidya, we're able to simply enjoy our memories as they bubble up without identifying with them or being defined by them.

Forward-seeing vidya is not merely about projecting, planning, or imagining a new future for ourselves. So often, our vision for the future is based on fear and desire. Forward-seeing vidya is about openness and possibility. It is not limited by the small ego self.

Present-seeing vidya is not ruminating, contemplation, or even zazen—although it may arise during zazen. With vidya, we're able to experience the present moment directly, without a filter that's based on our ideas, fears, and concepts.

As mystical as it sounds, when vidya arises, it feels ordinary and practical. It is a natural aspect of our true self.

I'll give an example of the practical aspects of backward-seeing vidya. My father is deceased now, but as he aged, he became more and more cantankerous. It was hard to be with him without becoming angry and frustrated.

I cultivated compassion by consciously bringing to mind those times when I was young and my father and I went hiking and swimming together. Back then, there was a positive energy between us, and warm feelings of interconnectedness. My practice, during the last years of his life, was to arouse those feelings, which were stored in my body. As I opened up, the warm feelings began to flow again, and compassion for this aging, cantankerous old man arose naturally. Instead of splitting off from my father, I was able to be fully present with him, regardless of his cranky mood.

Forward-seeing vidya—seeing through the present and into the future—is a matter of seeing how present moments permeate the future. If you want to know what your future will be, look directly at what you're doing right now. Your present thoughts and feelings, together with your aspiration or lack of aspiration, have a more powerful effect on your future than you might imagine.

Not long after I began practicing, Dainin Katagiri, a young Zen teacher from Japan, arrived at the San Francisco Zen Center. Katagiri Sensei, who years later would become my second teacher, frequently talked about his "dim vision" for the future. His aspiration was to plant the seeds of Zen in this country and encourage them to sprout. "Dim vision" was his way of reminding himself, and us, to hold our vision lightly so it doesn't become an obsession. Obsessiveness is an aspect of avidya, delusion.

There's a story about Suzuki and Katagiri on a plane flying over the Midwest. Suzuki pointed out the window and said, "That is where the real Americans live. They all have jobs!" He was referring to his experience with us early counterculture ne'er-do-wells in San Francisco. For Katagiri, this statement turned out to be prophetic. In 1972 a group of Zen practitioners from Minneapolis flew to San Francisco to meet with Katagiri Sensei and ask for his help. Suzuki was dead by then, but Katagiri remembered what he had said about the Midwest. He agreed to go to Minneapolis and lead a retreat.

By this time I had left California. By sheer coincidence, I was living in northern Minnesota. But I was not part of the Minneapolis group and knew nothing of their effort to persuade Katagiri to move there. As a matter of fact, when I left San Francisco, I never expected to see Katagiri again.

So I was surprised to hear he was coming to Minnesota and excited to see him. I drove down for the retreat, which was in the home of a guy named Erik Storlie. On the first day, I went in to *dokusan,* a private meeting with Katagiri. I couldn't believe I was seeing him again.

But he could. His first words were, "I thought I'd see you again, Tim."

This was the first Zen retreat in Minnesota led by a trained teacher. Among the small group of practitioners who attended was a man named Cal Appleby, who has since become my friend and is still very active in the Zen community in Minneapolis. He sat the entire retreat in full lotus, his back as straight as an arrow. I've never been able to sit in full lotus. Every time I glanced at Cal, I felt a stab of jealousy. Sitting that way seemed rude. He probably still sits in full lotus—and he's older than I am.

Throughout the retreat, Katagiri talked about planting the seeds of Zen and watching them sprout. I thought, *Oh, yes, that's his dim vision.* A few years later, he became the first Zen teacher to ordain priests in the Midwest. He ordained two students, Norm Randolph and me. We were a small part of his dim vision. Today Katagiri Roshi's seeds have sprouted all over the country. The Minnesota Zen Meditation Center, on Lake Calhoun in Uptown, is renowned because it was created by Katagiri Roshi's dim vision.

Present-moment vidya, the here-and-now aspect of deep seeing, is always the most difficult for us. It's such a struggle for human beings to stay present, without splitting off into the past or the future. When we are fully present, life is vivid and our actions are fresh and spontaneous. Present-moment vidya is the wellspring of abiding joy and true compassion.

Here is an example of how the struggle for vidya manifests naturally in the life of a four-year-old. My grandson Ethan lives in France, but he speaks English at home. Learning French was a struggle for him when he was four, since it was his second language. While my wife and I were visiting, we took Ethan and his little brother Logan to the park. Ethan noticed a stray cat hanging around that was thin and looked hungry. Even though he was very shy about speaking French, Ethan went to a family picnicking nearby and asked, in French, for food to feed the cat. No one else had even noticed the cat, but when Ethan saw it, his heart opened.

But two hours earlier, before we left for the park, Ethan had shoved his little brother into a closet and closed the door so he could have Grandma and Grandpa to himself. When I noticed Logan was missing, I said, "Ethan, where's Logan?"

Ethan said, "Oh, I put him away. He was bothering me."

I went to the back of the house and looked in the closet. There was my little grandson.

This is what we do as human beings; it's the human condition. Vidya one moment; avidya the next. When the desires of ego arise, we often overlook vidya, whether we're four or forty or sixty. But we can't beat ourselves up over it. Beating ourselves up is just more avidya.

Vidya is the ability to sense the interpenetrating nature of things. It is based on the premise of basic goodness. Not good in contrast to bad, but good because it is what is. Sure, there's good and bad in the world, but that's not primary. Suzuki Roshi said, "You are all perfect just as you are. But you can use a little improvement."

We can all use a little improvement, because cloudy seeing, based on fearful projections, preconceptions, instinctual drives, and painful memories is the human condition.

Even Suzuki Roshi was not immune to anxiety and worrisome thoughts. In the midsixties the San Francisco Zen Center bought property in Carmel Valley for a monastery. It would be the only Zen monastery outside of Asia. We purchased the property for a below-market price, but we were faced with a large final balloon payment due in 1972.

Once, shortly after the purchase had been made, I was driving Suzuki and a board member to an engagement. Suzuki surprised me by anxiously declaring he was worried about having money for the balloon payment. The board member replied that he, too, was worried. After a pause, Suzuki Roshi turned to him and said, "Of course, it is already 1972."

So that is the difference that a mature Zen practice makes in one's life. Suzuki was not immune to the natural impulses and worries of the ego, but when they arose, he noticed immediately. He remembered that the future is not separate from the present, and he let go of the anxiety he was projecting. He returned to a place of ease and calm, which is the feeling tone of present-moment vidya.

We all have the potential to be fully present. But it takes time, patience, and a sincere meditation practice. Letting go of anxiety becomes an option only after our mind slows down enough to see the thoughts that sustain it. For the worried board member, a sense of ease seemed out of reach. When Suzuki said it was already 1972, the board member retorted, "It may be for you, but it's not for me."

But let's not put too fine a point on this vidya teaching. Clear seeing also means seeing clearly into our own intrinsic dim-sightedness. Many of the Holocaust survivors Viktor Frankl studied had only a faint sense of what their future might entail. Furthermore, dim-sightedness, or, to use Katagiri's term, dim vision, is also intrinsic within enlightenment. How could it be otherwise? Enlightenment is not a state of going beyond our true nature; it is an authentic expression of who we actually are. Yes, we were enlightened before we were born, but that enlightenment is ever intimate with dim-sightedness.

Remember the verse from "The Sandokai"? "In the light there is darkness, but don't take it as darkness." Don't take it as darkness, because it is just an aspect of human nature. If we condemn our shadow side, we end up back in the Chatterbox Café, experiencing our life as a story narrated by our inner critic.

So moving from avidya to vidya is a matter of penetrating the levels of attention that overlay our natural ability to see clearly. The first is the level of ideas, images, memories, and evaluations. Here is where we spend most, if not all, of our time, squandering our attention on surface-level thinking.

We also have instinctual urges that we're unaware of, and yet they have a lot of force and drive. Below that is the level of our moods, which are subtler and longer lasting. Usually we are unaware that our moods are influencing how we see the world.

Our emotional state is made up of a constellation of feelings paired with our conditioned, instinctual drives. Through meditation we become familiar with these layers and the feeling tones that they arouse in the body. As the mind slows down and clarity arises, the mind naturally frees itself from unwholesome, unhappy states. It happens on its own, because freedom from conditioned processes is a naturally occurring aspect of vidya.

VIDYA AND EMPATHY

One characteristic of a free mind is empathy. We are constantly being presented with opportunities to experience and practice empathy.

Imagine leaving the grocery store with a bag of groceries in each hand. Suddenly, someone knocks into you. Your groceries crash onto the ground, spilling everywhere. You are startled and angry. Then you look up and notice the person who ran into you is blind. What happens? Where does your anger go? When we see that someone is blind, our heart opens up to the person.

But what about all the others who seem to have good eyes but whose hearts and minds are closed? In Buddhist iconography, the key image of someone suffering from avidya is a person with an arrow in his eye. We all have arrows in our eyes. Delusion is the human situation; we all suffer from it, again and again. We cultivate compassion by remembering that within the light there is darkness.

The Buddhist teacher and author Jack Kornfield tells a story about a man in India who was being severely beaten by a gang of thugs. He was on the floor in a state of total surrender, but the beating continued. Suddenly he tapped into something much bigger than himself. He was both inside and outside his body simultaneously. He was both experiencing the beating and also dispassionately observing it.

Then his penetrating consciousness expanded even more. He was the boot kicking his prone body, he was the flecks of green paint flaking off the walls, he was the bleating sound of goats in the distance, and he was the angry thugs giving the beating. There were no divisions or boundaries of any kind. He even passed through the division between life and death—and returned to his original nature. He saw how everything in the natural world is continuously giving birth, expanding, and dying, moment after moment. He was being beaten, but that was just one small dimension of his experience, which was one of great compassion for all beings, because he was not separate from anything else.

Experiences like this one have been repeated over and over, throughout human history. Sekito wrote, "Within the darkness there is light." This light allows us to penetrate to the core of our being, to the core of existence, and see that we are not separate, discrete beings.

In the fifth century, the Theravadin Buddhist monk Buddhaghosa wrote:

Suffering exists, but not the sufferer.
The deed is done, but there is no doer.
Peace exists, but not one who is at peace.
There is no walker, but there is a way.

In my twenties, I became convinced that there is no greater purpose in life than waking up to this huge consciousness. My inmost request went beyond an isolated enlightenment experience. To seek a personal experience can be petty spiritual materialism, which can be as limiting as physical materialism. I wanted to create a life that was beyond the confines of "little Tim." The significance of an awakening experience is that it shifts our orientation. It opens up a path and inspires us to look beyond our noisy thought stream so we can experience life in a new way.

THE SELF AS A SWINGING DOOR

What we call I is just a swinging door, which moves when we inhale and when we exhale.

—SUZUKI ROSHI

A swinging door is easily moved, but it always returns to a position of rest. We are emotional beings; our emotions bring depth and texture to our lives. We are affected by the events that pass through us, but our default position is one of calmness and equanimity. When we cling to our biases or strong opinions, we freeze up in a certain position, without regard to what's actually going on.

When we fixate on the object of our desire, our senses and sensibilities become distorted. We no longer respond to the world as it is but to the world as we *wish* it to be. Equanimity is lost, and without equanimity, clarity is impossible. Everyday life becomes dull and confused. When passing events are not free-flowing, when we cling to a particular thing, life becomes stale. The same thoughts cycle through our mind over and over.

Responding to the world according to a particular thought pattern creates suffering because we aren't responding in a way that's fresh and appropriate. Patterns color our perception. Even if our thinking works out, it is nevertheless demeaned. Each time we resort to patterned thought, we reinforce the pattern—at the expense of the ever-changing reality right in front of us. Patterns arise and take over so quickly that freeing ourselves from them is difficult. As we learn to embrace the unknown, we discover our innate goodness, our so-called buddha nature. This allows us to trust, to stay open to life, and to experience our own aliveness.

My friend Ken is ninety-one years old. He and his wife were living in an assisted living facility. When his wife went blind, Ken moved into the role of caretaker and was completely devoted to her until her death. Shortly after his wife died, Ken's son committed suicide.

When I visited my friend, I expected him to be distraught. I wanted to comfort him in any way I could. He was wealthy, so the facility where he lived was beautiful. But it felt like misery to me. It was sickness, old age, and death.

Ken invited me to stay for lunch. Afterward, he asked if I wanted to go for a walk. I wanted to talk about how he was doing, but he just wanted to go for a walk. I noticed an attentiveness and presence about him, and I was moved by it.

"We'll look at the flowers," he said, urging me to come with him.

Ken could barely walk. He was all bent over, but he didn't seem to mind. We walked along and looked at the flowers without talking. Just to walk and be together was all he seemed to want.

After a while, he said, "Let's stop and look at the sky."

So we stopped and looked at the sky. I regarded Ken for a moment as he gazed at the sky. He was surrounded by sickness, old age, and death, and yet he manifested clarity, stillness, and attentiveness. He had tapped in to his birthright, and there he stood, noble, upright, and accepting.

He helped me to come back to the swinging door. If Ken could be so open and available to life, appreciating the flowers and the sky—so could I.

Suzuki's swinging-door metaphor points to a mind that is boundless. His term was Big Mind, which is our true mind or buddha nature. To experience boundlessness is to experience *mu,* the Japanese word for no-thingness.

One Sunday morning I gave a talk at the Minnesota Zen Meditation Center about this famous Zen koan:

> *A monk asked Zen Master Joshu, "Does a dog have buddha nature?"*
>
> *The master said, "Mu."*

—CASE I, BLUE CLIFF RECORD

Though koans are often worded as questions, they are not meant to be answered; they are meant to be lived. Rather than looking for an answer, we look directly at the koan itself. We may ask, "What is the question really pointing to? How does it relate to my anxiety, to my relationship problems, to my job? What sort of felt sense, or feeling tone, is evoked by it?" Zen students have been known to immerse themselves in a koan like this one for years, just watching their reactions to the inquiry and how their inquiry evolves and deepens.

When I finished my talk on the mu koan, I asked for questions or comments. A guy in the back raised his hand. He said, "I've had my dog for so long he's like my child. And after all these years, there are two things that I know for sure. First, my dog *definitely* has buddha nature. No doubt about it! And second, whether he has buddha nature or not makes no difference to him. *Just throw the ball!*"

Six Persimmons, by Mu Ch'i Fa-Ch'ang, thirteenth century, China.

THREE

Becoming Who We Already Are

THE ZEN TEACHER AND AUTHOR John Daido Loori said that Zen art has one purpose: "to point to the nature of reality." According to Loori, Zen art "suggests a new way of seeing, and a new way of being, that cuts to the core of what it means to be human and fully alive."

In the sixties I frequently became discouraged with my practice. For inspiration, I caught a bus to the de Young Museum in Golden Gate Park, which, in those days, had some of the finest Buddhist art in the Western world. The wonderful spaciousness and immediacy I felt from the Zen paintings lifted my spirits.

Mu Ch'i is one of the best-known Chinese Chan (Zen) painters in the world. With nothing more than six persimmons and a great, spacious background, he depicts a path to openness. When we first begin a Zen practice, our mind is so full of personal opinions, prejudices, and ideals that light can't penetrate it. With practice we begin to empty out, becoming more transparent to the world as it actually is rather than how we think it is or want it to be.

Suzuki told a story about two professors who visited a Zen master. The professors were full of ideas and opinions about Zen. When tea was served, the master began to pour the tea, slowly and attentively. But when the cup was full, he continued to pour. Tea overflowed onto the table.

One professor exclaimed, "Stop! Look what you're doing . . . the cup is overflowing!" Calmly, the Zen master continued to pour.

The second professor cried, "You're spilling tea on everything!"

"Yes," the master said calmly. "The tea is overflowing onto everything, just as your mind is spilling over and contaminating everything. If you want to experience Zen, you must *empty* your cup."

In Buddhism, emptiness refers to a mind that is open and receptive to whatever is happening. In Mu Ch'i's painting, the two transparent persimmons depict emptiness. They are completely permeable to the surrounding light. According to D. T. Suzuki, "Zen art is meant to train the mind, to bring it into full contact with ultimate reality." By observing our ideas, concepts, and opinions as they arise during meditation, we begin to empty our cup and bring our mind into full contact with ultimate reality.

But an empty cup doesn't make us feel very secure.

BEING AT HOME WITH INSECURITY

There is a famous Zen story about Emperor Wu of the Liang Dynasty in China and a legendary, cave-dwelling Indian monk named Bodhidharma, an intimidating figure with red hair, a red beard, and bulging eyes. He is credited with the emergence of Zen in China.

Emperor Wu was a devout Buddhist who meditated regularly and devoted a lot of resources to Buddhist temples and monasteries. His reign was a golden age for Chinese Buddhism. The emperor wanted to be recognized for his dedication to Buddhism, so he sent for the great Bodhidharma.

As Bodhidharma stood before him, the emperor asked his burning question, "What is the significance of all I have done?"

Bodhidharma growled, "No significance!"

The need for recognition stems from deep feelings of unworthiness. Poor Emperor Wu—with all his power, he felt unworthy.

In the previous chapter I talked about the levels of attention that limit our ability to see clearly. The attitude of unworthiness arises from the deepest level, and it afflicts even the most powerful and influential. Bodhidharma saw that Emperor Wu was missing the essence of life, because he was driven by his need for approval.

Emperor Wu was looking to Bodhidharma for endorsement; Bodhidharma was offering him something of far greater value.

But the emperor did not understand. He was crushed by Bodhidharma's rejection after all he had done to promote Buddhism. "What is the first principle of your holy teaching?" the emperor implored. He was wondering, *If your first principle isn't creating temples and striving for enlightenment, what is it?*

Bodhidharma said, "A vast emptiness—with nothing holy about it."

This is one of the most repeated stories in Zen. "A vast emptiness with nothing holy about it" is the core of Zen thought. And it paved the way for a radical transformation of "religious" art. In Mu Ch'i's *Persimmons,* religious life is depicted without any religious symbols at all—no buddhas, bodhisattvas (enlightened beings), or any other celestial beings; no heavens or hells; no paradise scenes; and no mandalas. Just simple, unadorned, everyday objects.

But it was not a mere change in symbols, replacing buddhas with persimmons; this exchange between Emperor Wu and Bodhidharma represents a fundamental shift in Buddhist thought. Early Buddhism had little appreciation for nature. It focused on transcending nature. Bodhidharma's teaching, "A vast emptiness with nothing holy about it" cultivated the ground for a fusion with nature.

"Nothing holy about it" says, don't go searching for buddha nature anywhere else. The truth right before your eyes is all that exists. If your practice is about being holy, you are missing out on life. Don't try to be a good Buddhist. We were all enlightened before we were born. Just be who you already are. Let go of any ideas about lacking something or attaining something. How could we possibly be more than what we are already? There isn't any more. Nada, nada, nada, nada.

By contrast, the concept of holiness is just a convention to help us feel secure in an insecure world. But security is a delusion. Buddha said that one moment of clarity is better than a hundred years of delusion. If we want to experience clarity, we have to accept the truth of insecurity. We live in a world that is ever changing.

Mu Ch'i's six persimmons are surrounded by nothing but open space, yet they are upright and stable. Where does this stability come from? Not knowing where our support comes from creates a sense of vulnerability—but clearly, the persimmons are supported by some unseen something. We don't know what; we will never know; it's unknowable. By letting go of our ideas of being holy, we cultivate a capacity to be at home with insecurity. Without the pretense of holiness, we learn to trust.

Suzuki said, "Enlightenment is an accident. Zen practice makes us accident-prone." Over the years, I have come to appreciate this saying more and more. It points to an attitude based on trust—not trust in any particular entity or process, but unconditional trust that is not contingent on anything. We can tap in to this trust, but we cannot own it. It is not *my* trust or *your* trust; it is just trust in the basic goodness of the universe, from which we are not separate.

Trust in our basic goodness is foundational in Buddhist thought. It sets Buddhism apart from other major religions. In Buddhism no intermediaries are required to bridge the gap caused by sinfulness, because there is no gap to bridge, and no sin—only suffering and the causes of suffering. Even suffering is a part of our basic goodness. It brings us into direct contact with reality, cultivates compassion, and builds great inner strength when we deal with suffering skillfully.

OUR MISTAKES ARE IT

In order to paint bamboo, you must study bamboo for many years. Then you completely forget bamboo and paint it in an instant.

—ONE OF MU CH'I'S DISCIPLES

Zen painting is based on years of rigorous practice. Yet the style is free and spontaneous because Zen painting is not about meticulous, academic rigor or following precise rules. For a Zen painter, the practice is to still and focus the mind. A painter may take hours to still her mind. When she is ready, she paints the image within minutes.

When we completely forget ourselves and delve wholeheartedly into our activity, we don't become frozen by our mistakes and shortcomings. In Zen painting there's no going back to correct mistakes and no expectations of outcome. Expectations come from small mind, which could never create something as spacious, simple, and ordinary as Mu Ch'i's *Persimmons*, because small mind wants to be special.

If you make a mistake, the mistake is it. Dogen said, "A Zen master's life is one mistake after another." To draw lines around our mistakes and try to exclude them is delusion. In the wholeness of life, everything is included. If it's a ripe persimmon, enjoy the wonderful flavor. If it's a green persimmon, let it be green. If it's a rotting persimmon, enjoy the worms.

I inhabit a rotten persimmon right here, in this rotting-persimmon body of mine. I experience it every morning when I wake up, and some mornings I can't even get out of bed. Over the past few years, I've seen a dozen doctors about this rotting persimmon, and they can't figure out why it's rotting. I hate this delightful persimmon!

Yet right here, in this rotting persimmon, is a vast spaciousness. My opportunity to practice is not anywhere else but here. Can I be intimate with it? Can I open up to it? Buddha said that suffering and joy are not separate. Our joy is always right where we are, worms and all. The worms are painful, but they're *alive*. I have to appreciate each one of my moments, right here in this body that is constantly changing, getting soft, and bruising—it seems to be melting away, moment by moment. Can I stay right here with it? Am I willing to feel each sensation vividly? This is where my life is. Only here.

When Suzuki Roshi was in the last stages of cancer, he said, "I feel like I am being tortured." Yet he refused to medicate himself. He wanted to be fully alive, in whatever form that aliveness took.

Buddha said, "Good in the beginning; good in the middle; good in the end." Before we think, before we divide things up into good and bad, fair and not fair, right and wrong, there is wholeness, even in a rotting persimmon. Especially then. Because when you inhabit a rotting persimmon, there's a great appreciation for life.

The myth around Mu Ch'i is that he did zazen his whole life, without pause. Well, I don't know about that . . . but the truth the myth points to is one of deep sincerity, earnestness of practice, and resiliency. If you want to paint persimmons, you start by copying persimmons, over and over and over. If you want a sincere Zen practice, you start by coming to your cushion, over and over and over. You do it with earnestness, even though it doesn't feel earnest at first. If your mind didn't race around while you were trying to meditate, how would you learn to bring it back to the present moment?

It's the nature of the mind to judge, compare, and complain. It's the purpose of Zen meditation to experience the mind's gyrations directly. When we turn the mind back onto itself, it starts to slow down on its own. It becomes focused and concentrated. We do it by bringing ourselves back, again and again, with kind, patient attention. Without kindness and patience, the mind will never settle down.

When I first began my Zen practice, every time I sat down on the cushion, my mind shifted into high gear. One morning I shared my frustration with Suzuki Sensei. I asked for a technique to slow down my racing mind.

He said, "A busy mind is no problem. Just sit, Tim. That is all."

"Should I repeat something to myself?" I asked, thinking maybe a mantra of some kind might help.

"No, no, no. Just sit."

"But shouldn't I do something with my mind?"

"No, no. Just come sit with me," he repeated gently.

"Can't you give me some books to read?"

He shot me a puzzled look. "Why would you want to read a book?"

"Well, how often should I sit?"

"Every morning and every night."

"*Every morning and every night?!* And there's no *how*?!"

After I'd been with him for several months, Suzuki asked if I would help him start a sitting group in my hometown of Palo Alto. I was happy to do it. I found some grad students willing to let us use their house. Then I began spreading the word that a Zen master would come weekly to instruct us in meditation.

The first morning, there were about three or four of us when Suzuki arrived before dawn. After meditation he gave a short talk, and then he leaped up, rolled up his sleeves, and started cleaning the house. We cleaned while the guys who lived there slept—and for the first time, I actually enjoyed washing dishes.

Suzuki emphasized *no gap* between sitting meditation and working. So this became the routine. Every week we would do zazen and then clean the house.

After a while, cleaning the house became a chore. One morning I ventured a complaint: "We can't clean the house; we're students. We have classes to get to."

Suzuki replied, "Then we'll have to start earlier."

Shortly thereafter, I mentioned that I'd like to become a priest. Suzuki said, "Okay . . . but you seem to favor zazen over cleaning the floor. You'll never be a priest as long as you favor zazen over cleaning."

His point was that if you wholeheartedly clean the floor, it is zazen. There is no difference. Everyday life is Zen. Giving ourselves to something concrete, like physical labor, joins us to the world. Zen is about completely giving ourselves, and then there's no difference between work and zazen, or between work and play.

Every week Suzuki came to the new sitting group in Palo Alto, even though there were never more than three or four people present. Finally, I put a small announcement in the *Palo Alto Times*. That week a dozen people showed up. After Suzuki gave his talk, I raised my hand and asked if he would say more about how to do meditation. He had given instruction about posture and demonstrated the specific way we hold our hands, called the cosmic mudra, but nothing about what to do with the mind. I wanted him to offer a technique for calming the mind, like following the breath.

He replied that he could say nothing about it because it wasn't something that could be explained. He said that any technique would "miss the mark."

"Could you say something about breathing and following the breath?" I said.

"Breath breathes, Tim," he said, sharply.

Suzuki was generally not comfortable giving techniques, which he referred to disparagingly as "stepladder Zen." When we are given a technique, the practice becomes the perfection of a technique. But his metaphor about the swinging door was essentially a technique that involved following the breath. On occasion he suggested we might even count our breath. But his favorite technique was no technique. Just to sit and be open to whatever comes up is zazen. If we can do that with every breath, without even thinking about it, resiliency is cultivated. Zazen is the actualization of availability, openness, and resiliency.

"Breath breathes, Tim," was the only time Suzuki ever called me on the carpet. And it was the last time I asked him for a technique.

The next week the group shrank to our original three or four. I was annoyed with Suzuki. But gradually the group grew. One morning a woman named Marian Derby joined us. She started coming every week, and we became pretty good friends. The group, which later became the Haiku Zendo, eventually moved into Marian's garage in the neighboring town of Los Altos. Marian began to tape Suzuki's weekly talks, and later she transcribed them. These transcriptions became the first draft of *Zen Mind, Beginner's Mind.*

WHOLEHEARTED ENGAGEMENT

"Breath breathes" because when we are wholeheartedly engaged, there is no separation between the doer and the deed. If our full concentration is on the breath, there is only breathing. In wholehearted zazen, there is only zazen. Zazen does zazen. Dogen called this kind of absorption "the dropping away of body and mind."

For Zen painters, the dropping away of body and mind is the essential point of practice. A few years ago, I had an interesting conversation with Bob Jacobsen, the Asian art curator for the Minneapolis Institute of Arts. He shared his insight about Zen painters:

> Zen paintings were done as a practice. But it was not practice to gain a skill. They practiced to clear the mind and to focus on clarity of thought. For the Zen practitioner, painting was a direct avenue to the heart and mind. What makes a Zen painting successful is that it breaks through the exterior of its object. It goes beyond mere appearance to harmony and balance, to the heart and essence of the objects being depicted.

In Zen we practice meditation daily, and periodically we immerse ourselves through retreats. We tend to think the Zen way is exotic. But actually, the idea of wholehearted engagement or total immersion in each activity is not that foreign to the Western way of thinking. When I was in the eighth grade, I took a

Spanish class. The teacher said that to learn Spanish we would have to practice daily and periodically immerse ourselves. So I tried to practice every day. And several times I immersed myself by going to Mexico. But I went with my family, so I only partially immersed myself.

Many years later, my wife and I signed up for a Spanish immersion program. For ten days we lived with a Guatemalan family and were tutored separately for six hours a day. My tutor was a teenage boy from rural Guatemala. The assignment was to talk, one-to-one, with a teenager who spoke no English for six hours every day.

I neither heard nor spoke a word of English. But still, it didn't feel as if I were soaking Spanish in. Until the night before we left. That night I had a dream, and in it everyone spoke Spanish. I knew it was finally getting inside me. If something sinks down into your dream world, your whole life is affected—no doubt about it.

An opening was created by the immersion. Does that mean I can now speak fluent Spanish? Not at all. The next day we left. My interest in Spanish waned. Without persistence and wholehearted effort, we will always fall back on our old patterns.

Immersion is central to Zen practice. When we are fully engaged in an activity, we don't feel isolated and alone. With wholehearted engagement, we feel our connectedness; our dynamic, undivided nature is being manifested through activity. When I was fully engaged, I even felt a connection with a teenage boy from Guatemala whom I barely understood.

When we are sitting zazen, on the outside it doesn't look very dynamic. We are just sitting still and doing nothing. But wholehearted zazen is done with the whole body and the whole mind; every cell is doing zazen. Just seeing our thoughts and stories without believing them or suppressing them, just feeling our sensations and emotions without reacting to them, is possibly the most arduous thing for a human being to do. We are fully engaged in the activity of inner transformation.

The old Greek myth of Sisyphus is a good example of how isolating and miserable life becomes when we split our self off from our activity. Sisyphus angered the gods. As punishment, he was forever doomed to push a boulder up a mountain, allow it to roll back down, and then push it to the top again. This myth exemplifies the philosophy of three renowned existentialists: Søren Kierkegaard, Jean-Paul Sartre, and Albert Camus. It was also my father's philosophy. According to these guys, it is the human condition to struggle perpetually in hopelessness and despair.

Suzuki had a different take on life. One of his great loves was working with stones. At our monastery in Carmel Valley, during spring and summer, Suzuki gathered stones and used them to build walls. The big guys got to help, but I'm not a big guy, so I was always assigned some other duty—like taking out the garbage.

In Carmel Valley winter is the rainy season, so much of their spring and summer work was washed away by torrential rains. But Suzuki was never deterred. As soon as spring came, he was back out there moving stones. Whenever he could get away with it, he didn't even take the time to change clothes. It was a game between Suzuki and his wife. If Mitsu came along while Suzuki was working in his robes, he would step behind a tree or a boulder. If she saw him, she would say, "No, no, no. Change!" And then off he would go to change into his work clothes.

One day I watched as they worked on a wall along a shallow embankment. Suzuki was at the top of the hill pushing a large stone. Suddenly, he slipped and started rolling down the hill.

I thought, "Oh, no; he's old. He's frail. He'll be hurt. Oh, my!"

Down, down, down he rolled. When he finally got to the bottom, he leaped to his feet, dusted off his robes, and smiled.

"Just like a stone," he said.

TWO PITFALLS ALONG THE WAY

When trying to cultivate a Zen life, there are a couple of pitfalls to be aware of. The first is fear of intimacy. About twenty years ago, I started going to homeless camps with my friend Peter. Like many of those in the camps, Peter suffered from depression. He had difficulty sleeping, so he would go to the camps and help out however he could.

Peter told me two things about being in the camps: dress down and pay attention. And then, he said, just be with the folks; just hang out. If they offer cold coffee, take it. If their hands look cold, offer mittens. But if they reject them, don't make a big deal out of it.

For Peter, going to the camps was just something he did. He wasn't trying to be a Good Samaritan or do anything special. He was just visiting people who were suffering, whom he had great compassion for and who happened to live outside. So when it was cold, he brought mittens. If they were thirsty, he offered water. I never saw any self-consciousness or self-importance in Peter. Intimacy with his activity seemed to bubble up naturally from his humility and compassion. In the camps his depression was not a problem because he wasn't even thinking of Peter.

The other pitfall is intrusion of belief. We get thrown off balance so quickly when we glom on to beliefs that have been passed down to us. Often our most deeply held beliefs began as practical solutions to specific problems that no longer exist.

One afternoon a stray cat had the good fortune of being taken in by a guru who lived in an ashram. But during evening worship, the cat got in the way and distracted the worshippers. So the guru made a leash from a short rope. During the evening liturgy, the cat was tethered to a nearby post to keep him from disturbing the worshippers.

This went on for years. After the guru died, his disciples continued to keep the cat on the leash during worship. When the cat died, another cat was brought in and duly tied to the post each evening. Centuries later, treatises were written by scholarly disciples on the liturgical significance of having a properly tied cat during evening worship.

We all have cats tied to our altars, or in our basements or attics. I was raised as a Unitarian, so my cats are not tied to religious accoutrements. They are tied to cultural norms such as social status, gender roles, achievement, intellectual pursuits, and the like. The particular brand of our deeply held beliefs isn't important. When our biases lock us into a fabricated way of seeing and responding to life, they rob us of our spontaneity and aliveness.

In Buddhist mythology, the robber of life is Mara, the evil one. There's a story about Mara and his two attendants, whom I'll call Mayhem and Confusion. As they travel through a village, they come across a monk who is walking along in a very meditative state. His eyes are cast downward and his face is aglow. Confusion asks Mara what the man is seeing.

"A piece of truth," Mara says calmly.

"Doesn't it bother you when someone finds a piece of truth, O Evil One?" Mayhem asks.

"No," Mara replies. "Right after this, they usually make a belief out of it."

Freedom comes when we let go of our beliefs and undo the patterns that keep us from being intimate with life. We all have patterns—those that are imposed on us and those that we habituate ourselves to.

At Stanford my fraternity friends wondered what happened to their old drinking buddy. Not only did I swear off alcohol, but I also left the fraternity and moved into a small dressing room behind my parents' swimming pool. It was a tiny room, barely big enough for the single bed and desk I crammed into it. I thought the move would help me break my old patterns and foster my new meditation practice. I covered the mirror with a towel. I wanted to focus on inner transformation rather than the small ego self that I presented to the world.

It wasn't just my drinking buddies who wondered what was going on with me. My parents wanted their high-achieving son back. I'm from a long line of high achievers. My grandfather and both of my parents graduated from Stanford. My father was a lawyer and my grandfather a California Supreme Court judge. I was the first child and the first grandchild, so it was a given that I would graduate from Stanford, then go on to law school, like my father and my grandfather. Or as my father often suggested, I might prefer to become a doctor like my uncle. When he saw both of these possibilities slip away, he beseeched my mother to talk to me about at least becoming a dentist.

I graduated from Stanford and then took a job as a mail handler at the San Francisco Post Office. I worked in a basement a few blocks away from my father's high-rise corporate office. After the mail-handling job, I worked in a cannery and then a plant nursery.

The counterculture movement of the sixties was about getting back to the basics. It rejected the constant striving, materialism, and values of our parents and grandparents. At its core, the counterculture was a reorientation toward letting go of fixed ideas and accepting life's uncertainties. We celebrated life rather than things.

In my heart I'm still a counterculture guy. But I've learned to appreciate the values of others. And to see the limitations of all tightly held beliefs, including my own.

TOO MUCH EMPTINESS, A CUP OF TEA, AND FINDING A GOOD SEAT

After an eight-week retreat at our monastery in Carmel Valley, which was named Tassajara Zen Mountain Monastery, I returned to San Francisco and immediately took a bus to the de Young Museum. I was still in the afterglow of the long retreat. In a meditative state, I walked through the museum slowly, soaking it all in as I made my way to the Asian section.

When I came to the first Buddha statue, I stopped—or rather, I was stopped by it, captivated by the peaceful expression that seemed to mirror what I was feeling inside. I felt an incredible stillness emanating from it. When I looked into the Buddha's eyes, they seemed to open up into pure space. It felt as if I were teetering on the edge of something. Instinctively, I turned away.

But just a few feet away, there was another statue. Its eyes were also like deep holes into no-thingness. Again I turned away. But the statues were everywhere. Infinitely vacant eyes were everywhere. I was overwhelmed and, by now, completely disoriented. With difficulty I managed to get back to the bus.

Still disoriented, I headed straight for the Zen center. I stumbled up the stairs and plopped down on the couch in Suzuki's office. He greeted me in a friendly but mildly concerned manner, and then asked what was going on. I told him about the statues. The spaciousness emanating from their eyes had pierced me to my core. There were no thoughts bubbling up in my mind. My body felt awkward, unable to adjust to the sudden shift.

"Which statues?" Suzuki asked, which seemed totally irrelevant, but I told him where I had been in the museum and described the statues I saw there.

"Let's have a cup of tea," he said.

. . .

There is an ancient Buddhist saying: "In a single blade of grass, the universe reveals itself."

This saying points to a profound truth about the two realities we live within: relative reality, which is the ordinary world, and absolute or ultimate reality, the unknown and unknowable.

An intrinsic continuity exists between the relative and the absolute. They are not separate. Without that continuity, there would be no path and no possibility of experiencing our own buddha nature.

Because of continuity, the symbol becomes the symbolized. My friend Andrea Martin, who edited Katagiri Roshi's book *Each Moment Is the Universe*, said, "A metaphor is only a metaphor until you actually experience it. Then it's no longer just a metaphor."

All that's required for a symbol to open up into a profound realization is a still mind and an open heart. But this is not an easy path or a quick fix. It takes years of sincere practice to develop a good seat, the ability to still our body and mind. As my own students struggle to cultivate a good seat, they come to me with the same questions I had. Mostly I offer the same reassurance Suzuki offered me: Just sit.

Suzuki Roshi resisted techniques because we attach to them. However, techniques can also be helpful, especially in the beginning but also in times of emotional or mental distress. I encourage my students to be familiar with all the tools in the Buddhist tool bag and to use techniques whenever they need support. It doesn't matter which you choose—a mantra, counting your breath, using a *mala,* or visualizing a mandala. Whatever technique you choose, I recommend you stay with it. Settle into it. Trust it. When our practice is sincere, the mind slows down on its own. Guaranteed.

As Katagiri Roshi said:

The first point is that we have to practice. And then right in the process of practice, the huge universe moves and a magnanimous world comes up. Pop!

In part 1 of this book, we have focused on the three major components of a sincere commitment: inspiration, aspiration, and attitude. In part 2 we are summoned to a serious investigation of the phenomenon we call the self. As long as an isolated self exists, fear exists, and a need for protection. By looking directly at that which gives rise to the notion of me, myself, and mine, we see the fictional nature of an abiding self—and start to move beyond it.

PART TWO

Calling in the Shards

WE START WITH THE SELF

FOUR

To Study Buddhism
Is to Study the Self

WHEN OUR ANCESTORS LOOKED into the night sky, they were captivated by the heroes and villains who lived there. They traced lines around star clusters to create wonderful stories; told them, over and over; and then passed them down, generation by generation.

To this day, we look into the night sky and tell our children about the Great Bear, Ursa Major, who was grabbed up by a mighty king, swung round and round by the tail, and then flung into the sky to circle the Arctic forever. Perhaps we tell them he is being chased by three fearless hunters.

Ursa Major is prominent in the northern hemisphere, but the constellation Orion can be seen from all over the world. It is the most recognizable constellation in the night sky. Perhaps you know Orion as a great hunter. Over his left arm hangs a lion's skin for a shield. In his right hand he wields his unbreakable club. He is locked in battle against his eternal enemy Taurus, the mighty bull, with splendid long horns and fire darting out from his eye. Huddled behind Taurus are the Pleiades, the Seven Sisters, distraught and frightened.

However, if you live in the Middle East, you might point to Orion and tell stories about his adventures as a heavenly shepherd. In some European tales, he is a magic archer. The Vedic hymns of ancient India know him as Mriga, the Deer, who is surrounded by hunting dogs.

What stories we tell! Constellations are just stars, and stars are just whirling clouds of cosmic dust at very high temperatures. Most constellations are made up of smaller constellations, which in turn are made up of still smaller ones.

We know that the stories we tell about the stars are just fabrications. But what if someone said that *you* are just a fabrication?

According to Buddha, the world we live in and we ourselves are just whirling clouds of dust, completely unpredictable and ultimately unknowable. We are made up of constellations that are themselves made up of smaller constellations. Ultimately, we are composed of what appear to be isolated, elemental materials that are definitely not us—things like hydrogen, carbon, and oxygen atoms and the complex molecules they form. Buddhism teaches that we are a fabrication of the mind—and like the Great Bear and the hunter Orion, our world is made of stories.

SEEING THE FICTIONAL SELF

How lovely!
Through the torn paper screen,
the Milky Way.

—ISSA, BUDDHIST PRIEST, EIGHTEENTH CENTURY

Buddha saw *through* the screen we call a self. He saw that this fictional self was actually a constellation made up of five components he called *skandha*s, a Sanskrit word that translates as "aggregates" or "bundles." These five components are form, sensation, perception, impulse, and consciousness, or thought. Together they make up the self.

Bringing these components into our awareness is a key practice in Buddhism. When we bring the skandhas into view, we begin to see *through* them, as Buddha did, and see that we ourselves construct our experiences by the stories we tell about what happens to us.

We start by breaking our experience down into the five components. Here's a simple example.

My wife and I adopted a homeless kitten. He was not tame. One morning I awoke to the kitten pouncing onto my bare calf. It was fur, teeth, and claws attached to my leg.

The first skandha is form—my leg. The second skandha is sensation, which was a constellation of pain. The third skandha is perception: I had a fleeting perception of a ball of fur flying through the air and clamping down on my calf. The fourth is impulse. My impulse was to toss it off. And the fifth skandha is thought, the weaving together of a story: *It was a mistake to get a homeless cat. We should have gotten a tame cat. This cat will never warm up to us. This is my wife's fault! Why did she have to choose a feral cat?* On and on and on our stories go, creating dramas and squandering our attention on the fictional self.

In Buddhism we bring the five skandhas into our awareness, one at a time, to see them clearly. By looking carefully and attentively at each star in the constellation, we become less reactive. Our mind starts to slow down. Rather than despair over our sensations and perceptions, we begin to appreciate how bright and wonderful they are.

My perception of the kitten leaping into the air was vivid and clear, but immediately I went into a big trip about it. The fifth skandha, thought, is quick to trip out over things and refocus our attention toward the fictional self and all its travails. Our storytelling mind jumps in so fast that we're barely even aware of the first three skandhas.

In Buddhism, when we talk about direct experience, or immediacy, we are referring to the first three skandhas, to form, sensation, and perception. The last two are also important. Yet they become reactionary overlays, intermediaries, and it is here that we spend most of our time, squandering and scattering our attention.

In Zen practice we cultivate the ability to stay with our immediate experience. We do it by watching our minds and seeing how we spend so much of our time reviewing, regretting, and rehearsing. As soon as I saw the kitten leap onto my leg, I started reviewing how she was a homeless kitty and regretting that we'd chosen her. In another second, I would have been rehearsing how I might convince my wife to take her back. But I caught myself, and instead I just let it go.

A WONDERFUL/HORRIBLE GATEWAY

A commitment to Zen practice is made with every cell in the body, in the heart, and in the mind. Our commitment is to see through our constricting ego shell so we can open up to this oceanic life, with all its color, form, and sound. It is not about getting something or becoming someone different; it's about manifesting who we already are. We're not trying to get something, because there's nothing to get. We are *already* all that there is, all that exists. If we try to get it, we will miss it our whole life.

Our commitment is to open up to whatever arises. But this opening up is very subtle. An awareness of the feeling tone associated with opening up is cultivated over time—it takes patience. And courage.

For some practitioners there are two phases to this process. The first is about settling in, and it may be quite pleasant. As we settle in to a regular meditation practice, there is more bodily awareness, more awareness of breathing; some moments of real calmness occur, along with the realization that we can be calm regardless of what's going on. We begin to feel comfortable in our meditation and in daily life. Concentration becomes steady, and the ability to stay with the breath brings confidence. Posture improves. The mind still chatters, but it doesn't dominate quite so much. We feel lighter, less burdened.

As our thoughts slow down we may enter a second phase. A sense of separation and loneliness seeps into our awareness. Comfort vanishes. Anxiety bubbles up, and we begin to experience more psychic pain than we had before. We may even blame the teacher. We may want to find a new teacher. This can be a difficult time for both teacher and student. It is painful to lose a student just when his or her practice is beginning to yield something deeply significant.

Koan 16 in the *Blue Cliff Record* (a book of one hundred koans) compares the ego shell to an eggshell. The student is inside, pecking to get out, while the teacher taps from the outside. The metaphor is a very old one that helps us disidentify with the egoic thoughts and emotions that have always defined us.

Phase two can be disorienting. It is *meant* to disorient, so we can reorient to a self that is not contained within a rigid ego shell. This transformative stage is always marked by difficulty.

When students come to me and say, "My practice is going great. It's wonderful." I say, "Oh? That's good."

When they come to me and say their practice is going fine, I say, "That's good."

But when they come to me and say their practice is hard, that sometimes they think about quitting, I say, "That's great! Tell me more about it." As a teacher, this is where my job begins. The student is beginning to peck the shell.

It's painful to recognize that you're confined to a limited and constricted space, one that lacks abiding joy and spiritual freedom. To move through the pain, first you have to get very close to it. This is what's referred to as pecking the shell. As a teacher, my job is to help you stay with your difficulty and experience it fully without pulling back into the shell. Feeling our pain is essential, but when we feel it with our kind attention and with compassion, we do not suffer.

In Zen practice, we learn how to relax into whatever is happening, even our pain. We relax and release, over and over. With each release, our heart opens.

Openness is the heart's natural state. The shell is just a human fabrication, like the lines we draw around star clusters. The lines we draw in the sky impose a structure. The lines we draw around ourselves give us a feeling of security. But it is security based on fear. Fear creates rigidity and limitations. It isolates nation-states, religions, and families and creates a personal rather than a universal sense of self.

As long as we cling to that narrow space, our mind is not yet the way-seeking mind. We are not yet coming from a deep longing. Zen practice is not a trick we can figure out. Without sincerity, we spend our lives trapped within the ego shell. The shell may feel as impenetrable as steel or cement because it comes from our desire to be secure, to be loved, and to be successful. But actually, it is made from mere thought. How impenetrable can it be?

BECOMING DISENCHANTED WITH OUR IMAGE

In Greek mythology, Narcissus was the son of Cephisus, a river god, and a nymph named Liriope. He was a beautiful and proud hunter, but he wasn't very nice. To punish him for the way he treated those who loved him, Nemesis, goddess of revenge, lured him to a pond where he saw his own lovely reflection. Immediately, he became transfixed, turning his head this way and that, posing and posturing, interacting with his own image. He became so enchanted with himself he couldn't leave the pond.

Narcissus, whose name means "sleep" or "numbness," isn't a faraway mythological figure who has nothing to do with us. He is a universal archetype, an aspect of every human being. We are all fixated on the image we project onto the world. This is the human situation. As long as we are fixated on the small ego self, we miss out on the unbounded life going on around us and through us every moment.

In America, most of us who practice Zen are doing it because we have become disenchanted in some way. We were not born into Buddhism. Nor are there any cultural benefits to being a Buddhist—no power, status, or networking opportunities. Disenchantment is often thought of in a negative way because we like being enchanted. We go to great lengths to experience enchantment. But from an Eastern point of view, disenchantment is not negative.

In Sufism, there is a saying:

> Those that make you return for whatever reason to the spirit, be grateful to them.
> Worry about the others who give you delicious comfort that keeps you from prayer.

Delicious comfort is pretty nice. And it's fine to enjoy our comforts. After all, Buddhism is often described as the middle way; it isn't the way of asceticism. But too much comfort becomes an enchantment. In our consumer society, we are enchanted with materialism and celebrity. In other cultures, people are enchanted with gurus, martyrs, or royalty.

When I was three years old, I attended a progressive preschool in Berkeley where I was given an IQ test. The test labeled me as gifted. My parents were proud of me, and it felt good to make my parents proud. It was enchanting for me. When we are three years old, we believe what we are told. Buddhism teaches that we are imprisoned by what we believe about ourselves.

When I entered the first grade and didn't make it into the first reading group, I was confused. I began to feel the gap created by the label. It's incredibly painful to feel the gap between what we think we should be and what we appear to be. Labels convince us that we should be someone better, smarter, more ambitious, more disciplined. When we try to live up to a label, we lose our spontaneous joy of living. I worked hard to get into the first reading group so my parents would be proud. Before long I was promoted.

Typically, what follows enchantment is depression. I didn't think of myself as being depressed, but looking back I recognize that I suffered from depression throughout adolescence. In the eighth grade, I got my first bad report card. When school let out that day, I rode my bike to a nearby hotel and started up the dimly lit stairwell. I intended to jump off the balcony—because I had failed to live up to a label. I didn't really *want* to jump—and, anyway, the hotel was only about five stories high. But the pain felt inescapable. It was caused by a label.

Labels are inflexible. They drain away our humanity and the simple joy of being alive. Even positive labels like "gifted" can freeze us up, perpetuate fearfulness, and make us feel isolated and constrained. Through a regular meditation practice, we start to see the incredible complexity and rigidity of the ego, which is composed of an array of labels that make up our self-image. The Buddhist path is about going *beyond* our ideas about who we are. Disenchantment can be the beginning of going beyond.

SEEING THROUGH OUR STORY LINES

Once there was a young turkey living happily on a sunny organic farm. He spent his days scratching around in the dirt and roaming freely in his large, well-kept pen. He was fed only the best food and all his needs were provided for by the kind and compassionate farmer. The turkey lived a carefree life of ease and comfort. Life felt predictable, structured, and safe.

So what kind of prediction might this turkey make about his future? And what happens when the season of Thanksgiving and Christmas rolls around?

This story depicts two conflicting narratives. There's the turkey's narrative, one of predictability, structure, and safety—and then there's the farmer's narrative. The turkey can point to several obvious truths to validate his narrative, but in the end which narrative prevails?

This story is told by author Nassim Nicholas Taleb to demonstrate how we construct stories around facts and then fit new facts into our old stories.

Suzuki Roshi said, rather than seeing the world as we wish it to be, it's important that we accommodate ourselves to the world as it actually is. Often we don't do this. Instead, we try to fit the world into our stories, ignoring what doesn't fit and emphasizing what does. According to Taleb, we create narratives because we prefer a world that is predictable, structured, and safe. So we use our storytelling minds to create one. Taleb coined the phrase "narrative fallacy."

Taleb is not a Zen practitioner. His scholarly work focuses on randomness, probability, and uncertainty. His modern education and training have led him to the same conclusion Buddha came to more than twenty-five hundred years ago.

Paradoxically, the more we learn, the more wedded we become to our narrative fallacy. That's because we tend to rely on sources that support our beliefs. I get my news from Amy Goodman, a progressive broadcast personality. One of my colleagues watches the ultraconservative Rush Limbaugh. My "facts" come from Amy; his from Rush. The more we learn, the more justified we feel, because our facts reinforce our narrative. Problems arise because we concentrate on the things we know but fail to take into consideration the things we don't know. We are conditioned to simplify, categorize, and narrate instead of going beyond what we "know."

In ancient Hinduism, a *sannyasin* is a holy person. If a sannyasin broke his arm, he would go into a cave and meditate on the causes and conditions that led to his broken arm. He would review everything he'd done or not done until he could determine what bad karma had caused his misfortune. A sannyasin had the ability to remember past lives, so if he couldn't find anything in this lifetime, he would search previous ones. This was his belief, his narrative.

Our narrative becomes our identity. It arises from our sense of self, and once arisen, it defines us. So the stories we tell and our sense of an abiding self perpetuate each other. Sure, dwelling on karma promotes ethical behavior (as does fear of going to hell), but it goes against fundamental Buddhist thought. Buddha taught that everything is the cause of everything else, and everything is the effect of everything else. It's hard to develop a narrative about that. It's certainly not a narrative that makes us feel secure or gives us a sense of control. But this is the teaching of Buddhism. As practitioners, we do our best to wrap our minds around it and to live in accordance with it.

Toward the end of 1965, I had been practicing with Suzuki for almost two years. We sat zazen together. We did retreats together. I taxied him around. He always treated me well and was always very supportive and available.

After much thought and consideration, I decided to commit my life to Zen. I wanted to be ordained as a Zen priest and study under Suzuki Roshi. In Zen, ordination is the beginning of many years of rigorous, formal training.

I went into Suzuki's office, told him my heart's desire, and asked him to ordain me. I stressed how important Zen was to me and that I wanted to spend my life helping people experience a little calmness, a little peace in their lives.

He seemed pleased. We set a time to discuss it further. He even suggested I bring Linda, my fiancée, because ordination is a lifetime commitment and family support is important.

A few days later, the three of us sat in Suzuki's office. Linda and I were on the couch across from Suzuki. He asked a few questions and was very friendly and sweet, as he always was. There was nothing in his words or his demeanor to foreshadow the decision that I am certain he had already made.

In the end, he said, "You are very young, and I am very old." He explained that he would not be ordaining me.

What a shock! I was wedded to the idea of being ordained and working closely with Suzuki in a more structured and serious way. I had wedded myself to an image that had emerged from the narrative that I was telling myself. But the narrative had nothing to do with the uncertainty of reality. What if my aspiration to help people had been tied to this narrative? Often this is the case, and when the narrative fails, our aspiration shrivels up.

So what do we do, as Zen aspirants, when we realize that our story line is a fallacy? If we're serious Zen students, we begin to develop comfort with the unknown. Not that we avoid predicting the future, but we know our predictions are uncertain. The more comfortable we are with the unknown, the less we cling to a delusion of predictability.

According to Buddhist psychology, there are three stages to the development of a narrative: experience, perfume, and seed.

We have the experience, which creates a perfume, an emotional memory. That memory coagulates to form a seed that projects into the future. Our narrative is created and perpetuated by a waterfall of experience, perfume, and seed; experience, perfume, and seed; experience, perfume, and seed. As long as we cling to a narrative, our future is affected by the residue of the past.

Friends are those for whom we carry positive seeds. Our last experience with them left a wonderful perfume that coagulated into a positive seed, so we want to be with them. This tendency keeps our narrative going. For as long as our narrative runs, we experience the present through the past.

But with practice, we begin to notice when we are watering seeds from the past that will condition and limit our future.

Zen teacher Toni Packer was being interviewed once. The interviewer said, "You come from Nazi Germany. How does that impact your practice?" Toni replied, "I don't think it matters much, those details of the past—I don't give them sun or water."

FACING ONENESS

Zen Master Uumon is asked, "What is the teaching of Buddha's lifetime?"

Uumon replies, "Teaching facing oneness."

—CASE 14, BLUE CLIFF RECORD

The famous psychiatrist Milton Erickson had a unique approach to helping patients suffering from mental illness. Once, while working in a hospital, he was assigned a particularly difficult patient. His staff told him, "Don't waste your time with that fellow. All he does is talk to himself and pace. No one can reach him. He is beyond help."

But Erickson didn't believe it. He began by simply walking with the patient, keeping his distance because he didn't want to scare the guy, but staying close enough that his presence was felt. Whenever the patient looked a little freaked out, Milton backed off. Then, slowly, he moved back in.

From dawn till dust, they did this dance together. This went on for a few days. Noticing that the patient was a smoker, Milton bought a pack of cigarettes, which he slipped into his shirt pocket. When the patient ran out of cigs, Milton offered him one. The patient accepted it, and then they returned to their pacing.

Even during lunch, Milton sat nearby so they could eat together. One afternoon Milton didn't have a dessert on his plate. Noticing, the patient offered Milton his own dessert. Milton took it. When they finished their lunch, they got up and paced.

Gradually, through simple acts of kindness and attention, Milton cultivated a relationship with this person. Milton was simply available as a friend, without any demands or expectations. It was the beginning of the patient's return to the world. Soon he was even relating to the nurses and the staff.

We manifest oneness by giving ourselves without expecting anything in return and by receiving without feeling obliged. When we give in this way, there's no separation between giver, receiver, and gift. Milton Erickson was not a Buddhist. But he transformed his patients by teaching facing oneness.

When we are facing oneness, the image reflected back is the image of all beings. It's pretty easy to be one with someone we love or with a pleasant environment, but our practice is to *always* face oneness. Then that frozen narcissistic fixation on a separate self dissolves. Life becomes lighter instead of feeling so heavy, so woe-is-me so much of the time. It's true that life can be woeful, but we're all in this woe together, and joint woefulness is not so woeful. Our deepest woes are created by our fixation on self-image.

At every midday meal, the abbot of a Zen monastery would serve the meal to his students. Then he would dance and sing loudly, "Dear bodhisattvas, come and take your meal!"

This is teaching facing oneness. In a teacher-student relationship, there must be this kind of attitude by the teacher. As we enter into Big Life, which is a life beyond you and me, we enter into our togetherness. *Already* we are together, whether we enter into it or not.

I'll give two other examples of teaching facing oneness. The first involves my own teacher, Suzuki Roshi. I had been with him for a few years and, frankly, I had become a little bored. And disenchanted.

Well, enchantment is seductive, and as human beings, we crave enchantment. So I was getting tired of Suzuki's low-keyed way. Then something *very* enchanting happened. I was approached by another teacher who was quite well known. He was a very good teacher and seemed to have a genuine interest in helping me. Maybe he sensed my disillusionment.

This teacher was high-energy, exciting, and charismatic. He said he knew about my satori experiences and he could guide me to have more and greater ones. I felt sure he could help me to *permanently* break through the boundaries of my limited self. This is what I really wanted.

"Why shouldn't I change teachers?" I said to my wife. "Suzuki isn't even interested in me."

Then one morning I was walking down the hall outside the zendo and Suzuki was coming from the other direction. He stopped right in front of me. Then he touched the tip of his nose with his index finger, which seemed oddly significant, so I mirrored the gesture.

"You have a great treasure," he said, still touching the tip of his nose. "Someone might want to steal it. Don't let anyone steal it." That's all he said. And then he continued on his way.

I was bewildered. First of all, how did he even know? The only person I had told was my wife, and she didn't tell him.

Suzuki was teaching facing oneness. Through that small gesture, my fixation on permanent enlightenment and my boredom and disillusionment seemed to dissolve.

The second example of facing oneness comes from the life of Buddha. Shortly after Siddhartha had his awakening under the Bodhi Tree and became the Buddha, he encountered the five ascetics with whom he had practiced before abandoning self-mortification. Immediately they recognized that something was different about their old companion. "What has happened to you?" they asked. Buddha responded by touching the earth. He uttered not a word; but his former companions *felt* something. They were moved by his presence. The five ascetics became Buddha's first disciples.

When we're with someone who is facing oneness, we feel their serenity and calmness. If we are open, we may even get a taste of the deep joy of being part of an interdependent universe.

This joy is not contingent on anything. It's always available, as this Buddhist tale illustrates:

A woman was walking alone in the jungle when suddenly a tiger leaped out from the thicket and gave chase. It chased her to the edge of a cliff. Grabbing some vines, she cleverly lowered herself down the face of the cliff. But the tiger didn't give up. He gazed down at her, growling hungrily. She clung to the vine for dear life.

A rumbling noise issued up from below. The woman looked down. There, pacing eagerly and licking his chops, was a second tiger. He gave a mighty roar. The woman tightened her grip. Things couldn't get worse—or so it seemed, until a little mouse appeared and started chewing on the vine.

As hope waned, something caught the woman's eye. It was a beautiful, plump wild strawberry glistening in the sun. *How wonderful,* she thought. To taste it, all she had to do was let go of the vine. With delight, she reached out, plucked the strawberry, and popped it into her mouth. "*Mmmmmm.*"

FIVE

Making Peace with the Fear Body

THE BUDDHIST COUNTERPART TO the Christian devil is Mara, the evil one. Mara is responsible for all our emotional and mental anguish, malaise, and overall dissatisfaction with things as they are. Mara exists to protect the fear body, which is just another way of thinking about the ego.

We will never be free of Mara. He is unavoidable. But we can cultivate an intimate relationship with him—as Buddha did.

The relationship began when Siddhartha sat down under the Bodhi Tree and vowed not to get up until he discovered a way to alleviate suffering. But instead of the insight he was hoping for, he got Mara. If Siddhartha's aspiration had been tied to a certain kind of insight, he would have given up. But he didn't give up. He opened up.

First Mara tried to tempt him with offers of supernatural power. Power can be very seductive to the ego. But Siddhartha was not distracted. He studied the offers as they bubbled up, noticing their intensity, their feeling tone, their shifty and ever-changing nature, and how easily he was able to penetrate them with attentive and kind awareness. When he opened up to them in this way, the offers seemed to dissolve on their own.

Next Mara offered his beautiful daughters. Again, Siddhartha just watched without dismay, criticism, or judgment as the sexual images bubbled up. When offers of power and sex failed to deter Siddhartha from his aspiration, Mara called up armies of fearful demons. Over and over the images came. Over and over Siddhartha experienced his deepest fears and strongest desires without withdrawing, suppressing, or criticizing. Each experience he opened up to brought its own insight into suffering and the causes of suffering.

Siddhartha became the Buddha by sitting with Mara—not Mara the archetype, but Siddhartha's own personal Mara. Mara the archetype exists to protect the fear body. But when we look closely at our own personal Mara, we see that he actually reveals the fear body, allowing us to see it.

Mara is not separate from the basic goodness of all things. The big difference between the Christian devil and Mara is that Mara points the way to transformation. He delivered the very insight Siddhartha was seeking. After six days and nights of peering directly at the causes of his suffering, Siddhartha's mind fell silent. He gazed up at the morning star. It was like seeing his own face, but it wasn't *his* face, it was the face of the universe.

BEFRIENDING THE FEAR BODY

This being human is a guest
house. Every morning
a new arrival.

A joy, a depression, a meanness,
some momentary awareness comes
as an unexpected visitor.

Welcome and attend them all!
Even if they're a crowd of sorrows,
who violently sweep your house
empty of its furniture, still,
treat each guest honorably.
He may be clearing you out
for some new delight.

The dark thought, the shame, the malice,
meet them at the door laughing,
and invite them in.

Be grateful for whoever comes,
because each has been sent
as a guide from beyond.

—RUMI, "THE GUEST HOUSE"

We cannot push away the painful events of our life. Pain is part of life. Learning to accept it, even developing a relationship with it, is the path of transformation. This is what Buddha discovered. He spent the rest of his life teaching that the way to alleviate suffering is *through* Mara—not over, under, or around, but through.

Even though Buddha was an enlightened being, he was not free of Mara. Mara always comes back, giving us the opportunity to make peace with him over and over again. When we can make peace with our own personal Mara, we can make peace with anyone. Buddha took every opportunity to cultivate an intimate relationship with Mara, who came around so often Buddha's disciples learned to recognize him in all his disguises.

On one occasion Buddha was meditating in a cave when Mara showed up, skulking around outside the cave, seeking entrance. Buddha's disciples recognized him immediately and tried to shoo him off. Mara refused to leave, stirring up a big ruckus. Buddha asked one of his disciples, "What's all the commotion about?"

When a disciple explained what was going on, Buddha said, "Oh, my old friend Mara. Invite him in."

When he entered, Mara looked a little out of sorts. Buddha said, "How are you doing, Mara? How are things going for you?"

Mara sighed deeply. "Oh," he groaned, "it's so hard. . . ." He shook his head slowly, looking distraught. "It's *hard* being evil all the time."

Buddha said, "You think it's easy being a buddha?"

It's not easy being an ordinary human being either. Often when we first start to practice, we try to cut off our strong emotions because we want to go beyond the self. We want to be a buddha. But Buddha didn't separate from his emotions. That just creates conflict between who we are and who we think we should be. Buddhism is about acceptance. How are we going to see our negative emotions if we keep pushing them away with our judgments and criticism? Clear seeing—vidya—is the beginning of freeing.

THE NATURE OF FEAR

As Zen aspirants, our practice is to recognize how the fear body manifests in our own life. But so often we fail to recognize the fear body as not-me because it starts taking over at such a young age.

The fear body can manifest in three common ways. The first is withdrawal. When I was labeled as gifted at three years old, I began to contract around the idea of being gifted. Contracting is a form of withdrawal. As time passed, I contracted more and more. This is what we do as human beings.

As adults, we contract around our strongly held opinions, prejudices, political associations, and religion. We become so contracted that we can't appreciate the values of those outside the lines we've drawn. Instead, we try to force our own stories onto others.

I was having dinner once with Suzuki Sensei and Ruth, another Zen student, in our apartment across from the San Francisco Zen Center. In the middle of the meal, the doorbell rang. I answered it.

"It was just some folks from the Soka Gakkai Buddhist temple. I think they want to convert me," I told Suzuki and Ruth when I returned to the table.

Suzuki said, "I think they have a problem. I think they're selling liquor."

The second manifestation of the fear body is lashing out, either in anger or through competition, always needing to be better than everyone else. We all compete, but if we become obsessive about competition, it's the fear body.

My family lived in Palo Alto, a prestigious city about thirty miles south of San Francisco. But after my father got a promotion, Palo Alto was not prestigious enough for him. We had to move to Atherton. I inherited my father's competitiveness. It's been my lifelong companion, my personal Mara. When it comes up, I try to see it and direct its energy in positive ways.

The third manifestation of the fear body is going numb. We numb out through alcohol, drugs, sex, gambling. Or perhaps we develop a TV addiction or become workaholics.

I have a friend who, after a devastating divorce, became addicted to porn. Every day he set his intention to come home and meditate. But inevitably, the porn won out. He watched porn until he fell asleep. His road back to emotional and mental well-being was long and hard. He tried all the usual strategies to free himself. Finally, he became willing to face his loneliness head-on. Then the addiction dissolved.

In meditation it's okay to feel all of your intense emotions, even murderous rage. Just feel the sensation of it, breathe into it, and allow it to pass on without engaging in the thoughts that arise from the sensations. It is not our feelings that get us into trouble; it's our actions. When we learn to experience our emotions skillfully, we do not need to act on them. Instead, we transform their negative energy into positive, constructive energy. There's a lot of energy in our emotions—enough to save the world.

But first we have to become an expert on our fear—not fear in general but our own fear. When we try to analyze our fear, we are separating from it. We are pulling back, disengaging, avoiding the bodily sensation by focusing on a concept. Fear is not something remote, something we can turn over in our minds and look at from a safe distance. Fear is immediate. To study our fear, we merge into it, becoming one with it. If we can experience fear directly, in a calm and kind way, it loses its power.

When I was a little boy I was afraid of the dark. I slept with a light on, except for nights spent at my grandmother's. I had to sleep in the dark at my grandmother's. But it was great, because she let me sleep in her bed, so I felt safe. With my grandmother close, I could just feel the fear as it arose without being overwhelmed, because she was right there. Over and over, I felt fear move through my body, then dissolve, then come back and dissolve again. I became very familiar with it. After a while I no longer feared the dark. This memory has been very helpful to me throughout my life, and especially in Zen practice.

We have to learn to manage fear skillfully because fear is unavoidable. It is imprinted on us by our family and culture. From birth to death, we are being imprinted upon by our environment, whether we notice it or not. If we notice, we have the opportunity to bring choice into the equation. But if our mind is spinning all the time, we don't even notice all the ways we are being influenced.

The psychiatrist and author R. D. Laing said, "The range of what we think and do is limited by what we fail to notice." Too often what we fail to notice are the small-minded, fearful thoughts that keep us feeling isolated, limited, and constrained.

It is contrary to the nature of the fear body to extend itself. It can only contract, making us feel tight and small. We react to the fear body by clinging and holding on to things. We hold on to time, money, and status. We have no time to spare, no money to donate, and we rarely do what we truly want, because we have a reputation to protect. When the fear body is present, the first thing that goes is generosity, because sticking and clinging are the opposite of generosity.

When I was a student at Stanford, Suzuki Roshi was invited there to speak. I sat next to him in the first row as he waited to be introduced. Suddenly, he took my hand and squeezed it. "I'm scared," he uttered. But when it came time for his talk, he was calm and totally available. He did not fear the sensation of being scared. He didn't contract around it or cling to it. When it arose, he acknowledged it and felt it fully, and it passed on through. He freed up the energy of fear, so it could be transformed. He met fear with kindness, and then he was free to give himself wholeheartedly to his activity.

As long as we are breathing, there are infinite possibilities. A good starting point is with a question: What if I completely let go of the fear body and were released from the gloomy future it predicted? And then another question: In the absence of fear, what would I want my life to be about? And then another: In the absence of fear, what would motivate me toward that life?

As we ask these questions and feel the resistance they arouse, we begin to recognize how hypnotized we are by the fear body. Recognizing our own neurosis is the beginning of freedom. Once we learn to recognize how fear drives our choices, we can choose differently. Then we can ask: What specific activity would move me forward?

Deep questioning, combined with the skillful use of imagination, can help us to break through the hypnotic spell fear casts. Imagination moves our inquiry from the intellect to the experiential. We begin to imagine what the absence of fear might actually feel like in our body.

It takes practice. At first it may feel as if the question just bounces off the surface of our mind, like a math question we don't know the answer to. But we can practice deep questioning in the same way we practice returning to our breath in meditation. When we bring our awareness back to the question over and over and over, the question sinks deeper into our flesh, bones, and marrow.

It is contrary to the nature of the fear body to extend itself, but it is contrary to our true nature to stay small. Deep questioning extends us beyond the fear body. Just holding the question is enough, because it is the question—*not* the answer—that opens us up. The question becomes our koan, guiding us and informing us in insightful ways. When we ask deep questions, we are not anticipating an answer. Answers can be sticking places.

"What is the most important thing for me to do?" I asked Suzuki Sensei. I really wanted to do this practice. I wanted answers.

"Just get up," Suzuki said.

Just to get up in the morning and come to the Zen center for zazen—that was the most important thing. But that was not what I wanted to hear. I had an analytical mind, and I wanted some special instruction.

As time passed, my practice matured, and I felt good about it. So I went to Suzuki again.

"Now what is the most important thing for me to do?"

"Just get up."

SEEING THROUGH THE FEAR BODY

The land that became the Tassajara Zen Monastery was 160 acres of mountain property surrounding the Tassajara Hot Springs, deep in the mountains an hour and a half's drive from Carmel Valley. The below-market price was $300,000. But everyone thought acquiring it was impossible. The San Francisco Zen Center had few members and little money. We didn't even have jobs.

"Well, maybe it is impossible, maybe so," Suzuki said thoughtfully. "Or maybe not impossible. Let's try it and see." That was in the spring of 1966. In July of '67, Tassajara Zen Monastery opened its doors. It was the first Zen monastery outside of Asia.

About a decade later, Katagiri was the abbot of the Minnesota Zen Meditation Center. He wanted to purchase land for a country monastery. We looked at five different locations. The one Katagiri liked the most was the most expensive, the farthest away, and in contrast to other properties we saw, had not even a barn on it. Many were opposed to choosing that property. It was too risky, we said. We have to protect the Zen center. We can't afford it. We aren't big enough yet.

But when Katagiri saw it, he said, "Ah, look at this!" He turned full circle, soaking in the beauty. "I don't know. It's wonderful! Shouldn't we try it?" He named it Hokyoji. It became the first Zen monastery in the Midwest.

The fear body is terribly afraid of failure, so much so that it kills life. Thoughts that arise from the fear body always assume negative outcomes. They tell us we can't, we shouldn't, we aren't capable. They convince us we will be judged, rejected, or abandoned if we express our true heart's desire. Fear creeps into our mind and takes over our body. We doubt our gifts, squelch our creativity, and leave our dreams behind. But the voice of fear is not our true voice. Our true voice is covered by layers of acculturation.

Vidya, the practice of deep seeing, reveals that fear generally has two major components: thought and sensation. Together they perpetuate and calcify the fear body. Through vidya we begin to see how sticky the fear body is, and we see that grasping at things paralyzes us—even grasping at the desire to help people, to be generous, or to have a deep Zen practice. We can only do those things when we are open. When we are acting from the fear body, even generosity becomes self-serving.

We build a relationship with fear by feeling the underlying sensation without clinging to stories about it, trying to fix it, or trying to get away from it. Talking about it, to ourselves or with others, magnifies and exaggerates it. Sensations themselves are actually quite simple, even wonderful, because they are just energy, always changing and moving, never stagnating and never staying around if we don't sustain them with our judgments and complaints, which are just strategies for covering up the unpleasant sensations. But the sensations are *alive*. There's life there being covered over with stories, and the joy of *just being* is missed.

When I was offered the job as CEO of People Incorporated, the first thing I felt was far from jubilation. I was besieged by fearful thoughts. *I can't ask people for money! What if I fail? I doubt I can even do it. I'll get overwhelmed. I'll have to work too hard. The job will destroy the intimacy of my friendships. I'll be criticized. What if people think I am just out for myself and my agency?*

Scared, scared, scared! We always start with the fear body. So the first thing to do is to make peace with it. Sit with it in meditation. Bring it into the zendo. Offer it a cup of tea. Invite it to stick around awhile. See what kind of sensations come up.

During zazen, all sorts of sensations come up. You might notice a constriction in some part of your body; it's probably fear related. But don't think about it. Just notice it with your kind attention. Notice its heat, how it undulates, how alive it feels. Sensations are sharp, dull, fluid, or pulsing and always morphing into something else. Any constricted, rigid sensation has a seed of fear at its center. But don't do an intellectual trip about it. Just notice it.

There are nine thought patterns that sustain the fear body:

1. All-or-nothing thinking
2. Always-or-never thinking
3. Mind reading (believing we know what others are thinking)
4. Fortune-telling (believing we know what the future holds)
5. Magnification and minimization
6. *Should* statements
7. Personalizing
8. Focusing on the negative in each experience
9. Comparative thinking

When we notice we are thinking about our fear rather than experiencing it directly, we bring ourselves back to our immediate sensations. Over and over, we abandon our thoughts and move our awareness back into our body. When we lose our fear of the sensations, we are no longer bothered by fear.

Suzuki said, "When you do something without any thought of doing something—that is you yourself." Our true mind is like the mirror-like surface of a calm lake, where everything is reflected just as it is. The trees along the bank, the clouds overhead, and the moon reflect perfectly on the lake's surface. If a bird flies over, it is reflected. After it passes, the image vanishes without a trace. When the fear body is not present, this is how our mind registers the world.

But when a wind blows across the lake, the surface becomes choppy and chaotic. The images are fragmented and distorted. Clarity is lost. When we experience the world in this way, the fear body is present. But all we need to do is sink down into the lake and look up. Beyond the choppy surface, the sky is still there, vast, open, and serene.

LIVING BEYOND THE FEAR BODY

Once, as I was driving Suzuki home after our Palo Alto sitting group, he asked if I would take him to an area in Hillsborough. He wanted to visit a woman who'd contacted him about Buddhism. He had never met this woman, but he felt he should go visit her.

Well, I wasn't too happy about it, because I was supposed to be in class, but I did it anyway. His directions weren't good. We drove around for some time before we found the house. It was on a large, spacious estate in a wealthy suburb. Suzuki said, "You stay here. I'll go up." So I waited, but after only about five minutes, he came back.

"How'd it go?" I asked.

"Very interesting," he said. "But not the woman I thought. Wrong woman." Then he started to laugh. "She thought I was there to wash her windows!" he exclaimed with delight. "But I didn't bring my window-washing equipment," he chortled with great amusement.

It was easy to see how she'd made the mistake—a Japanese man, dressed in a simple black jacket and baggy black pants.

This was 1965, just twenty years after World War II, when many Japanese on the West Coast had been forced into relocation camps. They'd lost everything: their money, their property, their stature. Even twenty years later, the only Japanese folks I saw in the Bay area were laborers.

So when Suzuki went to the wrong house, it's sad but understandable that the woman thought he was there to wash her windows. The fear body would feel demeaned by this because it is always concerned about what others think. Suzuki did not feel demeaned. He lived beyond the fear body. He could accommodate himself to his environment without getting caught by it, because he was bigger than his environment. It was more as if he had pulled off a practical joke on her.

This wasn't the only time people had difficulty recognizing Suzuki for who he was. My Irish Catholic maternal grandmother was dismayed when my mother left the church, married an atheist, and sent all of her children to the Unitarian Church, which to my grandmother was "no church at all." She was the only family member to show interest in my "conversion" to Zen Buddhism. It stemmed from her strong interest in Christian mysticism. She immediately saw the similarity between Christian contemplatives and Zen practitioners.

Once I became absorbed in Zen, my grandmother and I became confidantes. She talked about the "dryness" of her own prayer life and confided her hope that using a rosary would help. I told her that using a rosary was much like using a mantra for meditation. She was very supportive of my commitment to Zen, so I asked if she'd like to come to dinner some evening and meet Suzuki. She seemed delighted, so the date was set.

My grandmother arrived first. Linda and I had a little black kitten, and when Suzuki arrived, the kitten batted at the corners of his robes. Suzuki was amused. He shook his robes playfully.

The kitten loved it. Before long, Suzuki and the kitten were rolling on the floor together, playing with great abandon. After a few minutes, he stood up and straightened his robes, and for the rest of the evening he was attentive, gracious, quite reserved, and yet very sweet and friendly.

For the next year or so, every time I saw my grandmother, she reminisced about that evening. It usually started like this: "That man playing with your kitten. . . . You did say he was a priest, didn't you, dear?" Her impression of Suzuki was one of amusement and bewilderment.

Suzuki Sensei liked the term Big Mind to express the openness and spaciousness of our true nature. When we're experiencing Big Mind, we are not attached to any special experience, such as excitement, lust, happiness, embarrassment, fearfulness, or composure. We are just open to whatever is happening, moment by moment. It is not *your* Big Mind or *my* Big Mind; it is not separate from anything else, so it includes everything, even our small, contracted fear body. The activity of the fear body is to separate and divide, draw lines, and tell stories. Big Mind sees these activities of the fear body, but it is not bothered by them.

Suzuki said, "Whatever bird flies through the sky, the sky doesn't care." When we experience Big Mind, we are as open as the sky. Our thoughts are little birds. Whatever little bird comes along, we remain calm and open. When we extend ourselves in this way, the fear body dissolves. It always comes back, but that's okay. We are not bothered by it.

SIX

Eating the Globefish

IN THE SATIPATTHANA SUTRA, Buddha gave precise instructions on meditation and moving beyond the fictional self. *Sati* means attentiveness to the present, awareness, wakefulness. According to early Buddhist literature, practicing sati means staying focused on the object of meditation without floating away from it. According to Buddha, if we practice sati we won't become "like a hollow pumpkin that bobs up and down in the water."

Patthana translates to close, firm, and steadfast, like floor planks. When the planks are close, there is no gap, so dust and dirt cannot get in. When our meditation is firm and steadfast, overwhelming emotions and incessant thinking cannot leak in. Another simile from early Buddhist literature refers to rubbing two sticks together to start a fire. We have to be steadfast and continuous in our effort. If we stop rubbing even for a moment, we have to start over. In meditation, each time our focus falters, we simply come back and begin again.

Meditation, as described by Buddha in the Satipatthana Sutra, is an arduous practice that sets the mind face-to-face with the object of meditation. For example, when we focus on our abdominal breathing, we're face-to-face with the sensations in our belly. If there's tension there, we're face-to-face with the tension. If contraction, we're face-to-face with the contraction. The more subtle the object of our meditation, the more attentive we must remain if we're to stay face-to-face with it.

If our meditation practice is sincere, we eventually come face-to-face with what Buddha called the three poisons, which are delusion, greed, and anger. The three poisons create and perpetuate the gap between who we think we are and our true interconnected self. Through meditation we begin to see how the three poisons, in all their iterations, dominate our lives and keep us churned up inside. The poisons arise from ignorance of the world as it is, and they drive us toward thoughts and actions that cause suffering. Like Mara the Evil One, who constantly reveals the fear body, the three poisons are unavoidable if we are on a Buddhist path.

A globefish is reputed to be a very tasty delicacy. But it has a little poison in it. Transformation happens only when we eat the whole globefish, not just the sweet parts. And not just the poison, as Buddha discovered. Seeking transformation through pain and asceticism is not the way.

REMOVING THE VEILS OF DELUSION

You, the richest person in the world, have been laboring and struggling endlessly, not understanding that you already possess all that you seek.

—THE LOTUS SUTRA

The first of the three poisons is delusion, a basic misperception that is rooted in our conditioning and incessant labeling. It results in both dullness and bewilderment. Our delusion keeps us looking outside ourselves for happiness, satisfaction, and solutions to our problems. As we do this, the fictional ego shell becomes harder and harder.

Happiness is the true nature of the heart. But for most of us, abiding happiness is not our experience. The poisons continuously weave veils that conceal the heart's buoyant nature and natural resilience. They keep us seeking and struggling for some illusory something that's always *out there,* just beyond our reach. Zen is the practice of removing, one by one, these veils, or overlays (the Sanskrit word is *varana*). There are three types: bodily veils, heart veils, and mind veils.

Bodily veils. One of the bodily veils is contraction. We contract to protect ourselves from the emotional memories stored in our body. In Zen practice these trapped memories are freed. It can happen quite suddenly. As old pains surface, we feel tension and anxiety moving through our body. Sometimes our whole body aches or even shakes during prolonged meditation, as mine did when I was a young student. Because our minds are still and focused, we are deeply aware of the pain of freed-up emotions.

Suzuki Roshi said the only thing to do about pain is to let it be painful. We notice how the aches and pains come and go if we don't attach our judgments and criticisms to them. When we watch with kind attention and feel the unpleasant sensations without judging, we experience the purity of each sensation. When we can just experience the purity of our feelings, it's okay, because there is no confusion. So the practice is simply to feel our aches and pains until the old hurts work their way out.

I had a lot of bodily veils. Just trying to sit with a straight back was painful. During retreats, my whole body shook. To make matters worse, others seemed to have no problem sitting cross-legged even for long retreats. It was as if their bodies were made of air. Comparing ourselves to others is just another veil (mind veil), and it always makes things worse.

Another bodily veil is the urge to move. When we first begin to meditate, it may take a couple of years or even longer for the body to settle into a state of stillness. Usually, we experience a lot of bodily resistance to just being still. We feel itchy, tingly, hungry, sleepy, achy, nauseated, sweaty, queasy. Typically, we respond to the whims, restlessness, and constant demands of our body by staying busy. Americans are busy, busy people. We are a frantic, multitasking society, and our concentration is becoming more and more fragmented. Zen is the practice of single tasking with one-pointed concentration. Seeing through the bodily veils starts us on the path to our true state of calmness.

Heart veils. Anger, grief, sadness, and loneliness conceal our true heart. In meditation, when we see these veils and feel the strong emotions associated with them, we feel discouraged. But they have been there all along. It is only we ourselves who cling to them. In the very moment that we see them clearly, in that same moment we sense some immediate release. "In the darkness there is light." The light is always there; it is not separate from the darkness.

"But don't take it as light." As one veil drops away, another one arises. Behind the anger veil may be the loneliness veil, and behind the loneliness veil, the grief veil, the sadness veil, or the veil of victimization. We think these veils protect us, but they rob us of life's energy. To reclaim our aliveness, practicing through difficulty is the key. The heart veils dissolve naturally as we move into and through our painful emotions.

Mind veils. The third type is the mind veil. Mental chattering, worries, habitual thought patterns, constant planning, manipulating, expectations, and the like make up the mind veils. Suzuki said there are limits to the amount of pain the body can endure, but there are no limits to mental pain. When I was having so much trouble with my body, I could not help but compare myself to others. It was frustrating and embarrassing, which led to a general feeling of discouragement.

When we say, "This shouldn't be," we become entangled and confused. Life seems unfair. Anger and self-pity may conceal our bodily sensations. Purity is lost. If we start telling stories, blaming ourselves or others, or thinking "What if . . . ?" then we are no longer experiencing either the emotion or its underlying sensation. Storytelling is an avoidance technique. By avoiding our emotional pain, we actually attach to the suffering. Suffering is not caused by emotional pain; it is caused by our avoidance. Furthermore, when we avoid our painful emotions, we may feel numb and lifeless.

Helen Keller, the deaf and blind author and activist, said, "Life is either a daring adventure or nothing." Our commitment to see through the veils is a daring adventure. Sure it seems tedious at times, but that's part of the adventure. When we penetrate the veils with our kind attentions, they drop away. The mind falls still, and something new appears. Then we move into that, too. There's always something new to open up to. Katagiri Roshi said, "At the pivot of nothingness, the next moment unfolds and a new world appears."

THE SPELL OF DESIRE

The second poison is greed. When greed—excessive desire— casts its spell on us, we become rigid: unable to live openly or see clearly, trapped in a cycle of repetitive thoughts and emotions.

Remember adolescence?

Remember falling in love for the first time or even the second time, being in that semiconscious, dreamy la-la land? Driving by your girlfriend's house over and over. When we meet someone we're attracted to, even their faults are appealing. We are not seeing the person at all; we are only seeing our own desire.

Often, in meditation, we are besieged by desire. One desire after another, they cycle though our mind endlessly. We're alone with them, with nothing to distract us and no way to fulfill them. We can only look at the endless parade of desires.

If you sit in meditation with devotion, you will have to see and endure your desires. After a while, we realize how irrelevant the object of our desire is. It is desire itself that perpetuates our suffering. We use desire to cover up all sorts of difficult emotions. If we're insecure, we set goals that will prove our self-worth. We use goal setting to cover deep hurts or painful memories. Avoiding difficult emotions perpetuates them. The cycle repeats itself with even more intensity.

Can you accept your desires graciously? When you sit on the cushion and see one desire after another and feel how consuming each is—if you remain on your cushion, then you are graciously accepting them. It may not feel gracious on the inside. But when the bell rings and the desire suddenly dissipates, we recognize how little it actually means to us. Often it was just a temporary distraction from the pain or boredom that was coming up. Developing a gracious attitude toward our obsessive desires is what Zen practice is about. Seeing the nature of desire is the beginning of spiritual liberation.

As Zen practitioners, we learn to carry our desires lightly, like butterflies alighting on our shoulder. We can just watch the delightful butterfly. When it flies off, another will come, then another. If we don't get clingy or judgmental, we can enjoy them.

If you learn nothing else from Zen practice, I hope you learn to hold your desires lightly.

WORKING WITH ANGER

When we transform anger constructively, we are left with clarity about what needs to be done and an intense energy to achieve our goals.

—THE DALAI LAMA

The third poison is anger. As Buddhist practitioners, it's important to know that we *can* understand our anger. It is telling us something, informing us that our mind and our heart are in pain. We understand that physical pain reveals something about our body, and we know to listen to it. But there's confusion around emotional and mental pain. We don't understand what it's telling us, so we become frustrated and feel thwarted by it.

My friend Tom worked with his anger for many years. He changed his diet and started eating all natural foods. He stopped watching television. He moved to a small town, hoping a slower pace would help. He tried therapy, massage, and encounter groups. But none of these helped much. Through anger management, he learned to control his anger, but he still had anger at his core. He felt deep and abiding anger toward the politics of the world, the way people treated each other, and toward capitalism.

Then he came to Zen practice with Suzuki Roshi. Suzuki said, "You can do all that other stuff. It's okay to watch your diet and not watch TV and go to therapy—but just come to the Zen center and sit with me."

Tom became a dedicated practitioner. He did tap into some calmness, which brought some peace into his life, but it was limited because below that was an undercurrent of agitation fueled by his anger. For months Tom worked with his anger in meditation, moving into it as it arose, experiencing the sensations in his body but refraining from indulging the stories attached to the anger.

Then, on the last night of a long retreat, Tom's heart and mind opened up into something new, a vast spaciousness that included everything, even his anger. He saw that there was no need to try to rid himself of anger. When anger arose, he was not bothered by it. He didn't identify with it anymore. It was not *his* anger. It was just anger. It was not even *his* bare awareness that saw the anger. It was just bare awareness. There was no Tom attached to it. By focusing on his anger, Tom realized his buddha nature or nonself nature. With bare awareness, the energy of anger became the energy of transformation.

A week or two after the retreat, I ran into Tom, and we went for a walk. I asked him about his experience at the retreat and whether he felt enlightened.

"Enlightened? I don't have any sense about being enlightened," Tom replied. "As I'm walking with you, it's quite wonderful. One leg is following the other. One leg is leading the other."

When our heart is at peace, one leg following the other is enough. More than enough—it is abundant. If we look with compassionate attention at our anger, there's the opportunity to go beyond it, as Tom did. The key is to bring it into our awareness without incessantly feeding or criticizing it. We notice the immediate feeling of anger and what we're telling ourselves about it. The basic components of anger and all other emotions are sensation, perception, and interpretation—together they form a web that traps us. But there's the possibility of seeing the web, and in the seeing is the possibility of freedom.

In 1965 the San Francisco Zen Center owned the apartment building across the street. I lived there, and so did Suzuki Roshi's son Otohiro. I envied him, growing up with a father like Suzuki. I told him once how lucky I thought he was.

Otohiro shook his head and spoke in broken English. "Not same man," he said, sadly. "Not father I had. He difficult. He mean."

I remembered this conversation many years later when I read David Chadwick's important biography of Suzuki, *Crooked Cucumber*. Chadwick describes a young priest and father who really struggled with anger. One of the things that made him angry was absentmindedness. It went against his ideals. Suzuki himself was famously absentminded and had been all his life. As a young man he was hard on himself, and seeing this same absentmindedness in his sons, he was even harder on them.

Suzuki's anger was covering up his shame over being absentminded. We all do this. Anger is always a cover for something deeper and more painful.

Often our painful memories are with us our whole life. Suzuki was a young priest when the Second World War began. Imagine what it must have been like to be a peace activist in Japan during the war. He never talked about it; some memories are just too painful.

One day as Suzuki gave a dharma talk, a woman asked a question about war, and Suzuki began to talk about how wars get started. Then someone asked why we were just sitting here while there's a war going on. Suzuki was having a difficult time understanding the question, so my friend John, who was one of Suzuki's students, repeated it.

Suddenly Suzuki leaped up from his cushion and stormed toward John with the wooden stick used by Japanese Zen masters. He whacked John several times on each shoulder. "You can't even tie your own shoes! How can you expect to stop the war?"

Then Suzuki walked back to his cushion and sat down. He gently straightened his robes, took a few breaths, had a sip of water, and went back to his talk. He was completely composed.

After the talk, I went to check on John.

"John, are you okay?" I asked.

"Yes. Sensei knows how to use the stick so it doesn't hurt."

Even the most compassionate among us is not immune to anger. It can feel like an out-of-control freight train. But as we learn to work with anger through meditation, our mind starts to slow down. Eventually, we begin to see the gaps between our thoughts, like the gaps between train cars. Within the gap there is a sense of ease and calm.

When anger flashes, if it is very deep, there may be a moment when we can't see the gaps. But a trained mind returns quickly, and we again see the space between our thoughts. We can move back into that spaciousness, as Suzuki did.

Anger arises for a reason out of our karmic past. In *Crooked Cucumber,* Chadwick writes about how difficult it was for Suzuki in Japan during the Second World War.

Suzuki apologized to John later, telling him that the question had reminded him of the horrors of war. When we can be compassionate toward our anger, it actually deepens our intimacy with life.

Suzuki said, "Let anger be a great bonfire that burns itself completely away. . . . I wish I could be like that." And he was like that; he was just humble about it.

Suzuki Roshi was asked, "If a person sees things clearly, is there no case in which he would be upset emotionally?" Suzuki answered:

Upset emotionally? I don't think so. But affected, yes. There is a big difference between these two. A buddha may be upset quite easily, in the sense of being deeply affected. But when he is upset, it is not because of his attachments. Sometimes he will be very angry. Anger is allowed when it is Buddha's anger. But that anger is not the same as the anger we usually have. If a buddha is not upset when he should be upset, that is also a violation of the precepts. When he needs to be angry, he must be angry. That is a characteristic of the Mahayana way of observing the precepts. We say, sometimes anger is like a sunset. Even though it looks like anger, actually it is a beautiful red sunset. If anger comes from a pure mind, from purity like a lotus, it is good.

One day when I was a young student at the San Francisco Zen Center, I lost my glasses. I looked everywhere for them—in my apartment, the zendo, Suzuki's office. I couldn't find them anywhere. Finally Suzuki came downstairs with my glasses. In his absentmindedness, he had taken them to his room thinking they were his. He laughed and laughed when he gave them to me.

The father Otohiro remembered from his childhood would not have laughed. That Suzuki would have been angry for failing to live up to his ideal about being a Zen teacher. But the Suzuki I knew had eaten the whole globefish, poison and all. Eating the globefish is the art of Zen transformation.

SEVEN

Healing
the Splits

Once, a child named Chien lived with her family in Han-yang. Chien played every day with her nephew, Wang-Chau. Chien's father teased them that they would marry someday. But Chien and Wang-Chau did not know he was teasing. To them, they were betrothed.

When Chien got older, a man of wealth and stature asked her father for Chien's hand in marriage. The father accepted. Chien and Wang-Chau were greatly upset. Wang-Chau decided he could no longer live in Han-yang. In the middle of the night, without telling anyone of his plan, he got into a boat and started up the river. As he paddled away from Han-yang, he heard a voice calling out, "Wait, wait!" He turned and saw Chien running alongside the bank. He paddled over and she eagerly climbed into the boat.

They lived happily for many years and had two children. But Chien missed her family. She longed to see her parents again. So

Chien and Wang-Chau decided to return to Han-yang. When they arrived, Wang-Chau went first to see Chien's father, as was the custom, while Chien waited in the boat with the two children.

Wang-Chau knocked on the door. He was greeted happily by Chien's father. "How much I have missed you!" he said. Wang-Chau was surprised at this friendly greeting. "I am here to ask your forgiveness for taking Chien away," Wang-Chau said. "I don't deserve your kind words."

Hearing this, Chien's father became confused. "What do you mean? Chien has not gone anywhere. She is here. She is upstairs in her room."

Now it was Wang-Chau who was confused. "Please don't tease me. Chien is waiting at the river with our two children. We have come back because she longs to see you. We wish only for your forgiveness."

Bewildered, both men stood facing each other in silence.

Finally, Chien's father drew a deep breath. "Follow me," he said. "I'm afraid my daughter is very ill. Since you left, she has not been herself. She cannot speak, nor does she ever leave her bed."

When Wang-Chau saw the young woman lying in Chien's bed, he was stunned. She looked like Chien, but she was thin and pale, only a ghost of her real self.

When he was finally able to speak, he said to Chien's father, "Please, come with me, for I have something to show you." He led Chien's father to the river, where Chien and the children were waiting. Now it was Chien's father who was speechless.

When he regained his voice, he said, "If you are really my daughter, then please come back to the house with me. There's something I do not understand."

They all started toward Chien's old home. As they approached, the sick Chien, who had not left her bed for all these years, walked eagerly toward them. The two Chiens ran into each other's embrace, and as they held each other, they became of one mind, one heart, and one body.

SENSING THE GAP

The story of Chien reveals something about the human situation, about how we split off from ourselves. Our vital psychic energy is dispersed whenever we are not of one body, heart, and mind.

When our thoughts pull us away from where we are now to where we'll be later or to the past, our experience is not one of wholeness. We are fragmented. Those fragmented shards of ourselves have sharp edges, because whenever we're fragmented, we're frustrated, confused, and fearful. We sense the gap between where we are and the present moment. It can feel like a kind of *bardo,* or purgatory, between being and nonbeing. If our body is in one place while our mind is another, or if our body and mind are engaged in an activity that excludes our heart, we experience a sort of nonbeing-being, a phantom-like being.

In many ways we are Chien, and from a Zen point of view, this is our illness. From a Buddhist perspective, most suffering isn't caused by physical illness. It's caused by splitting off.

A turning point began with Chien's longing to return home. This is what makes it a Zen story. At some point Chien began to sense the gap; she had neglected her home, and now she was far away from it. Her longing summoned her to return to herself.

In zazen we patiently refuse the domination of our opinions and fantasies that keep splitting us off. By bringing ourselves back to our breath, we can reunite with our suffering self and become whole again. It doesn't mean that we won't be sad anymore—but we won't be *split* in our sadness. If we're not split in our sadness, it's okay to be sad.

Suzuki was asked, "Do you still get sad sometimes?"

"Yes," he answered. "But when the tears land, they don't grow roots."

CALLING IN THE SHARDS

Far above the earth, in the frosty clouds of Nor, the Snow Queen lived in a beautiful ice castle. Everything was made of ice, so it sparkled and glistened like fresh snow. As she did every day, the Snow Queen looked into her mirror to admire her crystalline beauty.

But unbeknownst to her, an evil troll had cast a spell on the mirror. Now it reflected only the negative aspects of the human heart. Instead of her physical beauty, the Snow Queen saw deep into her heart. She saw sadness, anger, greed, loneliness, despair, bitterness, and confusion.

The mirror slipped from her hand. It fell to earth and shattered into a million pieces, some no larger than a grain of sand. Riding on the wind, the shards circled the earth, lodging in the eyes and hearts of human beings. One of these was the boy, Kai, who underwent a radical change in his personality, becoming hostile and mean. The story ends on a positive note, though. His sister, Gerda, cries in despair when she finds him, and her tears melt the ice shards in his heart. This causes him to cry as well, melting the remaining shards in his eyes.

The story of the Snow Queen is one of Hans Christian Andersen's most critically acclaimed fairy tales. It is not a Buddhist story, but it points to a fundamental truth in Buddhism. The magic mirror distorts the appearance of things. From a Buddhist perspective, the mirror represents the ego and the distorting effects of the three poisons—greed, anger, and delusion. Ego blinds us to the world as it is and to our own true nature. Shards that get lodged in the eyes and hearts of all human beings point to this same truth.

But don't worry. The shards are only made of ice. The warmth of our kind attention is all it takes to melt them away. This may be hard to believe, but it's true.

Shards create separation. We feel isolated and frozen. Staying with those feelings is difficult. But as we begin to feel whole again, the mere sight of a leaf falling to the ground can fill our heart with joy. We sense an affinity with the falling leaf. The components of consciousness no longer have big gaps between them.

In wholeness, consciousness becomes a wonderful mosaic. I was lucky to meet someone when I was young who didn't seem to be fragmented. With Suzuki Sensei, there was wholeness and warmth. He always seemed fully present and available.

As I mentioned before, when I told my father about Suzuki, he cautioned me about putting my trust in the idea of abiding joy. My father knew how people cover up their suffering with piety, by repressing, suppressing, and disassociating. He was a pretty good existentialist. As far as my father was concerned, life was pain and the rest was bullshit.

My father dulled the pain of life through achievement. Winning. Success. Moving up the ladder. But this was a strategy that left him filled with anxiety. I pulled away from the painful vibes I was picking up from my father. I needed to protect myself from the sharp edges of his anxiety shards.

Later in life, after several years of Zen practice, I worked hard to heal our relationship. But it meant accepting my father as he was. We don't have to be like that, hurting our loved ones and isolating ourselves. We can call in our shards and attend to them with our kind attention until they melt away.

Dukkha is the Sanskrit word for suffering, which includes general malaise and unsatisfactoriness. *Sukkha* means joy. The two words are separated by a single letter. Buddha taught that the path to sukkha is *through* dukkha. When we try to avoid our pain, we split off from our self.

Suzuki said that a regular meditation practice makes us sensitive to the suffering of others. So we may feel more pain than we had before. But it's okay, because with a regular meditation practice, we cultivate the inner strength to enter into our pain skillfully. With practice there is no rift, no splitting off, and therefore no suffering. Pain without suffering brings us home to our true self.

But we are fragile beings, so maybe we need to split until our meditation becomes more steady and supportive. That's okay. In meditation, just notice how you've split. Notice how the gap feels in your body. Allow the split itself to become the focus of your meditation. It doesn't matter what kind of pain it is; open into it with your kind attention and it will take you where you need to go.

In 1964, when I turned away from my father and toward Suzuki Sensei, I became infatuated with him. The bigger Suzuki became in my mind, the smaller I became. But he was a skilled teacher, and he always pushed me back to the cushion. So I didn't split off too much. He would say, You know, it's not about me; it's about doing the practice. It's about discovering that right in the middle of the worst ache, there's something wonderful, something beyond our stale ideas that split us off, something that is always alive, fresh, and whole.

When our body, heart, and mind are one, we can appreciate the simplest of things. Suzuki didn't think of himself as a Zen master. When people said he was good, he said, "If so, it's because my students are good." And that's how he truly felt. He was still absentminded. He wore two-dollar glasses from Walgreens because he lost them so often. But his absentmindedness no longer caused him to split off. When he became angry about something, it was not egoic anger, covering up some deep shame, fear, or insecurity. The ideals of his youth about what a Zen master should be had dissolved. He was free to be just who he was.

DON'T LEAVE ANYTHING OUT

In *Tales of a Magic Monastery* by Theophane the Monk, there's a story about an old Trappist monk who goes to a monastery seeking the true gifts of spiritual life. The monk had seen and learned much in life, but he was not interested in ordinary knowledge. "I didn't want any more of the little answers. I wanted the *big answer.*" So he went to the magic monastery and asked the guest master to show him directly to the house of God.

In the house of God, the monk sat down, determined to wait as long as necessary for the big answer. He sat all day and far into the night, looking God in the eye and wondering whether God was looking back. As dawn neared he heard a voice, "What are you leaving out?" He looked around but saw no one. Then he heard it again, "What are you leaving out?" Was it his imagination?

Soon the voice was coming from every direction, beseeching, whispering, demanding, and roaring. "What are you leaving out? What are you leaving out?" The monk wondered about his sanity. Had he lost his mind? "What are you leaving out?" roared the voice.

He leaped to his feet and headed for the door. He ran down the corridor to the first door he came to and knocked.

"What do you want?" came a sleepy voice.

"What am I leaving out?"

"Me," was the answer.

The monk turned, ran to the second door, and pounded on it.

"What do you want?"

"What am I leaving out?"

"Me."

A third door, a fourth, all the same. The monk thought, "They're all stuck on themselves." Feeling disgusted, he left the monastery. The sun was peeking over the horizon. He looked directly at it and beseeched, "What am I leaving out?"

The sun answered, "Me."

In despair, he threw himself to the ground.

The earth said, "Me, too."

My son married a wonderful woman whose family is of Indian origin. Several years ago my wife and I planned a trip to meet some of her relatives. We planned to stay in India for three weeks. I had always wanted to go to India, so I was excited.

I expected blissful vibes from the birthplace of the Buddha, which we did experience as we spent time with our new relatives. But the level of poverty was beyond anything I'd ever seen. Suffering was tangible. Beggars crowded around us, following us everywhere we went. We were told not to give them money, because many worked for crime lords, so giving would only perpetuate the problem. But it was so difficult to see their suffering and not do anything to help.

I found myself wanting to stay inside. I didn't want to go out and face the poverty and suffering of the people. It was too much. I thought I might watch TV to avoid going out, but that didn't work either. So I decided to visit the ashram of Amma, the hugging saint of India. *Amma* means mother, and she is known throughout the world for her compassion and love. She is devoted to alleviating the pain and suffering of others.

Several years earlier, Amma began routinely visiting the United States. I'd had a falling out with Katagiri Roshi and had left the Minnesota Zen Meditation Center. Even though I lived within a few blocks of the Zen center, I was practicing alone. I went with my friend to visit Amma two or three times and, along with hundreds of others, was hugged by her.

During the last time I visited Amma, after a long evening of focused meditation, I went back to my motel room and fell into a deeply tranquil state that lasted for hours—during which I felt a strong pull to return to formal Zen practice. Because of Amma, I was able to find my way back to the Zen center and complete my training in Zen.

Now years later, feeling overwhelmed by the depth of suffering in India, I felt compelled to see her again. When I arrived at her ashram, throngs were waiting for their turn to be hugged by her. I watched as she hugged each and every person with loving affection. She didn't shy away from those with open sores or other afflictions. She was totally open and available, hour after hour. She didn't stop until every person, including me, had been hugged.

I was deeply affected by this encounter with Amma. After that, I was able to settle in to the environment of India. I wasn't overwhelmed anymore. I was able to accept things as they were, as I'd seen Amma do, and just experience everything from the bottom of my heart. I began to enjoy India—the wonderful colors and smells, the hustle and bustle, the horns blowing, the shouts and whistles, the cows roaming freely in the streets. Yes, there was suffering. But there was also joy.

When I returned to my job at People Incorporated I felt compelled to do better at reaching out to our homeless clients when

I visited their camps around the Twin Cities. It was a privilege to be with them, learning about their hardships and travails, and giving them support.

FOUNDATIONS OF MINDFULNESS

At the same inn
play women too were sleeping;
bush clover and the moon.

—BASHO

Once when Basho and a friend were traveling to a sacred site, they decided to stop for the night at an inn. The walls were thin. In the next room were two play women—prostitutes. Prostitutes were really looked down on in Basho's time, like the untouchables in India.

The next morning Basho, his friend, and the play women were having breakfast. Talking together, they discovered that they were all going to the same sacred site. The two women were traveling alone and unprotected. These were dangerous times. So Basho and his friend decided to accompany them for protection.

Basho lived several hundred years after Dogen, but he considered Dogen to be his teacher. Basho was practicing whole-being buddha nature, which is one of Dogen's core teachings. Whole-being buddha nature means recognizing, acknowledging, and befriending the base emotions. If Basho had been afraid of his base emotions, he wouldn't have been able to extend compassion to the women in need of protection.

In the previous chapter I talked about the Satipatthana Sutra, Buddha's instruction on meditation. He describes four foundations of mindfulness, which help us to recognize when we're leaving something out:

1. Mindfulness of the body, which includes all the bodily sensations
2. Mindfulness of the feelings, including hatred and anger and greed
3. Mindfulness of mental formations, which includes our thoughts, ideals, concepts, and intentions
4. Mindfulness of our environment

Most often we are mindful of only one or two of the four foundations. But it's important to be attentive to all of them. When we ignore any of them, they will manifest in unwholesome ways—as they did for a great yoga master who was incredibly mindful of his bodily sensations but was sexually abusing his female students.

Then there was a Zen teacher who was great at explaining the dharma and always sat in full lotus to give talks. When the pain in his knees began, he ignored it. He refused to take care of his body because of his ideals about being a good Zen teacher. He ended up needing two knee replacements. He was leaving out Buddha's first foundation of mindfulness—mindfulness of the body. His body had something important to share, but he was not listening.

I have a friend who's been practicing Zen for about forty years. He's gay, but he didn't tell his Korean Zen teacher about this until he met someone he was serious about. Finally, my friend told his teacher he was gay.

His teacher said, "No you're not."

And that was the end of the conversation. What foundation of mindfulness was the teacher missing? What was he repressing?

Years later, I got a picture from my friend. He was standing next to his teacher. They must have worked things out, because I know my friend was still living with his partner. I hope they did. I hope the teacher isn't still saying, "No you're not." But who knows?

Relationships are complicated. And it's difficult to maintain awareness of all four foundations of mindfulness. But it's essential.

Dogen said, "Flowers fall even though we love them. Weeds grow even though we hate them."

The self is often disparaged by Buddhist practitioners. We look at the small ego self and see that it includes a lot of entangled weeds. But it's very important to take care of the small ego self. If you disparage it, then you're just creating another split. The ego self is a fiction, but we need that fiction to operate in the world. It may be weedy, but to split off creates weeds of fearfulness and self-loathing.

Supposedly, when the historical Buddha became ill, his disciples said, "Buddha, please heal yourself." Buddha answered, "People are getting too attached. They're acting like I'm a god. It's time for me to go." His final teaching to his followers was, "Become a lamp unto yourself."

To be a lamp unto ourselves, we have to be a lamp unto our *whole* self. Often we're afraid of our base emotions because we want to be good. We try to compartmentalize our world, both our internal world and our external world. If we think something doesn't support our practice, we push it away. When we split off from our emotions, we cut off from an essential part of ourselves. The more we open up to our entire being without denying or repressing, the more we realize we can shine our light of compassion and wisdom anywhere.

As Zen practitioners, rather than retreating into calmness, we discover calmness right in the center of our hurly-burly life. What good is our practice if we can't embrace a little chaos?

Instead of trying so hard to be unattached to things, we can mix things up a little and focus on developing healthy attachments. As long as we hold them lightly, we can enjoy them. To calibrate whether the attachment is healthy or not, ask whether it causes suffering for yourself or others. If not, then here's your opportunity to take your open heart and kind awareness into the world.

EIGHT

Bringing It All
Back Home

My love she speaks like silence

—BOB DYLAN, "LOVE MINUS ZERO/NO LIMIT"

BEFORE HE BECAME FAMOUS, the Buddhist monk, author, and peace activist Thich Nhat Hanh came to the Minnesota Zen Meditation Center to give a dharma talk. Katagiri Roshi, who was the abbot then, met him at the airport. "As I watched him get off the plane and come into the airport, I experienced nothing but stillness," Katagiri told us. His voice was filled with awe as he related the story. He told it over and over because he was deeply moved by the presence of this young Vietnamese Zen teacher, whom he had never met before that day.

It was Katagiri's own stillness that enabled him to be touched in such a profound way. That's what happens when we steep ourselves in silence. We recognize it when it blossoms, even in the middle of a bustling international airport. In the middle of chaos, the innate joy of the universe is always available.

When the mind becomes stable, we hear the great voice of silence wherever we are. At first the stability may be fleeting. That's okay, because a stable mind is not *of time;* the voice that speaks from silence is beyond time. You may think it lasts only a moment—but how long does an eternal moment last?

Zen practice is the effort of steeping ourselves in silence until we actually become the great silence that we are steeped in. When we first start to practice, and maybe for a long time afterward, it may not feel like silence. Obsessive thoughts continuously bubble up, tripping around in our head. They seem beginningless and endless. We try to return to our breath, but the noisy thoughts keep coming.

In the beginning, noise is what you have, so noise becomes your teacher. That's wonderful. Noise has something important to teach you. Steep yourself in it. Don't indulge it—just steep yourself. At first you may not know the difference. But if you sit with the endless parade of thoughts, bringing yourself back to your breath over and over, eventually silence speaks through the noise. Suddenly you know the difference between indulging and steeping, and you are no longer caught by *me, my,* and *mine.*

Noise becomes the compost for realizing the great silence that is always speaking to us, regardless of how much entanglement there is. The silence speaks *through* the entanglement. Our meditative effort is to shine our awareness directly on thought. Through this simple practice, our mind becomes steady, and at the same time patience is cultivated without any effort to cultivate it. Through our diligence, vigor and enthusiasm spring up.

That is how Zen practice works. Without the noisy thoughts to see and release, there would be no path to silence. For Zen students, the path and the destination are not different. There is no place to go and no one to become other than who you are right now. The path of transformation is the path to the bottom of your very self, just as you are.

MY LOVE-MINUS-ZERO MANTRA

After my first year of Zen practice, the austerity of sitting still and doing nothing did not seem to be working for me anymore. Even Suzuki Roshi was not working for me, though I kept sitting with him every morning and evening. To make the early-morning meditation, I sometimes stayed up all night. I sat at an all-night diner, drinking coffee and staring out the window into the fog and darkness until it was time to go the Zen center.

This was about the time Bob Dylan came out with his album *Bringing It All Back Home*. Four lines from two verses in the song "Love Minus Zero/No Limit" became my mantra:

My love she speaks like silence
Without ideals or violence
. . . .
She knows there's no success like failure
And that failure's no success at all.

The first line, "My love she speaks like silence," was about my teacher. Sensei seemed to speak like silence. Silence went with him wherever he went. It wasn't a rigid, heavy, reverent kind of silence. It was light and spacious: a brilliant silence, an ordinary silence. I was romanced by that silence. I sensed something wonderful in it and was drawn to it.

I'm still romanced by that silence. But not by the silence of any one person—by the silence that is present in all beings. After almost fifty years, I am still awed by the great silence that surrounds and imbues everything.

"Without ideals or violence." One reason practice became so hard for me was that I had an ideal that I was clinging to. My ideal was that I should do Zen practice with grace. But I was stumbling through it, with no grace at all. Ideals are frequently about *should* and *shouldn't*. They have nothing to do with what's actually going on. Too often they provoke violent thoughts. We are limited and bullied by them. Just showing up, each morning and evening, was all I needed to do. I didn't need to compare my Zen practice with some ideal. The more rigidly idealistic we are, the more violent we become on the inside.

We chanted the Heart Sutra twice a day, after morning and evening zazen. One day when I showed up for morning meditation, Sensei had posted a little note that read, "Please chant with your ears." It didn't have my name on it, but I knew the note was for me. I thought, Oh my! Oh my! I realized how little attention I'd paid to tune or rhythm. It didn't even occur to me to harmonize with others. I was so caught up in my ideal of giving myself wholeheartedly to the chanting that I wasn't aware of what was actually going on.

Ideals are okay if we can hold them lightly. But I was not holding my ideal lightly. I'd given up everything for this practice. By this time I had dropped out of Stanford; I'd been disinherited by my father and was estranged from him; I'd chosen Zen over law school; and here I was stumbling along without any grace at all. It was a very painful time. But I was doing it to myself, trying to be the ideal student and failing completely.

"She knows there's no success like failure." Zen practice is about stillness and peacefulness, and more than anything else, I wanted to reflect that in my practice. But just when I thought I was beginning to settle in, my body began to shake violently during long retreats. It became so embarrassing that I asked Suzuki for permission to sit outside so I wouldn't disturb others. He said no, that I should keep sitting in the zendo. He sent me to Katagiri Sensei because Katagiri "knew about exercise." Katagiri led me through a few calisthenics. But it didn't help.

"And that failure's no success at all." When I lived in an apartment across the street from the Zen center, Howard and I shared a room. We had been friends and attended Stanford together until I dropped out. One morning after meditation, Howard said to me, "You know, Tim, your zazen is so competitive." As every Zen student knows, being competitive in your zazen is the biggest failure of all.

And yet, in Zen we develop faith in failure. Having faith in failure means knowing there's no difference between failure and success. Too much success solidifies the ego. Failure cultivates bare awareness, and it inspires courageous effort. To endure failure is to succeed brilliantly. As Zen practitioners we encounter an equal amount of success and failure, so there is no difference.

When you become discouraged in your practice, as we all do from time to time, I suggest you try my mantra, gratefully lifted from Bob Dylan. I highly recommend it.

> My love she speaks like silence
> Without ideals or violence
> She knows there's no success like failure
> And that failure's no success at all.

The word *passion* comes from the Latin root meaning "to suffer." Whenever we feel passionately about something, suffering is always present. Nevertheless, life is short, and we need to do things we feel passionate about. The next part of this book is about cultivating equanimity and compassion so we can forget ourselves completely and manifest the enlightened activity of an open heart.

PART THREE

When Snow Falls, It Falls on Everything

CULTIVATING EQUANIMITY AND COMPASSION

NINE

Accommodating Ourselves to the Environment

"WHY DO THE JAPANESE MAKE their cups so fragile?" a student asked Suzuki.

Suzuki replied, "The problem is not that the cups are too fragile. The problem is that you do not know how to handle them. You should learn to accommodate yourself to what's around you."

Suzuki was very good at accommodating himself to the environment. He had been assigned by the Japanese Soto Zen hierarchy to the San Francisco Zen Center to serve the local Japanese congregation, who mostly lived in San Francisco's Japantown. Suzuki conducted weddings, funerals, and other traditional ceremonies, and the congregation members, in turn, supported the Zen center financially. But they didn't attend the meditations, dharma talks, or retreats he led. In Japan only the monks and nuns living in monasteries actually do sitting meditation.

Nonetheless, Suzuki seemed to move with ease between three different cultures: his own culture, as reflected in his Japanese congregation, which perhaps gave him the most difficulty; San Francisco's subculture, which must have been a total shock to his conservative sensibilities; and the budding American Zen culture, which was the culture he seemed most committed to and was nurturing.

On weekends Japanese movies were shown at the Zen center— high-action, class B samurai-type movies. The posters were lurid and violent. One Sunday as Suzuki was getting ready to give his dharma talk, he mentioned that he was sleepy.

"Sleepy?" I said, surprised.

"Yes," he said. "Every Saturday night, I go to the movie."

"You don't go to the movie in the auditorium, do you?"

"Yes."

"Oh, I'm sorry," I said, feeling bad for him, assuming that he was duty-bound to go. "Do you like any of them?"

"I like them all," he said cheerfully.

Suzuki was also able to accommodate himself to the Haight-Ashbury subculture that began in 1966–67. Every evening people drifted over from Haight-Ashbury to sit meditation with us. Bells, beads, bright colors, and pungent aromas filled the zendo. I'm sure Suzuki had never been exposed to anything like this in Japan. Yet he seemed completely at ease and welcoming.

By this time, many in the counterculture were picking up on the mystical side of Buddhism. Some were having LSD-induced experiences of oneness, but few were interested in committing themselves to a Buddhist practice. Suzuki called LSD-induced enlightenment experiences "dry enlightenment" because people were not being transformed by their experience. They didn't become more generous or compassionate.

But Suzuki didn't disparage dry enlightenment. Marian Derby asked him once whether he thought she should take LSD. He answered yes. He knew Marian would take it in a safe environment. He must have suspected it would help her experience an opening beyond the ego. And it did. But as far as I know, he never recommended LSD to anyone else.

Once, on a ride through town with Suzuki, the driver spotted a friend and stopped to pick him up. The guy snuffed out a joint, then crawled into the car next to Suzuki, reeking of marijuana. I looked over to gauge Suzuki's reaction. He sensed my question.

"I am not for or against marijuana," he said softly. "I am just trying to show people our way."

The third culture Suzuki accommodated became America's first authentic Zen culture. We were sincere—but not exactly what he envisioned before coming to this country. This must have been difficult for him, because he couldn't simply accommodate us and remain true to the teachings. He was fostering Zen in America. It was a big responsibility. But if he pushed too hard, we would run away, and he would lose a wonderful opportunity to share Buddha's teachings.

After we bought Tassajara, we began having Zen practice periods there, which lasted for three months. He wanted to show us how to steep ourselves in stillness. But between sittings, we were skinny-dipping in the hot springs. Initially, Suzuki accommodated it. He even joined us occasionally, cupping his genitals in his hands. His modesty was endearing.

Eventually, he put an end to skinny-dipping. But he did it gently. Consequently, we *wanted* his guidance and gratefully accepted it. If he had tried to impose his way on us too soon, we would have fled.

Suzuki was not the first Zen teacher in America. But he was able to spread Zen further than others partly because he accommodated himself to the environment. Dogen said, "To carry the self forward and illuminate the myriad things is delusion. That the myriad things come forth and illuminate the self is awakening."

Suzuki embodied Dogen's teaching. It seemed to bubble up continuously from the core of his being. A bodhisattva's compassion is not limited by the lines we draw around culture, race, class, or caste. Suzuki just extended himself. He didn't seem to see boundaries. He saw people.

In 1965 *The Three Pillars of Zen* by Philip Kapleau was published. It's all about big enlightenment experiences. Suzuki didn't speak out against the book, but it was apparent that he didn't think too much of it. Suzuki showed us, through example, that Zen was about something much deeper than having a big experience.

Zen practice is about taking care of our lives, helping others, and being open to whatever comes up. When we accommodate ourselves to others, the ego self is not so important. This change happens on its own, because our small self is sustained through self-centeredness and self-involvement. But accommodating ourselves to our environment is not an easy practice.

OFF THE CUSHION AND INTO THE WORLD

Not long after my son was born, my wife and I decided to leave California. We wanted to go somewhere new. We wanted an adventure, but we also wanted a wholesome place to raise our family. We packed up and moved to Minnesota, where we lived in the woods in a trailer home.

I went to work as a social worker for northern Saint Louis County, which includes part of the Nett Lake Ojibwe reservation. A dirt road runs through the center of a small town located in the middle of the reservation. I was the social worker for the south side of the dirt road, and a social worker from Koochiching County was responsible for the north side.

It was a totally new environment for me. I was a counterculture guy. For years I had protested against "the establishment." Now I owed my job to it, and I would have to accommodate myself to it in order to serve the Ojibwe people, a difficult culture to penetrate. Could I accommodate these two new cultures? I did my best, but in the counterculture, we focused on the culture we opposed, so I was unaware of my own strongly held beliefs and prejudices.

I had a few successes but many failures. On one occasion I worked hard to get a group of Ojibwe teenagers registered for tech school. I arranged for transportation and made sure they got the textbooks and supplies they needed. This was a great opportunity for them. All they had to do was show up. But they didn't.

The problem was that they never said they wanted to go to tech school. I thought I knew what was best for them. I wasn't able to accommodate myself to their environment, and no doubt the boys suffered because of it. When we contract around an idea, we are closed to other options. There are always other options, but I saw only one—tech school.

Suzuki Roshi said, "In the mind of an expert, there is only one possibility. In the mind of a beginner, there are many." It was the central teaching of his first book, *Zen Mind, Beginner's Mind*. It is also central if we are going to accommodate ourselves to the environment. In the early days at Tassajara Monastery, Suzuki didn't impose his way on us when he was trying to bring silence and stillness into our lives. But in my efforts to help the Ojibwe people, I had not yet imbibed that wisdom.

On occasion one of my clients would go on a drinking binge, and I'd get a call that their kids were being neglected. I drove over to figure out what was going on and to decide what to do. Typically, I found the kids and took them to one of our foster homes in the white community. But time after time, before the day was done, I'd get a phone call—the kids had run away and were back on the reservation.

As a social worker, the kids were my biggest concern. Every time we took them to a foster home where they would be cared for, they ran away. I suspected the kids were not treated well in the white community, but at least they were safe. They had food to eat and a bed to sleep in. So over and over, I picked the kids up and drove them to the foster home.

For a long time I missed the clues. The reservation was an extended family. If the parents were drunk, someone else stepped in and took care of their kids. The community was both interdependent and resilient. They were a third-world culture overtaken by a powerful first-world culture. They survived because they had their own way of doing things. I missed that, so I became part of the problem. It was harmful to rip these children out of their context and plop them into another one.

I was convinced that if the parents were drunk, the kids were being abused. It stemmed from my personal history. If I'd been able to see through my conditioned ideas, I wouldn't have been hauling kids off the reservation.

Viola Villebrun was a petite Ojibwe woman in her forties. She had long dark hair and wore big earrings and no makeup. She was friendly and intelligent, and she cared deeply about the kids on the reservation. I approached her about opening a foster home. She was cool to the idea at first. She feared retaliation from the parents whose kids she would be taking in. But in the end she gathered her courage, and the Nett Lake reservation got its first foster home. The kids and the community benefited greatly.

It took a while to see past my cultural baggage so I could help the Ojibwe people. Often our ideas about helping people get in the way of actually helping them.

When I was a child, I watched my mother get drunk and abuse my sisters. She wasn't abusive to me, only to my sisters. People say it's easier to suffer yourself than to watch someone you love suffer. I think it's true. There's confusion when guilt gets mixed in with grief. On an unconscious level, I linked being drunk with being abusive, and I wanted to protect the kids on the reservation.

Zen practice is about freeing ourselves from our conditioned ways of thinking and being in the world. Instead of accommodating myself to the environment, I was clinging to the past and projecting it into the future. Many years later I was able to look back and see the inner workings of my conditioned mind.

For many of us in the counterculture, mental illness was a blind spot. We rejected the reality of it. R. D. Laing talked about psychosis as being a journey. Rather than taking medicine, you go through it and become an enlightened being. At Stanford I had a professor who said he'd had a psychotic break and used it as a learning tool. Then there was the *One Flew Over the Cuckoo's Nest* theory that mental illness was just a social construct, a way for society to put away people who were irritating. There was the belief that Ezra Pound was a brilliant poet who was institutionalized because of his political beliefs. There were a lot of ideas being floated around concerning mental illness.

So when my sister Yvette called to tell me that our younger sister, Charlotte, had had a psychotic break, I didn't think too much of it. The diagnosis was schizophrenia. I dug in my heels against what I saw as negative labeling. My suspicions and aversions toward the establishment came roaring to the fore. If this was some sort of inner journey Charlotte was engaged in (à la R. D. Laing), perhaps it would help her to get away from the city and immerse herself in nature. "Send her here," I told Yvette.

A few days later, I drove to the Hibbing airport to pick up Charlotte. She seemed okay. A little off-kilter maybe, perhaps because it had been a long flight. When we got home, she bounded out of the car and into the small trailer where we lived. She was thrilled to see my wife, Linda, who was pregnant with our second child. But Charlotte didn't see Linda. She saw our childhood neighbor, Noreen, and when Linda told her she was not Noreen, Charlotte looked at Linda very carefully; and then said it was obvious Linda was suffering from amnesia.

There's a saying in Buddhism: If we accept reality, things are just as they are. If we *don't* accept reality, things are just as they are. My sister was not on a journey of transformation, and it wasn't open space and fresh air that she needed. All my ideas about mental illness were naive. It is not a social construct. And only rarely is it a spiritual journey.

Charlotte stayed with us in northern Minnesota for about a month. During that time I was forced to accept that the sister I had grown up with was gone and that she was not coming back. At times I still contract against this reality. It is human nature to close down when our pain seems overwhelming. I did not want to accommodate myself to this environment. It is still hard for me.

Those times when accommodating ourselves to the environment seems too difficult, we can acknowledge that our heart has closed up to protect itself. You are not truly a Zen student until you have practiced through difficulty. A technique such as following the breath or repeating a mantra or visualizing the self as a swinging door is most helpful during times of despair. We can focus our kind awareness on our breath or a chant, or move fully into our painful emotion, allowing ourselves to be moved by it, and then return to a place of rest.

When I can do this, I'm able to enjoy my memories of the sister I once had. I can also enjoy Charlotte just as she is.

CULTIVATING THE BARE GROUND

Instead of food from the refrigerator, we should be interested in producing food from the field, from the bare ground.

—SUZUKI ROSHI

There's something about growing your own food that arouses great generosity. But before we can produce food from the field, we have to cultivate the bare ground, the ground of our being, from which little shoots of freshness, spontaneity, and authenticity sprout. Suzuki said, "The most wonderful thing in the world is dirt under your fingernails." It means you are cultivating the bare ground and something is growing, unfolding, opening up, and blooming.

It doesn't matter what kind of fruit is produced. There will be varied amounts of suffering and joy, so it doesn't matter how red your tomatoes are or how yellow your corn is. The point is to produce your own vegetables and fruit. When the next season comes, the snow falls, and we are back to bare ground again. Problem after problem, mistake after mistake, we continue to seed, water, and aerate. Wonderful fruit arises from our effort. Then winter comes and snow makes everything the same again. The snow is always falling, and sameness is always here.

When you truly cultivate the bare ground, you want to share the abundance that arises. Share everything, without picking and choosing. Even the worms have something to offer—life is manifesting, and worms are part of it. You may not want to eat the worms, but you don't have to. Already, the worms are totally you, and you are totally they, when you're in contact with the bare ground.

After two years in northern Minnesota, living in a trailer and working as a social worker, I quit my job. My family, which had grown to four, moved to Two Harbors, a town by Lake Superior. For five thousand dollars we purchased a homestead that included forty acres of land and an old farmhouse. We lived semicommunally with another couple.

Homesteading in winter in northern Minnesota is all about accommodating oneself to the environment. I got up at 5 A.M., sat zazen for an hour, and then went out to milk the goat. After breakfast there was wood to cut and snow to shovel and Jed to get to kindergarten. I put him on my back and skied from the farmhouse down a hill, across a bridge, and up through a field to the paved road where the school bus picked him up. Once, I took a tumble and Jed went airborne. He landed in deep snow, but it was not a problem. He hauled himself back onto my back, and on we went.

Accommodating oneself to the environment means taking care of whatever bubbles up. When a mother goat refused to nurse her baby, we took him in and nurtured him. It was March—too cold for him in the barn, so we brought him inside and fed him with a cloth soaked in goat's milk. We named him Nemadji, after a river close by.

Nemadji quickly outgrew his accommodations. Finding a home for him proved difficult. No one wanted a male goat. We ended up giving him to another farmer, hopefully for breeding, but we didn't ask any questions. It was traumatic because our children, Jed and Erin, loved him. Nemadji had become our friend.

With Nemadji, as with life, there were varied amounts of joy and pain. Our practice is to make the most compassionate choice possible in each circumstance and then experience fully whatever arises from our decisions. Life is a series of ever-changing situations, so accommodating ourselves happens moment by moment.

Zen Master Ryokan said, "What is right today is wrong tomorrow." We look at each situation anew, with fresh eyes. When we're cultivating the bare ground, there is always something new to deal with.

UNCOMMON SENSE

There is a story about Buddha throwing his bowl into the river. It traveled upstream. The Buddhist path is not the common way. From the outside, it may look foolish.

My in-laws certainly thought Linda and I were foolish. A lot of folks in America thought the counterculture was foolish. Often we were. But cultivating the ground of our being is not the common path, especially if you're living in northern Minnesota, where the bare ground is red clay. Instead of planting seeds, Linda and I should have been making pots.

My wife's brother, Phil, who was an accountant from California, and his wife, Barbara, came to the farmhouse to visit us. We were eager to show them the wonderful wilds of northern Minnesota. We loved the sound of wolves and coyotes in the night, and we loved living in a place where bears and moose roam freely.

One of our favorite things was going to the dump to watch the bears. Unfortunately, Phil and Barbara didn't share our fondness for the bears—especially when they snuggled up against the car. When a bear and I went nose to nose against the window, Barbara totally freaked out.

After that, Linda and I tried to redeem ourselves by taking them on a peaceful walk through the woods along the goat trails. But we had become so acculturated to northern Minnesota, we forgot how bad the mosquitoes were that time of year. Later that evening, Phil told Linda, "You and Tim lack common sense."

It's true; we did lack "common sense," where life is packaged, routine, and predictable. Cultivating the bare ground is never common and never predictable—especially when the ground is red clay. But actually, we always start with red clay; it's the human condition. You may think your red clay is denser than anyone else's. You sit and sit and sit, just following your breath, hour after hour, year after year, and there's no aeration. Your thoughts keep coming in big dense chunks, with no space in between.

But the space is there. It's all the same soil. Our soil is not different from Suzuki Roshi's soil, which is not different from Shakyamuni Buddha's soil. Eventually, if our practice is sincere, it becomes rich and nutritious. All sorts of wonderful plants spring up. And what they produce is always fresh, delicious, and quite perfect.

Suzuki Roshi said that waking up to Big Mind is a very simple process. It's a matter of caring for the soil. We learn to live from the ground of our being, the bare ground, so we can experience openness and availability. The joy that comes from that cannot be packaged. It can't be stored and saved up for later. We think that if we can stay in the right environment and hang out with the right people so no one bums us out, we'll be able to keep it. That's stale food from the refrigerator. It's not fresh; it's not alive.

Every tradition has its stale foods. My mother was Irish and grew up Catholic. But in college she left her church. "All the stuff they repeated to us became so trite," she said. "The clichés covered up what was actually going on. We lived through the Great Depression, and we were being told that it was God's will."

Well, it didn't seem to my mother as if God were responsible. When she resisted this idea, she was told, "We are all sinners, dear."

Hollow truisms, like those my mother rejected, are just food from the refrigerator—dead and lifeless. They may pacify, but they cannot nourish. How can hollow truisms possibly help us uncover the stillness and joy of our true nature? Eventually, my mother returned to her own presence of mind and her own heart.

Unfortunately, she didn't have a community for support, so she felt alone and isolated.

When I was a young man, I put words of inspiration from Suzuki's talks on the bathroom mirror. But after a while I wouldn't even see them, and when I did, they didn't inspire. They became dull and stale because they were food from the refrigerator. They had bubbled up, fresh and alive, from the bare ground, and then I packaged them on little pieces of paper to save for later.

Each generation tries to pass down their values by packaging them up. There's a Buddhist saying that captures the theme of the sixties counterculture: Don't be the second half of a cut melon. The counterculture resisted the values of the generation that came before us. We were not pacified by platitudes that divide people by religious beliefs, bloodlines, and citizenship, drawing lines around meaningless and totally random constellations, creating divisions where none existed.

We wanted something different—an authentic life, one we cultivated ourselves, one that arose naturally from the ground of our being. For some of us, the quest for such a life led to Zen.

TEN

Touching the Heart
That Suffers

PATACARA LIVED IN INDIA AT THE time of the Buddha. She was a strong young woman who always followed her heart. When she was sixteen, her marriage to an older man was arranged by her father, and the wedding day was set. But Patacara was in love with one of the family's servants, who also loved her. To marry out of class was forbidden and dishonorable. So Patacara and her lover ran away.

Traditionally, when a woman married, she left her own clan and moved into her husband's home. But her husband had no family, no home, and no security. So the couple lived in a small hut made of clay and dung with earthen floors. Patacara chose a hard but peaceful life.

When she became pregnant, she wanted to return to her parents, as was the custom, but her husband refused to make the trip. She gave birth to their son at home, alone, on an earthen floor. The next year she became pregnant again. She longed to visit her parents. Again, her husband refused her request. Finally, convinced he would not change his mind, Patacara set out on her own with their young son, and with her unborn child near full term. But the delay meant the rainy season was upon them.

Realizing Patacara had left, her husband rushed to catch up, and the three of them continued their journey together. Soon a great storm blew up. Patacara sent her husband to find wood and palm leaves to build a shelter. While he was gone, she went into labor. Sheltering one child from the terrible storm, she gave birth to the other. Then she waited throughout the night for her husband to return.

But he didn't return. The next morning Patacara bundled up her two children and went looking for him. She found his body by a tree. He had been bitten by a poisonous snake while gathering wood. Patacara collapsed in grief. She remained with his body throughout the day and night. The following day she gathered her children to return to her parents' home as a widow.

But when she arrived at the river, the storm had turned it into a torrent. She couldn't possibly cross it with both children. She left the newborn under a tree for protection and carried her son across, holding him high above the water while looking back over her shoulder for reassurance that her newborn was safe. On the other side, she placed her son on the bank and then started back across the river.

Suddenly, a hawk appeared overhead circling her newborn. Patacara screamed frantically and slapped at the water to scare it away. But the hawk continued its downward spiral. Patacara watched in horror as it dropped down and stole the baby away. On the other shore her son, hearing his mother's screams, thought she was calling him and he started into the river. Immediately the current swept him away. Within moments, both of Patacara's children were gone.

Numb with pain, Patacara continued toward her home village. She happened across a traveler she recognized from her youth. They ran toward each other and embraced. Grief stricken himself, he spoke of the terrible storm that had devastated their village. Patacara asked about her family.

"Oh, please don't ask. It is such a tragic thing."

But Patacara beseeched him to tell her of her family.

"The terrible storm caused the roof of their house to collapse. They were killed."

At that moment, Patacara's mind slipped away. She became a crazed spirit. Days passed into weeks. She became an outcast among outcasts, untouchable even among the untouchables. When her threadbare clothes fell away, she became known as the "cloak walker." People threw garbage and mud at her to keep her away. She wandered aimlessly, growing more and more remote, thinner and thinner, and more and more filthy.

Finally, she wandered into Buddha's camp. His disciples found her frightening and appalling. "Leave the lunatic alone," his disciples pleaded. "Do not get close to her."

But Buddha saw that she was so completely broken that she was very close to being whole. Every desire she once cherished, even the desire to follow her own heart, was gone. Any anger she once harbored had long since dissolved. Her mind was gone, but so were her delusions.

Buddha rose and moved to place himself in Patacara's path. As she approached, he said, "Sister, it is time to recover your presence of mind."

Hearing these words, Patacara immediately returned to clarity. It was not just the voice of Shakyamuni Buddha that spoke, it was the timeless voice that calls to all beings to wake up. Void of the three poisons, Patacara was able to hear the summons with her whole body and mind.

"Help me," she pleaded. "Save me from this pain." These were the first words she had uttered since meeting the traveler and learning of her parents' death.

"I can't save you from loss and grief," Buddha told her. "You are clutching at something you cannot keep—something you could never have kept."

Patacara was accepted into the women's sangha (Buddhist community), and she quickly became a great teacher and leader. By some accounts, she had thirty disciples; by others, over a hundred. But does it matter? She was a remarkable disciple whose story still supports people, more than twenty-five centuries later.

Yet though Patacara was able to comfort others who were suffering, she could find no comfort from her own pain. How could she accept that her children, her husband, and her parents were all dead? Her grief seemed too deep and her heart too wounded to heal.

One day it was raining lightly as Patacara sat alone on a hillside. She became engrossed by the many streamlets of water cascading downward. Some ran quickly, others slowly. Some covered a great distance before being absorbed into the earth, while others lasted only moments. For a long time, Patacara watched as streamlet after streamlet disappeared into the bare ground. Suddenly, her heart opened. In that moment, she finally accepted the death of her family.

BARE AWARENESS

Bathing my feet, I watched the bathwater spill down the slope.
I concentrated my mind the way you train a good horse.
Then I took a lamp and went into my cell, checked the bed and sat down on it.

I took a needle and pushed the wick down.
As the lamp when out, my mind was freed.

—PATACARA'S ENLIGHTENMENT POEM

Touching the heart that suffers and staying with it is the most difficult thing we do as human beings. Most often, when tragedy strikes, we try to protect ourselves by creating distance. *Thinking* about our pain numbs us to the actual feeling—so we analyze, rationalize, blame, and deny, spinning a web of confusion and getting caught in it. The more we do this, the more closed down we become and the more alone and isolated we feel.

A core Buddhist teaching is that everything is the cause of everything else, and everything is the effect of everything else. This is hard to wrap our mind around. It's impossible to contract around this teaching. We have to *open* to it.

The best tool in the Buddhist toolbox for opening up is bare awareness. There are four components to bare awareness: recognition, acceptance, restraint, and return.

Recognition. After Patacara joined the women's sangha, she became a teacher and leader. She could be available to others—but not wholeheartedly. Something was still blocking her openness and causing a feeling of disconnect.

We all get caught in a painful mind-set or reactivity that blocks our openness and increases the feeling of disconnectedness. First we have to recognize where we are. Then we begin to notice the types of thoughts that are swirling around, perpetuating our negativity, magnifying it, intensifying it, and holding our attitude in place. We stay with this recognition until it opens up into an underlying feeling tone or emotion. Notice whether the feeling is one of sadness, anger, fear—or maybe it's still too vague and ephemeral to distinguish. We just recognize that and then try to stay with it as it moves around. Notice whether you are identifying with the feeling tone or just seeing it. Recognition involves deep and subtle investigation. Often the underlying emotions are quite elusive. Not always. Sometimes the force of an emotion that we were totally unaware of knocks us off-kilter. But we can always return to our place of rest, like a swinging door.

As Patacara gazed at the streamlets running down the hillside, recognition began to emerge because, at last, she was able just to see her deep pain without identifying with it and being carried away by its force. She did it by just watching and allowing herself to open. She did not contract around the powerful emotions. Instead, she moved into bare awareness.

Acceptance. The second component of bare awareness is acceptance. I often refer to it as radical acceptance because it involves the whole body and mind. We begin to relax into the facts before us. Then, as our reactive thoughts and emotions arise, we relax into those, too. As Patacara sat in the rain, she went into a meditative state and relaxed into her feelings. Perhaps she thought, *I wish it wasn't so.* And then she relaxed into her feeling of wishing it wasn't so.

With understanding, things are just as they are. Without understanding, things are just as they are. As Patacara watched each streamlet disappear into the earth, she began to understand something. She noticed how some lived a long life and covered a great distance. Others lived only a moment. But they all vanished into the same place.

Patacara became known for her ability to help those who suffered terrible losses. But she was also known as a great teacher of impermanence, one of Buddha's core teachings.

Restraint. The third component of bare awareness is restraint. But there is a caveat regarding restraint. It's important to be clear about *what* we restrain from. We restrain from getting overly involved in thought. We do not restrain from attending to the sensations and feelings that arise in the body. Thoughts continuously pull us away from our strong feelings and emotions and back into the Chatterbox Café, where we feel safe and protected. But we don't need to be protected from our emotions. To experience them directly restraint is necessary because the pull of habituated thought patterns is always with us.

A second caveat involves the sequential nature of the four components of bare awareness. First we recognize that we are grieving. Then we open into the multitudes of sensations and feelings with kind awareness, which leads to acceptance. Recognition and acceptance have to come first; otherwise we are not restraining—we are repressing. If we move directly from recognition to restraint, bypassing acceptance, we become brittle and cold.

For Patacara, perhaps very little, if any, restraint was needed. As a crazed spirit, she completely lost her presence of mind—which included her habituated thought patterns that veil our true nature. According to the story, as Patacara sat on the hillside in the rain, she was able just to watch and open up to a profound truth that was being revealed.

The truth of existence is always being revealed to us. This is a fractal universe; it speaks the language of patterns, revealing its wholeness in every fragment of nature, even in a blade of grass or a drop of water.

Returning. The fourth component of bare awareness—returning—arises naturally from the third. We restrain by moving our awareness from our thinking back into our body, which is returning. We make a conscious decision not to let the pattern keep running. Then we immediately return to the sensations in the body or to the breath. Over and over, we return.

The acronym for the four components of recognition, acceptance, restraint, and returning is RARR, the sound a lion makes when it roars. When strong emotions threaten to overwhelm you, just RARR—recognize, accept, restrain, and return. When you RARR, you won't contract and shrivel up like a prune. Whatever happens, we can RARR our way back to bare awareness, which is our natural state of openness.

FIERCE GRACE: RAM DASS

I am more at peace now than ever, and that comes from settling into the moment.

—RAM DASS

I first heard Ram Dass speak in the midsixties, when he was Richard Alpert. He came to Stanford to talk about LSD and tell us all to turn on. Without LSD, it's doubtful the Zen movement would have caught on in the United States. The sixties and seventies were a time of experimentation, and people like Ram Dass were the models. Soon after his speech at Stanford, he moved away from chemicals and into a true spiritual practice. His transformation came about through meditation and with the guidance of a guru. His seminal book *Be Here Now* was published in 1971, and it had a huge influence. It is sometimes referred to as the counterculture bible. I later saw Ram Dass in the mideighties, when he came to the Twin Cities to speak.

Then, in 2001 his film *Fierce Grace* came out. It was made after his debilitating stroke, which happened in 1997. I was very touched by the film and by his deep spiritual transformation. The film reveals how thoroughly Ram Dass has internalized his meditative practice. He doesn't use the term *bare awareness,* but he practices it.

Throughout the documentary, you see how completely Ram Dass recognizes and accepts his limitations and works within them. He doesn't piss and moan about his difficult recovery from the stroke; he restrains, moment by moment. Wholehearted acceptance allows him to be with his limitations without complaining. He returns, time and time again, to the present moment. In the film he patiently lifts his leg with his hands to get in and out of a car. Each movement is slow, precise, and cautious, with no hint of frustration or crankiness toward his attendants.

When I'd seen him in the sixties, it was a different Ram Dass. From a Zen point of view, it was total ego identification. It was LSD narcissism. Twenty years later, when I saw him a second time in the Twin Cities, it was still a lot about Ram Dass—*his* practice, *his* guru, *his* trips to India. I'm not saying he wasn't a spiritual adept; certainly he was. But from a Zen perspective, the *his* was extra. Both times I heard him speak, he was quite glib.

But in *Fierce Grace* his words are few and far between. The glibness is totally gone, replaced by an incredible grace and sincerity. Time and time again, he uses his physical limitations to help him return to what's real. His emotions bubble up spontaneously, and he expresses them in a warm and touching way. In an interview, he reveals that he combined "fierce" with "grace" because he sees the stroke as a gift.

Zen practice is about returning, over and over, to *just this*— this moment, this reality, with no obscuring overlays created by our judgments, criticisms, and ideals. We use whatever we have to help us return, moment by moment. But we can use adversity only if we have accepted it with our whole heart.

Fierce Grace is about the discipline of living our impediments. We all have some impediment we live with that can help us return to bare awareness of our true nature. The ego disidentification that comes with bare awareness comes only through practice. It comes on its own; we can't force it—because the dis-identification is from the practitioner. When we focus our kind attention on living our impediment, moment by moment, we *become* the bare awareness. We dissolve into it. Here is Ram Dass talking about living his impediment:

> For years I worked as a Karmi yogi, the path of service. I wrote books about learning to serve, about how to help others. Now it's reversed. I need people to help me get up and put me to bed. Others feed me and wash my bottom. And I can tell you it's harder to be the helped than the helper. But this is just another stage. It feels like I died and have been reborn over and over. In the sixties I was a professor at Harvard. And when that ended, I went out with Timothy Leary spreading psychedelics. Then in the seventies I died from that and returned from India as Baba Ram Dass, the guru. Then in the eighties my life was all about service, cofounding the Save Foundation, building hospitals, and working with refugees and prisoners. Over all these years I've played the cello, golf, drove my MG. Since the stroke, the car's in the driveway, the cello and golf clubs in the closet. If I think I'm the guy who can't play cello or drive or work in India, I would feel terribly sorry for myself. But I'm not him. During the stroke I died again, and now I have a new life in a disabled body. This is where I am. You've gotta be here now.

In *Fierce Grace*, Ram Dass tells a story that puzzles me. He says that all he can remember about having his stroke and being taken to the hospital is lying on the gurney, looking up at the ceiling, and seeing the crisscrossing pipes. This memory disappoints him. "Here I was, Mr. Spiritual, and I didn't have a single spiritual thought. I didn't orient to the spirit. This was the test and I flunked it. All that was on my mind were the pipes in the ceiling. This showed me I had more work to do."

This is puzzling because, from a Zen point of view, Ram Dass was experiencing wholehearted engagement in the moment. He completely forgot the self and dissolved into bare awareness. Body and mind dropped away. From the point of view of Ram Dass's own book, *Be Here Now,* seeing the crisscrossing pipes in the ceiling is the whole deal. So I'm puzzled by his comments about failing the test.

But this is the human situation. Even the best teachers often feel that they have failed. We get caught in wanting to intellectualize each situation.

In 2005 I was involved in a car accident. I got broadsided by another car. My own car was totaled: the windshield shattered and the driver's side crushed in. Emergency responders had to pry me out of the car, and then I was taken to Regions Hospital in Saint Paul.

I have vivid memories of the patterns in the ceiling. As I lay on the examining table, a wonderful experience of bare awareness seemed to arise on its own. There was a delightful and fascinating dance going on. I didn't have a single spiritual thought. But from a Zen point of view, thought is extra. The dance itself is the great mystery of life.

Life is a dance, but it's a brief dance. Just a few days ago, I was in the third grade, riding my bike with my best friend. I blinked, and here I am, seventy years old.

The season of our lives is short. The opportunity to really experience life with bare awareness is fleeting: to do the things we really care about—to love the people we love, to become willing to touch the heart that suffers—there's not much time.

Each of us, in every moment, faces the inevitability of death. In that same moment, can we seize the opportunities of life? Can we appreciate the pleasures and joy in the midst of all the angst? If we can, then we become brave enough to risk further insecurity by returning to just this moment, even when the heart is suffering.

Maybe we can manage only one breath. If we learn to do one complete breath with bare awareness, then we're ready for death. Because on the out breath, we let go of everything—everything known and everything unknown. Then on the in breath, there is new life, new opportunity. And then the out breath. Life/death. Death/life. There's no difference. Everything is constantly transforming into something else.

When we are completely ready to die, we are completely alive. We can't separate ourselves from the life and death that is happening all around us. We are made of life and death. Our bodies are full of life and death. If we can accept life/death, death/life, then we are ready to explore the mysteries of the suffering heart.

But we are not doing it alone. We aren't separate from Siddhartha Gautama, who became the Buddha; or the Zen poet Basho, who wrote about mountain paths, missing Kyoto, and play women; or Suzuki Roshi. We're not separate from Ram Dass, who exemplifies the teachings of "The Sandokai": "Within darkness there is light"; or from Rainer Maria Rilke, who delved deeply into the mysteries of suffering and shared his wisdom in this poem:

You darkness, that I come from,
I love you more than all the fires
that fence in the world,
for the fire makes
a circle of light for everyone,
and then no one outside learns of you.

But the darkness pulls in everything:
shapes and fires, animals and myself,

how easily it gathers them!—
powers and people—

and it is possible a great energy
is moving near me.

I have faith in nights.

—RAINER MARIA RILKE, "YOU, DARKNESS"

THIS BLESSED CANCER: TRUDY DIXON

Without bitterest cold that penetrates to the very bone, how can
plum blossoms send forth their fragrance all over the world?

—DOGEN

Trudy Dixon, the editor of *Zen Mind, Beginner's Mind,* was one of Suzuki Roshi's earliest and closest students. She was there when I started. Her dedication to practice throughout her struggle with cancer was inspirational for all of us. She had long blond hair, a quiet but friendly demeanor, and clear eyes that seemed to get clearer as she sat with her illness.

I first met Trudy on a Wednesday evening shortly after I began to practice with Suzuki. On Wednesdays, after zazen, we turned to face the center of the room. Suzuki gave a short talk, and then we had tea together. Trudy usually sat opposite me. I didn't know her well.

Suzuki and Richard Baker, Suzuki's head student and only direct dharma heir, were invited to accompany Trudy to her family ranch in Montana. When they returned, I picked them up at the airport. As we drove back to the Zen center, Suzuki talked about going horseback riding with Trudy.

"I didn't know you knew how to ride horses," I said.

In typical Suzuki fashion, he replied cheerfully, "I don't, but the horse knew how to carry me."

Soon after that trip, it seemed that Trudy's cancer started progressing rapidly. One morning when I arrived for zazen, there was a small chair alongside the cushions, facing the wall. The only time chairs were ever in the zendo was for public talks on Sundays—never for morning meditation. So for a moment I was taken aback. Then I thought, *Oh, that must be for Trudy.*

It was such a small thing, but its impact filled the room. I settled in on my cushion, and a few minutes later, I heard Trudy shuffle in, walking very slowly, so different from her old vibrant and energetic self. She crossed to the chair and eased into it. Like everyone else, I was touched by her determination and by the quiet, compassionate way Suzuki supported her.

After a while the small chair disappeared and a bigger, more comfortable one took its place. When Trudy entered the zendo, she crossed painfully slowly. The rustling sounds as she settled herself into the chair reverberated through me, softening my heart and opening it.

Throughout Trudy's decline, Suzuki was able to be with her suffering in stillness and with composure. He loved Trudy deeply, so it must have been terribly painful for him. But he didn't get caught up in his own pain. It's impossible to support others if we're stuck in our own anguish.

For decades Suzuki repeated his bodhisattva vow "to help all beings." He repeated it with his whole heart and mind. When we support our bodhisattva vow, it will support us in times of need. So Suzuki was able to keep his heart open and be available for Trudy.

When I was a kid, my sister and I used to go to the beach and gather shells. The sea anemones were always closed, so I poked them with sticks, trying to get them to open. One day my sister touched one softly. I watched in fascination as it suddenly opened up. I'd never seen anything like it—beautiful and fragile. It was breathtaking. For a long time afterward, I secretly followed my sister around, hoping to learn how she did it.

When the human heart opens, it is so tender and immediate that there is no difference between great sadness and indescribable beauty. If we penetrate it, the pain of existence will take us right down to the nexus of life, where pain and joy, sadness and awe, are not separate. I felt this nexus fleetingly as a kid when I gazed into the exquisite beauty and tenderness of a sea anemone. I felt it again when Trudy eased her wounded body into the big chair and settled into the stillness of zazen. This is life's great paradox. Trudy's words "this blessed cancer" contain life's greatest koan, and she resolved it completely.

I don't remember much about Trudy's funeral. Suzuki wore formal robes and a large Japanese headdress. In the liturgy, he talked a little about Zen teachings, and then he talked about Trudy. But what is emblazoned forever in my mind is Suzuki's mighty farewell cry to his beloved student. He sent Trudy off with a great roar: "*Gooooo my disciple!*" It seemed to contain all the pain that ever existed in the universe. And all the triumph. Tears rolled freely down his face.

YIELD TO THE WILLOW: MY ONLY BROTHER

Yield to the willow all the loathing, all the desire of your heart.

—BASHO

I was sitting in my office on the corner of Nicollet and Franklin in Minneapolis when my mother called. I knew by her voice that something was terribly wrong.

When I hung up, I turned away from my desk and looked out at the sky. It seemed to go on forever, and I breathed deep sadness into it. I'm not sure how long I sat there, staring out the window and breathing into my body as the reality of my brother's suicide sank down into me.

I was ten years older than my brother. Growing up, I hardly knew him. When I moved away, Chip was only sixteen and already heavily into alcohol. I came down hard on him about the way he lived his life. I saw only his behavior. I never appreciated the depth of his depression.

Once in Santa Cruz when he was drunk and acting up, I stopped the car and told him to get out. These are the memories that flooded in as I sat there, breathing sorrow, regret, and guilt into the vast blueness outside my window.

My mother said nothing about a funeral. She was too distraught and overcome by her own guilt. I began to think about going home and making all the arrangements. It gave my mind something to focus on. For the next few days, I immersed myself in the myriad details.

When I returned from California, I walked to the Zen center for morning zazen. There was nothing more to distract me from the new reality I was living. It was just me, my cushion, and the blank wall.

After zazen I walked along Lake Calhoun, taking deep breaths and exhaling out toward the lake. With each inhale, I recognized and accepted the feelings of confusion and guilt. With each exhale, I yielded all to the willow—to the trees and flowers, the morning breeze, sunrise, the haze over the lake, birdsong. With each breath there was a sense of spaciousness, solace, and grief, all mixed together.

Basho's verse applies to all of us in all situations, regardless of how painful, how horrible, how earth shattering things seem.

Basho tells us that in our yielding is our strength. Losing my only brother to his own demons gave me a new empathy for others with the same struggle. Great suffering either shrivels us up like a prune or opens us up to Big Mind.

To yield to the willow is to accept that it is not *my* pain or *your* pain; it is the pain that permeates life, and we are entrusted with it. We don't give birth to it. Pain has always existed. It is not separate from anything else, not bad or good, right or wrong, just or unjust. It simply is. Like all things, when conditions call it forward, it arises.

We can yield our pain to the willow because we *are* the willow. Likewise, the pain of the willow as it withers and dies is not separate from us. To yield to the willow is a radical affirmation of interdependence.

For years I struggled to come to terms with my sister's lifetime schizophrenia, my brother's suicide, and the stigma associated with these tragedies. Then I read in *Crooked Cucumber* that Suzuki had a daughter in Japan who hung herself after spending nine years in a mental institution. I was stunned. It happened around the same time that I began to practice with him in 1964. He never spoke of it. He didn't go to Japan to attend her memorial. He didn't place her picture on the altar for forty-nine days in accordance with Buddhist tradition. His tears flowed in secrecy.

For me it was much easier to talk about my sister than my brother. At functions relating to my job at People Incorporated, I often talked publicly about Charlotte's schizophrenia. But for about ten years after my brother's death I never said a word about him publicly. Partly because I felt responsible and didn't want other people to know.

I still feel responsible. I still get angry. And sad. Dogen said, "Without bitterest cold that penetrates to the very bone, how would plum blossoms send forth their fragrance?" Living with Chip's death has helped me to become one-pointed, both in my Zen practice and in my other aspiration, to break through the stigma associated with mental illness.

People Incorporated is seven times the size it was when I was hired. Our growth is related to start-up programs that simply didn't exist because no one wanted to talk about or even see the most vulnerable among us. But when it happens in your own family, you have to see it. You need to talk about it. And no one should have to cry in secrecy, as my mother did, and as Suzuki Roshi did.

ELEVEN

Forgetting the Self
Is Our Only Refuge

DOGEN SAID, "TO STUDY BUDDHISM is to study the self. To study the self is to forget the self." When we forget the self, we experience our nonself nature, which is often referred to in Buddhism as *heartmind,* a word that evokes a sense of boundlessness. It is the mind and heart of the universe, but it also includes our small mind and our constricted heart. If our small ego-driven heart and mind were not included in heartmind, there would be no path to awakening.

THE BOUNDLESS NATURE OF HEARTMIND

One is no other than all; all no other than one.
Misunderstanding the great mystery, people labor in vain for
  peace.

—ZEN MASTER SENG-TS'AN

The Chinese Zen master Seng-Ts'an thought about heartmind as being composed of five dimensions:

1. Physical
2. Mental
3. Emotional
4. Openness
5. Full/empty

The physical dimension is the source of our energy and the main focus of our effort as Zen practitioners. We anchor ourselves in tactile sensation, smell, texture, taste, sound, and sight so we can experience the world with more immediacy. We pay attention to our relationships with the objects and people in our life. How we move a chair across the floor or handle our teacup or coffee cup affects the quality of our life. We determine for ourselves what has value and what doesn't. If we value all things, then everything in our life adds value.

I came across Suzuki on his way home one afternoon. He was carrying a big bag. He lit up when he saw me. "Look what I have!" he exclaimed, holding the open bag for my inspection.

Immediately, I was affected by his aliveness and presence. I gazed into the bag. Green spinach, red tomatoes, yellow squash, purple onions—it was filled with a myriad of colors and textures. Delightful! I was seeing with Suzuki's eyes, so everything looked fresh and wonderful. When we are immersed in the physical, before the intrusion of judgment, criticism, or ideals, there's a vitality that is both direct and uplifting.

Then Suzuki said, "Only two days old. Almost fresh!"

What! *Almost* fresh? My inner critic rushed to the fore. This was discarded produce from the grocery store. I was appalled. I glanced back down. Everything looked awful—brown and shriveled, maybe even moldy and wormy. Disgusting! Immediately, I was pulled into the Chatterbox Café, listening to my inner critic telling me how appalling those vegetables looked. Delight was replaced by disgust—big time! What if he invited me to dinner? I rushed off.

The physical dimension invites us to open up and experience life directly. If I hadn't been swept up so quickly by my inner critic, perhaps I could have shared a bowl of vegetable soup with my teacher that evening. Almost-fresh vegetables are fine in soup—better than fine, they are just right. But the inner critic rushed in and took over. There was no opportunity to choose. Until we slow down our mind, freedom is not possible for us.

One morning when Suzuki arrived to give his weekly talk to the Los Altos group, he brought along a young Japanese monk who had just arrived from Japan. Suzuki introduced him as Chino Sensei. We were all drawn to Chino. He had a gentle, sweet nature and a quick, natural laugh. He moved in attentive and precise ways, which somehow gave the impression of transparency. He seemed fragile.

Having held a position as ceremony instructor at Eiheiji monastery in Japan, Chino Sensei embodied ritual. It was like a dance for him. Suzuki was not as good at ritual, so he was happy to have Chino Sensei as his new assistant. I wasn't good at ritual either. So I knew why Suzuki was so insistent that I become Chino's attendant while he was at Tassajara. He was hoping Chino would shape me up, though he didn't say that. Instead, he said, "Chino Sensei will show you something every day."

Being an attendant was difficult. I tried to follow along and pay attention: see where Chino put his cup down so I could get it back to him when the moment came. When you're an attendant, you are completely immersed in the physical because you're attending someone else. But I didn't care much about the physical dimension back then. So the job was difficult but rewarding.

The first evening, I went to Chino's room to see if he needed anything. He invited me in and whipped up a very strong ceremonial tea. It was delightful to watch him whip the tea into thick foam and then serve it in such a delicate way. This became our routine—it was as if he were attending *me*. Every evening we drank tea together and talked. He asked questions about American culture or about books I was reading. Suzuki hoped Chino would teach me about ritual, but I discovered that Chino didn't even like ritual. Neither of us had much interest in it, so he didn't teach me anything about ritual.

But when Chino *did* ritual, he completely gave himself to it. At Tassajara we ate our meals in a ritualized way, as they do in Japanese monasteries. It's called *oryoki*. It is a highly stylized and formal ritual that involves three nested bowls that are wrapped in meal linens. I hated oryoki, but Chino taught it in a wonderful way. Oryoki flowered when Chino was doing it.

The most interesting thing about Chino Sensei was that he taught without speaking. He taught with his body. He immersed himself in the physical. When he moved, it was as if his whole being were moving with one-pointed focus. At Tassajara there was a stream with a log across it. Chino didn't have better balance than anyone else, but he was able to move across the log with ease. There seemed to be no intrusion of thought or fear. The rest of us would be freaking out, struggling to stay on the log and worrying about falling off. But Chino didn't seem to worry about anything. He just walked across the log.

> *To realize pure mind in your delusion is your practice. If you try*
> *to expel the delusion, it will only persist more.*

—SUZUKI ROSHI

The mental dimension includes both clear thinking and clearly deluded thinking. Everyone wants to get away from clearly deluded thinking. But the boundary can't really be found. So the practice is to notice, with bare awareness, whatever comes into our mind without trying to divide it up into clear or clearly deluded. We let it come, then let it pass.

Each thought in the story we're telling ourselves becomes the object of our bare awareness. We can honor each thought and let it pass. As the story changes, we just watch it, staying with it without criticizing or getting caught by it.

When we first start to watch our mind, we are always amazed by all the stories and how quickly they change. No matter how closely we're watching, it seems as if thoughts slip into our mind fully developed. How do they do that? Where are they coming from?

It may seem that the constant mental yammering will prevail until we die. Not so. Not so if we practice bare awareness. Not so if we practice with kind attention. Eventually the storytelling slows down. Stories, comparing, criticizing, and complaining are replaced by simple presence.

In the sixties it seemed to me that all the serious students were going to Japan to spend time in a traditional Zen monastery. After a retreat at Tassajara during which I had fallen into a wonderful stillness, I decided that I would go to Japan also.

I began talking to Suzuki about which monastery would be the best for me. He thought I should go to Eiheiji, the famous

Soto Zen training center where he, Katagiri, and Chino had trained.

I didn't really want to go to Eiheiji. There were too many tourists there, and too much ritual. But Suzuki would talk only about Eiheiji. So I started asking others who had spent time in Japan. I carefully weighed the pros and cons of different monasteries. I wanted to find the best place. More than anything, I wanted to deepen the delicious silence I had fallen into at Tassajara. Out of courtesy, I kept Suzuki informed about my investigation.

One morning he and I were having breakfast in the kitchen at the Zen center. I began telling him what I'd learned about the different monasteries. He seemed interested, but when I finished, he seemed more interested in his collection of raku teacups. I followed his gaze. Each cup was slightly different in shape, color, and size.

Suzuki said, "If you try to find the best cup, you will not appreciate any of them."

Nothing more was said about going to Japan. When I got home that evening, my obsessive thoughts about finding just the right monastery seemed to slow down. I was not so driven anymore. Within days, I dropped the idea entirely.

Soon thereafter, I was approached by a sangha member. Suzuki had told him I was no longer planning to go to Japan.

"Is it true?" he asked.

"Yes," I said, a little mystified.

I had not told anyone that I had changed my mind.

The emotional dimension is the affective component of stories we tell ourselves. It's often the underlying current or mood from which our stories arise. Sometimes it is quite viscous and long lasting. Other times it's more fluid and changes rapidly. We need to be aware of this emotional component. But I don't think that's possible until the mind slows down, allowing some space between our thoughts. It doesn't have to slow down much. Just a little space creates a big opening.

One morning after several days of rain, I woke up and saw the sun. I was delighted. Wonderful! My mood immediately lifted. Then the story arose: I'll walk to the Zen center this morning. It will feel great to get out in the fresh morning air and hear the birds. Or maybe I'll ride my bicycle and go along the lake. I got dressed, went downstairs, and began telling my wife my plan for the morning.

"Tim, it's really cold out there," she said.

What happened to my mood then? It took a nosedive. The story I was telling was glued to my mood, so it changed immediately, turning gloomy. I watched this direct relationship between the emotional and mental components. When we see how fluid our moods are, we don't get so caught by them.

OPENNESS—THE FOURTH DIMENSION

For the most part, we tend to experience partial awareness of only the first three components of heartmind. Some people are just naturally aware of their bodily sensations, but often these same people are unaware that they are experiencing the outer world through an intermediary—an inner critic or a narrator. Mentally they are in the Chatterbox Café. Other people are more aware of their thoughts but fail to notice their underlying mood.

In many cultures men are conditioned to split off from the emotional component. Years ago I taught couples communication in my work as a therapist. When we got to the emotional component of communication, I had to list the emotions on the wall for the men. Not that they didn't have them—they were just not aware of them as they arose.

When bare awareness is present, nothing gets left out. We are open to the physical, to the mental, and to the emotional dimensions of heartmind.

Openness is the fourth dimension. It's the disappearing-picture-frame dimension. When the frame disappears, the picture includes everything. We begin to experience this openness as our nonjudgmental, kind attentiveness to the first three dimensions increases. Whatever comes up, we just experience it.

That is where our freedom comes from—the willingness to experience our lives fully, without trying to split off from what is happening. When we resist, we contract, which is a form of imprisonment. We shrivel up in our prisons, and our world gets smaller and smaller. We see this in the elderly all the time. But it doesn't have to be that way. Suzuki Roshi knew how to live both deep and wide.

One afternoon Suzuki and I were on our way to Tassajara for a Zen practice period. I had been purifying my body so I'd be ready for it, drinking a lot of water, no coffee or caffeinated tea, and eating only fruits, vegetables, tofu, and grains. We were about halfway into our three-hour drive when Suzuki said, "Let's stop for coffee." He pointed to a roadside café that we were coming up on.

I was eager to get to the monastery. It seemed wrong to drink coffee when we were on our way to a practice period. Reluctantly, I pulled in and parked the car. We sat in a booth. When the waitress came over, Suzuki ordered coffee. I ordered water.

As he sipped his coffee, the waitress passed by with a banana split for someone at the next table. Suzuki's eyes grew huge. "What is that?" he asked eagerly.

"A banana split," I replied.

"I want one of those!" he exclaimed.

I sighed and gulped down my water.

When the banana split arrived, Suzuki took several moments to take it in with his eyes. "Just like America," he said, finally. "Everything mixed together."

Then he took a tiny bite of the whipped cream. Next he sampled the ice cream, one color at a time. He looked at the cherry, but he didn't touch it.

Then he pushed the whole thing over to me. "This is for you."

How could I resist? I ate the whole thing.

As we practice with the first four dimensions of heartmind, our small ego identification starts to dissolve. We get a taste of interconnectedness. It's an experience that happens in our bodies, in our emotions, in our mind, and in all our activities. It happens on its own. We are moving from openness to what master Seng-Ts'an called the fifth dimension of heartmind.

The full/emptiness dimension is totally uncharted territory, where form is none other than emptiness itself and emptiness constantly manifests as form. Here is where we see for ourselves that the seemingly tangible stuff of life is just a fabrication. What we're involved in is more like a dance, an ever-changing flow where there's actually *nothing* to grasp on to.

Consciousness divides, separates, and reifies things. Buddhism teaches that the universe is thoroughly pervaded by the quality of emptiness, meaning everything is empty of its own independent being. Everything that exists is thoroughly pervaded by everything else. It is the nature of all things to be both individual and undivided. Seng-Ts'an said, "One is no other than all; all no other than one."

The purpose of Zen landscape paintings is to evoke the mystery of the great unknown. Often a Zen painting is composed of five elements: a waterfall, mist, a steep mountain framed against a blue sky, and in the background usually a tiny human being.

Everything in the painting feels mysterious, ephemeral, interconnected, and therefore unknowable. The artist is trying to depict the true nature of things, the beauty and mystery of the universe. We are encouraged to disidentify with the small being standing alone in the background.

The mystery of the fullness/emptiness dimension is something we have to enter into. We can't know it with our intellect because it's bigger than our intellect. But we can know it experientially by entering into it. Often we think we want to experience the mystery, but when we stand on the edge of it we get scared. It may feel like standing on the edge of a cliff. What will happen to us if our ego dissolves?

There's no need to worry. We are already where we want to be. Already we are the great unknown—ungraspable and uncharted. We are supported by it and totally imbued with it.

A practitioner came into *dokusan* (a private meeting) and told me about an experience he'd had. He had been sitting in his office looking out the window when a hawk suddenly appeared against a cloudless blue sky. Watching the hawk soar, dive, and coast on the wind, the practitioner suddenly slipped into the fifth dimension of heartmind.

"I was in total awe! There was no gap between me and the sky and the hawk. There was no observer."

"That sounds wonderful," I said.

"Yes, it was. And then my iPhone rang."

Suzuki Roshi never talked about his beliefs concerning an afterlife. But shortly after the death of the great teacher D. T. Suzuki, I drove Suzuki to the first practice period at Tassajara. Our conversation turned to the loss of D. T. Suzuki.

Suzuki said, "He will be at Tassajara, too."

I shot him a surprised look. "What?"

"He will be at Tassajara, too," he repeated, in the same soft but firm tone.

THE WAY OF VOW

Sentient beings are numberless; I vow to free them.
Delusions are inexhaustible; I vow to extinguish them.
Dharma gates are boundless; I vow to enter them.
Buddha's way is unsurpassable; I vow to become it.

—THE BODHISATTVA VOWS

In Buddhism one way we forget the self is through the Bodhisattva Vows. A vow is powerful because we can call it to mind quickly. Suzuki repeated the Bodhisattva Vows every day. He embodied them. When we live in vow, we don't get lost in our heartbreaks and sorrows. Our vow is always right before us, beckoning us onward, refusing to let us get mired in our tragedies. Our vow always brings us back to our place of rest, of equanimity, available for the next sadness or the next joy.

However, merely repeating your vow is not enough. You can acknowledge your karma and repeat your vow thirty times a day, but what are you going to *do*? How are you going to manifest your buddha nature? How are you going to actualize your vow?

If we are bodhisattvas, we actualize our vow by not getting caught in our sorrows, not allowing our heart and mind to close up. No matter what, we do not shrivel up like a prune. We remain open and available to life and to other people.

The Chinese Zen teacher Yumen said, "With realization, all things are one family. Without realization, all things are separate and disconnected." When we still our mind and open up to heartmind, we know all things as one family.

Yumen added, "Without realization, all things are one family, too." It doesn't matter how much time I spend regretting the past or lamenting over my tragedies—it is still the same interdependent universe. I'm just not acknowledging it because I'm stuck in my own stuff. Yumen is pointing to a deep truth about the human situation and how our mind creates our experience.

FORGETTING THE SELF: REFLECTIONS ON COMPASSION

Betty Wong, a concert pianist, suffered from depression, and often there were long stretches when she could not come to the Zen center. But she was a very good tennis player. One morning, instead of his customary black robes, Suzuki turned up wearing white shorts, tennis shoes, and a ridiculous-looking hat to protect his bald head from the sun. He was going to play tennis with Betty.

"You know how to play tennis, Sensei?" I asked.

"No," he said. "But Betty does."

I couldn't resist going along. Sensei was all over the court, swinging his tennis racket without the least bit of self-consciousness or frustration. Every now and then he even hit the ball. Betty was radiant. And Suzuki beamed with the simple joy of being with his student in her suffering.

Another time a traditional ceremony was coming up at the Zen center that involved a procession. Richard Baker, one of Suzuki's senior students, would be the drummer. But shortly before the ceremony, Richard seriously injured both wrists. There wasn't enough time for his wrists to heal, but Richard was determined to meet his commitment. He worked very hard to rehabilitate, and when the time came he was in the procession. Everyone was impressed.

Some time later, Richard was having some major life difficulties, as we all do from time to time. One morning when he showed up for meditation, he was met by the two drumsticks he used in the procession. Suzuki Sensei had placed them next to his cushion to remind him of his own innate resiliency.

The Vietnam War was raging in the sixties. I was both a Zen student and a peace activist. The possibility of getting drafted into a war that I protested was a big concern for me. I applied to the draft board for conscientious objector status and asked Suzuki to write a letter in support of my application. He agreed but said I should write the letter myself and then he would sign it.

When I finished pulling everything together, I gave the envelope containing all the required documents to Suzuki so he could sign the letter. When he returned it to me, my birth certificate was missing. He looked everywhere but couldn't find it. I was dismayed over this. It meant I would have to obtain a new birth certificate before I could mail the application.

In his talk the following Sunday, Suzuki told the story of being a young monk struggling with his Zen practice. His teacher constantly chided him for being absentminded and forgetful. Then he revealed the nickname that his teacher gave him: Crooked Cucumber. He said that he had worked his whole life on his forgetfulness. But he was still just a crooked cucumber.

I have always felt that losing my birth certificate prompted that talk. Learning about his nickname made it worth it.

Later that night, someone slipped into the kitchen and placed a bowl of crooked cucumbers on the counter. We never learned who did it, but the sentiment was shared by all of us.

In a conversation once, a fellow practitioner expressed a deep concern that Suzuki Roshi was lonely. After all, his entire family was in Japan. He was here alone. I rejected that idea. I didn't believe that Sensei was lonely. He seemed to be beyond ordinary human emotion. He was always so composed and available.

Not long after that conversation, I happened to walk by the opened door of Suzuki's office. He was holding a letter in his hand, but he wasn't reading it. He was gazing off into space with tears on his cheeks. I was surprised and a little worried.

Suzuki was supposed to give a talk that evening. I told a senior student that I thought he should find someone else to give the talk. I didn't think Suzuki was up to it.

"Why? What has happened?" he asked.

I told him what I'd seen.

"Oh," he said, "Don't worry. He'll be all right."

That evening Suzuki was the same as always, lighthearted, humorous, and totally present.

Eventually Mitsu Suzuki, Sensei's wife, joined him in San Francisco. The first time I saw her, she was walking up the stairs of the Zen center. She wore a beautiful flowered kimono. I'd never seen one before outside a Japanese restaurant. Her hair was styled in the traditional Japanese way. I thought, *Wow! How lovely.*

Suzuki called her Okusan, Japanese for wife. And before long we were all calling her that. She and Suzuki had a playful, flirtatious relationship. He treated her with fondness and lightness. And Okusan always looked out for him, often chiding him in a playful way when he worked too hard or didn't take good care of himself.

Once a couple of us were talking with Suzuki in the hall outside his office when Okusan started up the stairs. She was returning from the beauty shop where she got her hair done.

"Oh!" exclaimed Suzuki, in a voice loud enough for her to hear. "My fair lady," he intoned cheerfully.

Okusan looked at him and beamed. Then she gave him a flirtatious, dismissive wave.

Suffering, when we turn toward it rather than away from it, cultivates compassion and equanimity, which in turn supports us.

Suzuki Roshi seemed to turn toward suffering. His kind attentiveness was always subtle and always just enough. It was never contrived or sentimental. There was no self-involvement. Dogen said, "To study the self is to forget the self."

"Forgetting the self" is a refuge that is itself spiritual freedom. We embody spiritual freedom through all our activities and through the five dimensions of heartmind, put forth by Zen Master Seng-Ts'an. Here they are again:

1. Physical
2. Mental
3. Emotional
4. Openness
5. Full/empty

The American poet, author, and philosopher Henry David Thoreau said, "Surely joy is the condition of life." And surely it is. As Buddhist practitioners, we have the possibility of becoming experts in one thing: happiness. By now it is apparent that Zen practice is austere and rigorous, and it requires discipline—but for what? For the opportunity to experience abiding happiness.

We cannot pursue happiness directly. Suzuki Roshi said that Zen practice was like walking a railway track. The sights we see are ever changing, but the track itself remains the same because of our sincerity. It has no origin and no destination and, therefore, no goal and nothing to gain. Just walking the track one step at a time is enough.

The next part of this book is about cultivating the endurance and fortitude to remain on the path, moment after moment. It is the beginning of advanced practice.

PART FOUR

Staying on the Track

EVEN WHEN THE SUN
RISES IN THE WEST

TWELVE

Five Hindrances
That Point the Way

A S WE WALK A SPIRITUAL PATH, the weaknesses
and difficulties we encounter are waking places.
Entering into our vulnerabilities allows us to grow in a more
genuine way. The Pali texts, which are the earliest Buddhist
scriptures, identify five universal difficulties, or hindrances, that
come up in a meditative practice:

1. Sensual desire
2. Ill will
3. Sloth and torpor
4. Restlessness and worry
5. Doubt

Every serious Zen practitioner will encounter these hindrances over and over. Some of us are predisposed to one or two
in particular based on our personality. Some of us move among

them all. The point of separating them out and looking at each one separately is to get to know them. As we work with the hindrances, our practice matures.

SENSUAL DESIRE

Sensual desire has to do with the immediate gratification of our senses and appetites. Instead of enjoying the simple activity of being alive in this moment, feeling the sun on our face or smelling the rain, we desire some other experience. It seems to be the human condition that we spend a lot of time wishing for a different experience. If we can't put our desire aside during meditation, we may as well be watching television. But with sincerity and patience, we can learn to put desire aside.

When my daughter Erin was eight months pregnant with her second child, she was tired a lot because she couldn't get comfortable lying down. My grandson Ethan was three and beginning to realize he would soon be sharing his mama. He was very clingy. Erin had a strong desire to get some rest. But she put her desire aside because Ethan wanted her attention.

During meditation, we can be completely overcome by desire. Instead of bare awareness, there's no awareness at all. We're in la-la land, one-pointed with the object of our desire, having what is called a *samadhi* romance.

I'm being a little loose with the term *samadhi romance*, but it points to the depth of our preoccupation with sensual desire. Here's an example: I am sitting in retreat when I smell spinach cooking in the kitchen. In a retreat, which is basically self-imposed sensory deprivation, food becomes very important. It's easy to become obsessed with food, especially on long retreats. So when I smell the spinach, I start thinking about how wonderful it smells and how much I love spinach. I think about the last time I had spinach pie and about when we might have it again. We could invite people over to the house for spinach pie and lemonade, perhaps on a summer night when we could eat out on the deck. The thoughts go on and on and on until the bell brings me back to the cushion.

True samadhi is total absorption in the present moment. The small self drops away, and there is only awareness. When we are one-pointedly focused on the object of our desire, we are totally absorbed by the ego. Unless we are highly skilled at meditating, a technique such as a mantra or following the breath is a good idea. Otherwise, sensual desire can dominate our meditation practice for years.

We also have the if-only desires. If only my mind were not busy. If only my life were different. If only I were taller, smarter, or richer or had parents with better parenting skills. The very process of wanting is painful because we don't feel complete. So we strive to avoid the actual feeling of desire by losing ourselves to some obsession. We lose ourselves to alcohol, drugs, food, TV, shopping, or perhaps we try to ignore our desire. But then it comes up in some twisted way.

The best-kept secret about desire is what actually relieves it. We have to look closely to recognize it in action. We think our desire is relieved by fulfilling the desire, by getting something we want. But the secret of desire is this: Getting something has nothing to do with the relief we feel. Our new possession is not the source of our relief. It is actually that the state of desire has ended. We are freed from the painful sensation of desire.

I'll give you a simple example. Suppose I have a craving for chocolate. Off to the store I go. I can't get through the checkout line fast enough. I take the first bite, and there's a great sense of delight. But the delight has nothing to do with chocolate. The wanting has stopped.

In our mind, we have associated the cessation of desire with chocolate. In America we are bombarded with consumer advertising that constantly reinforces this mental confusion. Actually, going for a run, meditating, writing a letter, or any other activity that we wholeheartedly engage in will interrupt the fixation on sensual desire.

In my example, the sensation of craving was just an expression of sensual desire. Chocolate was the fantasy that arose with it. Next time it could be something else. The temporary release I felt by fulfilling the fantasy actually reinforces the cycle of desire. I invited it back. This is the cause of so much of our suffering.

Being caught in a state of wanting is painful. Looking outside ourselves for relief is a delusion we engage in again and again. From birth till death, our consumer culture promotes our entanglement with sensual desire. But real freedom comes from seeing the desire and just being with it, fully experiencing the sensations as they move through our body. Eventually, the painful sensations dissolve. They come back, but now we know what to do.

ILL WILL

In retreats dislikes and irritations come up all the time. During one retreat a student came to see me. She wanted to move to another cushion because the person next to her was breathing "like a steam engine." But the meditation room was full, so there was no place for her to go.

I said, "Can you just put it aside?" She wasn't happy with this suggestion. She twisted up her face in a kind of pissed-off way.

When we fixate on the object of our ill will, our heart and mind become constrained. We become cantankerous. We can even develop ill will about the ill will. But having an aversion to the aversion is a good starting place. It can motivate us to meditate more seriously.

When ill will is present, there is anger. It is held in the body as tension, heat, and contraction. Jack Kornfield tells a story about going to India and telling his teacher that he was angry about how someone was behaving in the sangha. Jack was really upset with this person. The teacher, who was wearing sandals, got up, stormed across the room, and kicked a table leg. Then he held his injured foot in his hand and hopped around for a while. Finally, he sat back down and massaged his foot. Then he looked up at Jack and slowly shook his head. That was all it took to show Jack what he was doing to himself.

As I've mentioned, I was a peace activist in the sixties and strongly opposed to the Vietnam War, and when I asked Suzuki for a letter supporting my application for conscientious objector status, he asked me to write the letter for him to sign.

When he returned the letter, he had rewritten it, word for word, by hand. "Except I added one word," he said. Where I had written that I was a follower of the Buddha, Suzuki added the word *strict*. I was a *strict* follower of the Buddha. It made me feel good that Suzuki thought of me that way.

Not long afterward, Vice President Hubert H. Humphrey came to Stanford to speak. I went with a group of other activists. We suspected Humphrey was privately against the war, but publicly he was a mouthpiece for President Johnson and an apologist for the war. The longer he spoke, the madder we became. We wanted to confront him and demand he confess to all the needless killing our government was perpetuating.

When his security team slipped him out the back door, we ran after him. They ushered him into a car, but we were angry and determined to be heard. We rushed the car. When it sped off, we gave chase. We were an angry mob chasing after the vice president.

The ill will I harbored for those responsible for the war had spilled out and taken over so fast. Afterward I was embarrassed and ashamed. I was a *strict* follower of the Buddha. How could I let this happen?

I was stunned by the strength and depth of my hostility. What happened to my calm heart and clear mind? I decided I wouldn't go to any more rallies or political events until I dissolved the ill will I was harboring. I recommitted myself to my meditation practice.

The four mindfulness practices in the Satipatthana Sutra teach us how to move our attention around so we discover where we are harboring ill will. Is it in our bodily sensations, our feelings, our thinking, our fundamental attitude? Is it primarily just one of these or a combination? It takes a lot of patience to do this work, but we've made our commitment and this is part of it. It helps to realize that having ill will is not a personal failing; it is just what comes up.

But there is a caveat here: If we try to use the four mindfulness practices in order to rid ourselves of something, it won't work. Mindfulness is about seeing, about awareness. If we try to repress or suppress ill will, it just comes back in a twisted way, aimed inward instead of outward. And self-loathing is just another form of ill will. With kind attention and mindful awareness, the freeing happens on its own.

SLOTH AND TORPOR

The third hindrance is sloth, sleepiness, torpor, dullness, the habit of going unconscious. One reason we struggle with this one is that we live in such an on-the-go culture. We don't get enough rest. Even in our meditation, sleepiness shows up. It is possible that we are so unaccustomed to stillness that when the psyche becomes still, the body is cued that it's bedtime.

The problem can be very discouraging in retreats. We notice sloth and torpor so much in meditation because our daily lives are so frenetic. We often come to the retreat exhausted from chasing after our desires and chasing away ill will.

Sloth and torpor drain our vitality and limit our effort. We become weary and lethargic. But experiencing sloth and torpor does not mean the energy is not available. An endless supply of energy is always present, but we are not accessing it.

My grandson likes to ride on my shoulders. "Carry, Grandpa," he says. And I put him up on my shoulders. It's great. But sometimes I wish he would walk. I might say, "Ethan, you should walk." Then he says, "I tired, Grandpa. I tired."

Once he hadn't walked at all, and I was the one who was tired. But I'm just so happy to have him as a grandson and a friend, and he said he was "very tired," so I put him on my shoulders.

After we'd walked about ten feet, he saw the ice cream truck. He wanted down, and he ran to the truck singing, "Ice cream, ice cream, ice cream!"

I said, "Ethan, you're too tired for ice cream."

He said, "No, Grandpa! No tired. You have ice cream, too."

The energy is always available, but it's based on how we evaluate our situation. If we say our situation is boring, then we're going to have sloth and torpor. But there is nothing inherently boring. The feeling of boredom is often connected to self-identity. We feel energized when we're accomplishing something that we desire or getting away from something for which we have ill will. But when the self has nothing to do in the way of desire or aversion, we may feel dull or bored.

Energy rises and falls for all of us. When it falls, we don't abandon our meditation. When sloth and torpor are present, we practice with sloth and torpor. Everything is included. This is a good time for walking meditation.

Sometimes sloth and torpor are used to cover up something we simply don't want to face. About twenty years ago, I was coming to the Zen center every morning to meditate, but I felt dull and lifeless. Everything seemed fuzzy, and there was no calmness in my heart. I mentioned it to my wife.

Linda said, "Well, what month is it?"

I became irritated and said, "It's October, Linda. Come on, I'm absentminded, but I'm not that absentminded."

"What about October? Whose birthday was this month?"

Then I realized. My brother's birthday was in October. I was protecting myself with sloth and torpor because I didn't want to feel the guilt and anger that were still present.

So sometimes sloth and torpor aren't what they seem. If we investigate deeply, there is the opportunity to see what lies underneath the mood.

Chronic sloth and torpor could also mean clinical depression, and we need to deal with that by working with a professional. Or it could mean that our life has lost its meaning. Perhaps we're not doing what we deeply care about. If you have chronic sloth and torpor, investigate it. What do you want to do with this short life you have?

RESTLESSNESS AND WORRY

Restlessness is especially prevalent in our country. My friend was always encouraging me to get more TV channels. Finally, I got cable, but it was just basic cable. I immediately started clicking away with the remote. My friend said, "Tim, basic cable is not enough."

That was years ago. Now it's an iPhone and iPad—and my friend says, "Come on, Tim, you should be on Twitter, Facebook, and LinkedIn." One might think a Zen teacher enjoys continuous stillness and calmness, but no one is free of restlessness. As Zen students we even get restless and agitated about achieving calmness. It's the human condition. Zen practice is about seeing our restlessness so we are not controlled by it.

We Americans seek constant activity. We have accomplished a lot through our restlessness, but restlessness has become a cultural norm. We even program our vacations to fit in as many activities as possible. We program our beach time, museum time, lunchtime, afternoon walk, and dinnertime.

In meditation we may notice that sometimes our energy is just bouncing around. The practice is to enter into the restlessness to see where the Ping-Pong ball is bouncing—where it bounces from and where it bounces to. What stories are we telling ourselves?

A key aspect of restlessness is worry—concern about imagined futures, possible failures, and damage to our self-image. We may feel threatened by shame, guilt, or regret. Trying to put aside our worry doesn't generally work. But we can open up to it, feel it physically, watch its movements in the body, and observe what triggers it. Chronic worry can mean agitated depression or anxiety disorder and may require professional support. But in many cases, worry can be managed through exercise and getting enough sleep, and through ethical behavior.

When worry is present, our meditation needs to be more about letting go than about striving. If we criticize our meditation, we are just creating something else to fret about. Judging the quality of our meditation when our mind is restless can make us feel like frauds. So letting our meditation be what it is is important. Let restlessness or worry come on in. Then notice the moments, however brief, that worry is not present. Take those moments into your heart and your whole being.

DOUBT

Doubt can be a confusing topic for Zen students because it is often talked about in two ways. The first type is one of the five hindrances: the small, mundane, ego-driven doubt that constantly questions our abilities and the path we've chosen. It is a mental preoccupation that creates indecision and causes vacillation.

Such doubt may involve deep inner conflict. It usually arises based on defeatist stories from the past. We feel incompetent and unworthy. Doubt constantly asks: *What should I be doing with my life? Am I with the right partner? Should I have this job or that job? Should I practice Zen or should I go to a Christian church?*

Doubt is the human condition. We talk a great deal about freedom of choice in America. It's a wonderful freedom, but we make it into a curse with all our doubt.

In Zen there is also a second kind of doubt called Great Doubt. It is not to be confused with the small doubt of the five hindrances, even though small doubt can blossom into Great Doubt if we are able to penetrate it. Zen Master Hakuin popularized the term to mark a certain phase in practice, usually after we've been meditating regularly for some time. We begin to see the lack of solidity in our story lines. We realize that our stories can't support us. The world we carry around in our busy mind starts to dissolve. Great Doubt can be an important phase of Zen practice, but it is not pleasant when you start to question everything—including your so-called self.

SHINING OUR LIGHT OF AWARENESS ON THE HINDRANCES

The hindrances abide in the shadows of our personality. When we recognize them as they arise, we know where to aim our light of awareness. With kind and focused attention, we follow our restlessness, doubt, desire, ill will, and sensual desire all the way down into the cave beyond our conscious mind.

The hindrances reveal the darkest crannies. We may hesitate to go into them. No one likes dark places. What if we can't find our way back? What if we are overcome by our pent-up emotions? Fear is always present, whispering words of inadequacy and unworthiness. In these intense times of spiritual development, there is a deep reconciliation with our ghosts. The Christian mystic Saint John of the Cross called this the dark night of the soul.

In zazen our one-pointed focus is like a flashlight. It doesn't illuminate the whole cave at once. That would freak us out. Openness without a perimeter can be frightening. The flashlight narrows our awareness, giving us time to ease into the dark places at our own pace. We *can* persevere, as Buddha did. He was just a human being like you and me.

THIRTEEN

Training with
the Hindrances

I N AN INTERVIEW, THE RUSSIAN DANCER Vaslav
Nijinsky was asked about his technique. He said,
"It's really quite simple. I merely leap and pause. Leap and
pause."

The pause is important in dancing. It's the same in life. We
have to learn to pause. But to *really* pause, to completely still
the body and mind for even a moment, is difficult. Yet without
the pause, the leap loses its connection with reality; it loses its
meaning. As we train with the hindrances, we are learning how
to pause.

Zen training happens on the cushion. We train with whatever
arises—and what usually arises is one of the hindrances. From a
Zen point of view, these are opportunities for practice. We can
see that the hindrances *are* the path. They become the path as
soon as we see them as a means to study the self at deeper and
deeper levels.

Here are five ways to train with the hindrances, particularly on retreats where everything is intensified:

1. Putting aside
2. Letting go, or just letting be
3. Opening through the center
4. Expanding our field of attention
5. Cultivating a full awareness of feelings

PUTTING ASIDE

My friend Jack is an emergency room surgeon. We share an interest in meditation, but our ways of practicing it are quite different. Jack is not Buddhist and he doesn't do sitting meditation. He does, however, have a rigorous and regular meditative practice. He shared this story with me.

One day Jack and his partner were having a serious and heated argument. It wasn't a small thing; it was a fight with far-reaching consequences. At the worse possible moment, he received an urgent phone call from the hospital. There had been an accident involving multiple cars, and immediate surgery was required to save the lives of several people.

When Jack got to the hospital, he was able to slow down his turbulent thoughts and put them aside. For the next several hours his focus was one-pointed, with no intrusive thoughts swirling around. His ability to do this required years of training.

For my friend, the ability to put aside intrusive thoughts was literally a matter of life and death. It may not seem like a matter of life and death for us—yet a lot of the time we feel half-dead, so weighed down are we by our fantasies, doubts, and regrets. What should I have done that I didn't? What might have been if only? We beat ourselves up and project our anxieties into the future.

In meditation we practice living beyond our habits of thought. We practice living a life of freedom.

Meditation is an opportunity to train in putting aside whatever comes up and returning to one-pointed focus on our breath. We are aware of the hindrance, but we don't focus on it. Whatever it is, it can wait. That intense conversation I had with my partner last night was important and I need to process it, but it can wait until my meditation is over. Won't it help my relationship to do that? Isn't it healthier to put it aside and come back to it with some distance and clarity, and after my partner and I are getting along better?

It's important to communicate. It's important to share and deal with our difficulties in an up-front, assertive yet compassionate way. But in meditation we put it aside. It may feel impossible. But we do it by just doing it.

LETTING GO, OR JUST LETTING BE

Most of the time we have the choice to just let go of the story that we are telling ourselves right now. Then another story starts up. We let that one go, too. When our mind finally slows down enough that we can see the stories as they arise, we may see several stories vying for our attention simultaneously. Some are more colorful than others; some are really juicy, others drab and repetitive. The juicy ones are tempting. But the practice remains the same: just let the story go.

In Christianity there's the phrase "Let go and let God." But often the reason we don't let go is that we feel secure and protected when we're all wrapped up in our stories. They make us feel safe. But when we let them go, we discover something much bigger. You can call it God; you can call it Buddha; you can call it emptiness. It's always been here. It's never going to leave, never going to abandon us. If we just let go a little bit, we can experience it a little bit. Or we can let go a lot and experience it a lot.

It's easy to cultivate a mistaken idea about letting go: "Well, I can't really do anything, so I'll just let the roof leak" or "I'll just passively accept the situation." That's the kind of letting go that Suzuki was dismayed about in the early days of Zen in America. The future was irrelevant, the past was irrelevant, the leaky roof was irrelevant—we just let everything go. Because we were in the *now,* man! But that small-mindedness is just the ego's way of letting go. It is not the Zen way at all, and it is very uncompassionate to ourselves and others.

However, there are times when letting go doesn't work, and then we just have to let it be. Sometimes we try over and over to bid good-bye to the guest who's telling us a fascinating story. But the guest won't leave. No matter what we do, the guest won't stop telling his story. Well, then we have to just let it be.

Letting it be can be difficult for a Zen student. It feels like failure. But as long as we are attentive to whatever comes up, it is not failure, even if it means leaving a retreat.

A student went to her teacher during a long retreat. She was a serious student and ardent in her practice. But now she was confronted with an unsolvable dilemma because she was also the retreat leader. She said to the teacher, "I'm sick. I have a fever."

For the teacher, it was simple. He said, "Well, go home and be sick. Take care of your sickness. Be a sick Buddha. That's all. Just let the sickness be."

Often we are so filled with doubt and worry over what we should do or what someone expects of us that we don't even allow ourselves to be sick when we're sick. My poor father didn't allow himself to take a single day off from work for forty years, even when he was ill. If you allow yourself to be sick and you're really present with your illness, you can discover some wonderful things about your body and its need for rest, about your emotions and feelings and how you respond to pain.

So there's no need to do anything else. Just let it be.

OPENING THROUGH THE CENTER

Sometimes a hindrance is so persistent that nothing seems to work. It won't be put aside or let go of, and when we just let it be, it takes over everything. Then we just open up through the center of it. Even if we can open up to it for only a few minutes at a time, that's okay. We can notice how strong the pull is. Sometimes it's subtle, other times it isn't. We notice how consuming the preoccupation is. If the hindrance won't be put aside, then the practice is to notice all the different ways it reverberates through us and all the different stories it tells.

At Tassajara when Suzuki introduced oryoki, I didn't like it at all. Instead of teaching us how to eat a meal mindfully using the knife and fork, we were being forced to engage in a Japanese monastic ritual using chopsticks. I thought, *This is not relevant to Zen. Alan Watts never wrote anything about this.* At that time I considered the author Alan Watts and Suzuki to be my two teachers.

My problem with oryoki was that I couldn't do it well—I'm left-handed, and the ritual was designed for right-handed people. I was told to do it the right-handed way. It brought back memories of my first-grade teacher, who tried to force me to write with my right hand. I'm not very dexterous, so I was clumsy and felt awkward.

I felt like quitting, but I didn't. Instead, I gradually opened into the center of the difficulty, which meant accepting my awkwardness. I accepted that I would always be the last one to unwrap my bowls and place everything properly on the table, as well as the last one to wrap everything back up again. Perhaps the only reason I didn't quit was my love and appreciation for Suzuki. If this was what he was going to teach, silly as it was, I would just stick with it.

Finally, they decided we left-handed people could do oryoki a little differently. After that it became easier. Today I actually enjoy the meals served in the elegant and stylistic way of oryoki. And like Suzuki, I insist that people I ordain be well versed in the ritual.

I was always encouraged by watching Suzuki and Katagiri deal directly with their difficulties. They had a hard time with English. All the other non–English-speaking teachers I heard speak in the 1960s and '70s used translators. They would prepare long written lectures and have someone translate them. But Suzuki and Katagiri faced the language barrier head-on and continued through it, doing their best to communicate in our vernacular. It was very touching sometimes, boring other times, but I was always impressed by how they opened into the center of this difficulty and never gave in to the doubt and humiliation that plagued them.

Suzuki said once that he didn't want to talk on the radio ever again. He'd been interviewed by Pacifica Radio, broadcast throughout California, and felt he'd done an awful job. Just imagine what it must have been like—finally, a Zen master comes over from Japan, where nobody paid attention to him for years. Then all of a sudden public radio picks him up. His interview is broadcast to thousands of people, and he sounds ridiculous. It was humiliating. But he stuck with it and attracted many students because of his sincerity and openness. He opened through the center of his difficulty and moved through it.

Eventually, Suzuki's talks became quite wonderful because he used English in a fresh and spontaneous way. And Katagiri, too. Their talks were delightful.

Of all the hindrances, doubt can be the most debilitating. We can neither let it go nor let it be. We have to open up into the center of it, as Suzuki and Katagiri did. Doubt is such a powerful saboteur of our efforts. When besieged by doubt, we might start by saying, *I have the ability to follow my next two breaths,* or *my next one breath,* or *my next inhale.* Then notice the sensation of the breath entering your nostrils, going down your throat and into your chest. Notice how your chest rises slightly to receive it, then the belly rises and then falls as the inhale becomes an exhale. Stay very close to this one breath. Such a small effort is all that is needed.

Another hindrance we have to open into the center of is sloth and torpor. We will experience a lot of boredom in Zen practice. We can try to put it aside, but often we're too bored to bother. If we can't find a skillful way to face our boredom, we will become discouraged and seek out a new activity. This pacifies for a while, but when it becomes boring, we move on to something else. Instead we can open up through the center of boredom, as the poet John Berryman did in his poem "Dream Song #14":

Life, friends, is boring, we must not say so.
After all, the sky flashes, the great sea yearns,
we ourselves flash and yearn,
and moreover my mother told me as a boy
(repeatedly) "Ever to confess you're bored
means you have no

Inner Resources." I conclude now I have no
inner resources, because I am heavy bored.
Peoples bore me,
literature bores me, especially great literature,
Henry bores me, with his plights & gripes
as bad as achilles,

who loves people and valiant art, which bores me.
And the tranquil hills, & gin, look like a drag
and somehow a dog
has taken itself & its tail considerably away
into mountains or sea or sky, leaving
behind: me, wag.

In this poem, Berryman recognizes that boredom manifests itself as a self-centered dream in which he is caught. He recognizes that there's a picture of how things ought to be and how we're supposed to respond to them: *great* literature, *great* art. But he is bored by it all. He is even bored by his alter ego, Henry, with all its plights and gripes and complaining. But at the end of the poem, boredom suddenly drops away and Berryman experiences a moment of Zen.

Like everything else, boredom can be a dharma gate that opens into something wonderful. So when we feel overwhelmed by boredom, we don't have to leave Zen practice and go seeking something new. Our Zen is right here.

EXPANDING OUR FIELD OF ATTENTION

Again we can turn to the Satipatthana Sutra: mindfulness of the body, mindfulness of the feelings and sensations, mindfulness of thoughts, and mindfulness of our basic attitude. Usually when we have a difficulty, it's because we're stuck in one modality, like pain in the body or some feeling we have or some thought. If we can expand our awareness to include another modality, the difficulty loses some of its power.

I have a friend who used to get sick during retreats. We did a lot of seven-day retreats in those days, but she got nauseated on the first or second day and couldn't stay. Which hindrance was getting in the way? It may have been restlessness and worry. Worry is often an aspect of restlessness. But this was extreme, so there was probably a combination of hindrances involved.

My friend was physically nauseated, so she began her work with her body. For a year or so, she worked to expand her field of attention beyond her body. She came to retreats, stayed as long as she could, and then left. I admired her dedication and perseverance.

Eventually, she uncovered something interesting. She began to notice feelings she had never been aware of. They arose with the nausea. As she expanded her field of awareness, she realized the nausea was covering up her fear of abandonment. Her father had died of cancer when she was in adolescence. She was very close to her father and had never dealt with the pain of losing him.

Gradually, she was able to stay longer in retreats. She stayed close to the painful emotions of loss and grief. As the intensity of her strong emotions increased, the nausea decreased.

She confessed to me later that her general attitude had been that she had no one to love and that she herself was unlovable. Curiously, she had not even been aware of this attitude. It was covered up by the feelings of restlessness and worry that she held in her body. Expanding her field of awareness beyond her body enabled her to see it. Seeing is always the beginning of freeing.

CULTIVATING A FULL AWARENESS OF FEELINGS

In meditation the opportunity arises for us to experience fully the feelings and sensations involved with each of the hindrances. To experience them fully, we allow the sensations to expand and fill us up. We experience the permeability of the self and of the sensations that move through it. But if we allow our attention to move away from the actual sensation—for example, from the sensation of desire to the object of desire—then we are not actually experiencing desire. We are avoiding it. When we cultivate a full awareness of the uncomfortable, even painful, sensations of desire, we experience the stillness that is also present. It may be hard to believe that desire is permeated by stillness, but this is one of Buddha's fundamental teachings.

While sitting or doing walking meditation, we always have some feeling coming up. Often there's a constellation of feelings swirling around, below or outside of our consciousness. In chapter 11 I told the story about wanting to study in Japan. Now I'm going to tell another facet of the same story.

At Tassajara I had a satori experience. I believed that if I practiced hard enough, I could live permanently in this place of complete and utter freedom. This desire drove my obsession to practice in Japan. But underneath the obsessive thoughts was a fear that I wasn't fully aware of. It was the fear of being prone to anxiety my whole life.

I feared becoming like my father, too driven to take a sick day, too anxious ever to be satisfied. I sensed my father's anxiety inside me, and below that a churning fearfulness that I would be like him all my life. The satori experience revealed a way of being in the world that was not dominated by anxiety, and I wanted more of that.

When Suzuki pointed to his collection of raku pottery cups and said, "If you try to find the best cup, you won't appreciate any of them," something opened up inside me. As I followed his hands gesturing toward the cups, each with its unique shape, markings, and imperfections, my desire to be anywhere other than where I was fell away.

Avoid covering up the hindrances with busyness. Rather than ignoring them, pay close attention to them. They are waking places. They show us our stories and how hypnotized we are by them. Training with the hindrances helps us realize that it's okay to experience anxiety. It's okay to have a busy mind. It's okay that our parents did a lousy job. Regardless of all that, we can open up to our true nature right now.

With just enough faith to do the practice, we start to notice our patterns. Do we tend to get angry or harbor ill will? Do we become restless, doubtful, and confused? Do we get caught up in desire?

Jack Kornfield used to ask, "What are the top ten tunes?" What are the popular patterns? We need to know them. These popular patterns have probably been with us for a long time. When things are not going well and you say it's time to look for a new partner, be careful. This could be a pattern. If we don't see our patterns, we may lose someone precious. As we befriend the hindrances ingrained in our personality, we will see what triggers them and how they expand, move, and affect our behavior. As we bring them into view, they dissolve, releasing their pent-up energy and making it available.

Of all the hindrances, anger from pent-up ill will is possibly the most difficult to work with. It's so strong we get swept away by it, even if we've been practicing for forty years. But we can start by working with mild irritation. All it takes is to notice it and be with it with kind attention. If we can stay present with mild irritation, there is a good chance we won't get broadsided by anger and do something harmful.

When a hindrance arises, it's usually covering some basic, fundamental fear about life, about existence. We hold on to it because it's preferable to fear. But clinging to a hindrance causes us to lose our center. We become unsteady, as if we were skating on ice. In a sense, we *are* skating on ice because the hindrance creates an icy sheath over our fear and protects us from it. We don't want to break through. But we are separated from our life, from our vitality. Training with the hindrances is about breaking through the ice and meeting whatever it is that isolates us.

FOURTEEN

Continuous Practice

THE CIRCLE OF THE WAY

C ENTRAL TO DOGEN'S TEACHING is the idea that
each moment of Zen practice is a moment of
enlightenment, and each moment of enlightenment is a moment
of practice. Thus, continuous practice is undivided. This means
that the path and the destination are inseparable. Dogen wrote:

> Between aspiration, practice, enlightenment, and nirvana there
> is not a moment's gap. Continuous practice is the circle of the
> way. This being so, continuous practice is undivided, not forced
> by you or others. The power of this continuous practice con-
> firms you as well as others. It means your practice affects the
> entire earth and the entire sky in the ten directions.

There are two components to Dogen's continuous practice:
bare awareness and wholehearted exertion or engagement. When
I was a young practitioner, I preferred the term *exertion*. But

now, I much prefer *engagement*. In this chapter, we'll look at four ever-deepening stages of advanced practice:

1. Conceptual and nonconceptual language
2. Consciousness
3. Existence
4. Returning

Because continuous practice is undivided, each stage is thoroughly penetrated by the others and each opens organically and naturally into the next without a moment's gap. So there is no need to strive—continuous practice is not forced by you or others. When our practice is wholehearted, we just relax into it.

LANGUAGE AS A TOOL FOR AWAKENING

In Zen retreats we practice silence because verbal language tends to cover up the more subtle things that are happening all around us all the time. Our body expresses itself through movement— for example, the way we sit on a cushion or walk. Yet often we are unaware of our body language and the body language of others.

And what about the language of the trees outside our windows or the language of grass? Across from the Minnesota Zen Meditation Center is beautiful Lake Calhoun. It constantly changes color, speaking in its own voice, as Dogen would say. We practice silence so we can experience language at the deeper, subtler level of nonconceptual language. Dogen calls this "wholehearted expression," which is a key component of continuous practice. As the Zen teacher and poet Norman Fischer says, "All language is singing."

All language is singing—even conceptual language. But the problem arises when we hold on to words as if they refer to objects that really exist. When we do that, we suffer. If we're attentive to the language of our body while holding on to words in this way, we may feel a contraction. Our world becomes smaller. From a Buddhist point of view, this contraction is a source of suffering.

In meditation we pay attention to our internal language so we can break free of the belief that our story is the one true picture of the way things are. If we're not holding tightly to that one true picture, we can open up and relax. It requires continuous practice to break free of our need to reify, or solidify, our thoughts as if they represent truths. We have to see them as they are arising so we won't get caught in the stories they weave.

During a retreat a student came to see me in dokusan. She wanted to discuss the different ways she talked to herself during meditation. She realized she talked to herself in four ways. The first way was problem solving—sorting things out step-by-step, in a very practical and logical way. The next way was in the form of thoughts that seemed to arise from her subconscious—mostly irrelevant, waking-dream-type stuff. She observed that these waking-dream thoughts bubbled up and dissolved immediately.

The third and fourth ways were the most sticky—she noticed that she tended to cling to them and contract around them. The third way, circular obsessive thought, seemed to illuminate the obsessive-compulsive nature of her mind. The fourth way was daydreaming and fantasizing. The last two types, she acknowledged, could easily dominate her meditation.

In one of his discourses, Buddha made a similar observation. He used the analogy of four horses. The best horse runs at the shadow of the driver's whip. A good horse runs at just the slightest touch of the whip. A poor horse runs only after it feels the whip penetrating its skin, and the worst horse runs only when the whip penetrates to the bone.

In meditation we notice which horse we're on. Even if we're on the last horse, in that moment of noticing, bare awareness is present. In the next moment, we may be back on the last horse again— but the moment we notice, we have returned to bare awareness. The practice is just to notice which horse we are on. Suzuki Roshi said, "If you want to tame a horse, give it a large pasture."

In Zen it sometimes seems that we disparage language—but language is important. Like any powerful tool, it can be used to move us toward enlightenment or toward delusion.

Every day the Zen teacher said to himself, "Don't be fooled by anything."

"I won't be," he replied.

SEEING INTO CONSCIOUSNESS

Sigmund Freud, the founder of modern psychology, was a master of language. Psychology departments are not very interested in Freud anymore, but literature departments are. He knew how to use language to penetrate the psyche and bring it into awareness. Psychologists don't use Freud's terms much these days. But whether they know it or not, they *are* using his basic teaching. For instance, instead of talking about the superego (Freud's term), they talk about the internal parent, who is all about *should* and *should not,* which is the same to me as the internal critic talked about in Zen. One could argue that Freud was expressing ancient Buddhist concepts without knowing anything about Buddhism.

Freud postulated three forms of consciousness: id, ego, and superego. Id is our instinctual reactivity. It develops first; then the ego and superego develop simultaneously. The ego arbitrates the struggle between the instinctual drives of the id and the superego, our internalized parent. In Buddhism the word that describes our primal impulse is *samskara,* the fourth of the five aggregates discussed in chapter 4.It includes our impulse toward food, shelter, affection, comfort, and sex.

In Zen we talk a lot about how we drive ourselves with thoughts about what we should or shouldn't do. These are the obsessive thought patterns of the inner critic. In Freudian terms, ego is the arbiter, always trying to maintain balance between the id and the superego. Ego does its work through internal dialogue; it is the maître d' in the Chatterbox Café, trying both to keep the primal impulses in check and to prevent the internal parent or critic from spoiling everyone's meal.

Buddhist psychology asserts the possibility that we can free ourselves from these limited forms of consciousness. When we penetrate them, we see they don't refer to anything real. They are just mental constructs. They can be very helpful ones, but their helpfulness depends upon our ability to see them clearly and not be fooled by them.

When my eldest grandson, Ethan, was four years old and his brother Logan was one, they flew in with their parents from France for a visit. Ethan brought his entire Thomas the Train set, which included the tracks, tunnels, and several bridges. He had to bring it because he couldn't leave home without Thomas. He set it up in his room at my house, which is not very big. It took up the whole room.

Logan wanted to play with Thomas, too. Ethan was furious about this. "All he does is suck on the cars. He can't come in! Stay out, Logan!" Ethan's belief is that train cars are not to be sucked on. When he saw Logan suck on Thomas the Train, Ethan had an id response, or in Buddhist terms, a samskaric one.

In a four-year-old, the arbiter, the ego—the second layer of consciousness—is just developing. I overheard Ethan saying under his breath, "Why's Logan doing that?" When Ethan gets older, he will ask these questions internally rather than out loud. The third layer is the superego. "Mama said I shouldn't be mad because he's just a baby." This layer, too, was still being formed in little Ethan.

As this scenario was unfolding, Grandpa sat in the corner watching these developing mental constructs and thinking, *This is how we develop in the world. Maybe when Ethan gets older, he'll study Zen and be able to see all of this. But I shouldn't wish for it, because if I do, he won't do it. But if he does, he'll see how these layers are* always *expressing themselves, moment after moment—no matter how old we are.*

PENETRATING THE LAYERS OF CONSCIOUSNESS

You try so hard
But you don't understand
Just what you'll say
When you get home

Because something is happening here
But you don't know what it is
Do you, Mister Jones?

—BOB DYLAN, "BALLAD OF A THIN MAN"

The fifties was the era of the superego in American culture. It was all about *should* and *shouldn't*. Then came the sixties, and in the counterculture we said *Screw that!* The sixties were all about id, or libido: being in the now—sex, drugs, and rock 'n' roll—losing your mind and coming to your senses. You have to be my age to remember that. "Something's happening here, but you don't know what it is, do you, Mr. Jones?"

Bob Dylan, the troubadour of Hibbing, Minnesota, and Suzuki Sensei were my mentors. That was an interesting combination. Suzuki told me I should listen to my parents. But the troubadour said the opposite. "You try so hard, but you don't understand just what you'll say when you get home." In my eyes, my parents were all about authority, accomplishment, status—all the things I disparaged. The troubadour was right. I totally dissed my parents.

So I dropped out of Stanford the year I was supposed to graduate and moved to San Francisco, right across the street from the Zen center, where I could devote myself to Zen practice. But when I told Suzuki that I'd dropped out of Stanford, he was not happy. I explained that I wanted to devote myself fully to my sitting practice and that my father was a materialist. He said, "Material is good! You should pay attention to your parents."

This seemed to be an endorsement of the superego, which I was trying to shed. But what about the time when Suzuki interrupted our drive to Tassajara for a stop at a roadside café—where he ordered a banana split? That seemed to be an act of pure id. I was pretty confused.

Was Suzuki trying to help me penetrate the layers of consciousness? I don't think so. He was just being who he was. In the process, he taught me something about living beyond the ego, the id, and the superego.

In the counterculture, we didn't want anything to do with the values of our parents. We had nothing but contempt for materialism, status, and position. We thought we saw through the superego, that we'd transcended it. So we developed our own communities based on sharing and love.

A few of my friends were building a communal dome to live in. They wanted their home to be one of love, harmony, and community. The next thing I knew, they were fighting over how big the dome should be and whose design was the best.

The antics of many Zen masters poke fun at our attachments to status and position, which seem to persist regardless of which culture we identify with. Here is an example:

One day at the market, Zen Master Fukai walked through the streets ringing his handbell and begging everyone he saw to give him a robe. Everyone offered him one, but he rejected them all. On and on he continued, ringing his bell and begging.

Finally, Rinzai, the head monk, presented Fukai with a coffin. "Here! I had this robe made for you."

Fukai promptly shouldered the coffin and walked through the market calling loudly, "Rinzai had this robe made for me. I'm off to the east gate to enter transformation." (In Chinese calligraphy the character for *transformation* also means "die.") A crowd followed him to the east gate and gathered around, eager to watch him enter the coffin.

Fukai paused, then shouted, "No, not today. Tomorrow! I shall enter transformation at the south gate tomorrow."

The next day a crowd assembled at the south gate. Again Fukai said, "No, not today. Tomorrow! At the west gate."

The next day, he exclaimed, "Tomorrow, tomorrow!"

Well, on the following day, no one showed up. Fukai climbed into the coffin and asked a traveler who chanced by to nail it down. News spread quickly. People rushed to the coffin. Opening it, they found that the body had vanished. From high up in the sky, they heard the ring of Fukai's handbell.

In this story, Fukai and Rinzai are making fun of our attachments to status (robes represent a certain spiritual status), to the body (or to leaving the body), and to our ideas about transcendence. But they do it in a lighthearted way. It's a wonderful joke. But the joke is on all of us. It's life itself.

We could also see it as a story about dying to id, ego, and superego. In Zen we say that every moment encompasses life and death, without a moment's gap. If this weren't true, transformation would be impossible. Each moment that we die to ego, something bigger and wonderful is born. The power of this continuous practice confirms you as well as others. Then the moment dissolves into the next moment. It means, as Dogen said, that your practice affects the entire earth and the entire sky, in the ten directions.

THE NATURE OF EXISTENCE: OUR MULTIPLICITY OF SELVES

Ego, as the arbiter between id and superego, is based on patterned behaviors we learned in the past and project into the future. Most patterns are fear based, but they may also be based on a range of other emotions. These emotions may be either positive or negative, but it's the negative ones that give us trouble. If you keep finding yourself in the same situation over and over, some pattern is getting in your way.

In Zen there are specific cognitive and behavioral practices that help to free us from our conditioned patterns. In meditation, just watching our thought streams as they arise can enable us to identify a pattern. The next step is to imagine resisting the pattern and noticing what emotion comes up. Moving into that emotion may help us discover whether there's an underlying imperative. Usually the imperative takes the form of *I should, I shouldn't,* or *I can't.* Stay with the fear in the imperative, feeling how it resonates through your body until it dissolves on its own.

Patterns work most strongly in situations of adversity, which is why Zen retreats have an ordeal component. I've been practicing Zen for a long time, but in adverse situations I can easily revert back to old patterns. It doesn't matter how long you've been practicing—it's human nature to revert back to our conditioning during hard times. So don't be too greedy to get rid of these patterns. They could be with you for life. But once you learn to recognize them as they arise, you won't be controlled by them.

Early Buddhist thought described six psychological patterns that we constantly move among. These universal patterns are referred to as the six realms of existence:

1. Hell realm
2. Animal realm
3. Hungry-ghost realm
4. Human realm
5. Fighting-spirit realm
6. God realm

These are often divided into the three lower realms and the two upper realms, with the human realm right in the middle. It's in the human realm that we can do our work. In the lower realms, we are unable to focus on practice because there's too much suffering. In the two upper realms, there's no motivation to practice meditation because things are too good.

According to Buddhist psychology, we constantly move back and forth through these six realms until we learn to recognize them and free ourselves from them. Buddhist psychology uses several strategies for working with the realms. The teacher and author Ken McLeod pulled together a mountain of information about the realms and presented it in a well-organized way, matching each realm with its predominant emotion.

In the hell realm, the predominant emotion is anger.

In the animal realm, we fall back on our base instincts: food, sex, survival.

In the hungry-ghost realm, neediness is the predominant emotion. A hungry ghost has a long, narrow neck, barely wide enough for a single grain of rice to pass through, and a huge, protruding belly. The poor ghost is starving. But its throat is so tiny and its belly so big it can never get enough food.

In the human realm, the primary emotion is desire—we're concerned with getting what we want and avoiding what we don't want—and the primary way of dealing with desire is strategizing using our intellect. In the human realm, there is an equal amount of suffering and contentment, so this realm is most congenial in which to practice.

In the fighting-spirit realm, the primary emotion or driving force is jealousy. We want to get ahead, to be the best, pushing ourselves to achieve even at other people's expense.

In the god realm, we have everything we want. We're living in the stratosphere. The primary emotion is pride.

To determine which pattern you're trapped in, notice what you're striving for. In the hell realm, you are often striving to oppose the person making you angry. Then you might move into the animal realm, where it's all about your physical desires: food, comfort, sex, drugs, booze, partying. Addicts of all types dwell in the animal realm. If you're hungry-ghosting it, you're striving for attention, support, love, recognition.

In the human realm, you're striving to get what you want in life. In the fighting-spirit realm, you're striving to be the best, and you're not quite there yet. If you're a Zen student living in this realm, you want to be the most enlightened and the calmest and to have the best zazen. In the god realm, there's no striving; yours is a life of leisure and pleasure. Your desires are satiated, and you have everything you could possibly want.

Frequently our strategies in any of these realms don't work. So we do the opposite. If I'm in the hell realm and my anger isn't getting me what I want, I may give up and become deflated. If I become despondent in the hell realm, anger turns to hate. I move from hot hell to cold hell. My heart freezes. At least in cold hell, there's some control. There can be some feeling of calmness, which may feel comforting for a while, because in hot hell, my anger was so destructive that there was no sense of control. But the calmness I feel in cold hell is not the calmness of an open heart. Far from it! My heart is frozen.

In the animal realm, we strive to control our compulsions for food, sex, drugs, or alcohol. We can control them for a while. But then comes a situation of adversity and we blow it.

In the hungry-ghost realm, when our strategy doesn't work, we deny our neediness. Then it gnaws into us because we're not acknowledging it.

In the human realm, we work toward fulfilling our desires, but if things aren't working out, we get busy. Human beings are very good at getting busy. We say to ourselves, *Do you even have time to be reading this? Shouldn't you be doing something else, going to a yoga class or cleaning house? Busy, busy, busy!*

In the fighting-spirit realm, if you're not beating everyone out, you are failing. But no one can beat *everybody* out, so in the fighting-spirit realm, failure is always close by.

In the god realm, there's no opposite to go to, because you're just complacently satiating and congratulating yourself. It works— until it doesn't. Then you fall down into the hell realm. The god realm always leads directly to the hell realm.

In meditation it's easy to recognize what you're striving for. When you're trying to follow your breath but keep finding yourself lost in thought, what is the theme? Move into it with bare awareness instead of letting it carry you off. Identify which realm it's coming from. Then begin to imagine doing the opposite. What emotions come up? Stay with the unpleasant sensations.

Notice when you've moved into your head to avoid the strong feelings. Remind yourself: no mediator. Nada, nada, nada!

It takes perseverance to do this work. Over and over, move your awareness back to your immediate bodily sensations.

An emotion is a product of a multitude of sensations, each with its own intensity, heat, pulse, fluidity. Notice how they come and go. Eventually, they go and don't come back. The emotion dissolves because you stayed with it without fueling it with thoughts of blame or self-loathing. This is how the process works. It will never fail you if you do it with sincerity, compassion, and patience.

Through continuous practice, the realms become more nuanced and fluid. When we learn to hold our thoughts lightly, it's possible to express our multiplicity of selves without being dominated by them. It's possible to move freely between them without feeling trapped or confused.

The great American poet Walt Whitman was not bothered by his multitude of selves and he had no need to differentiate them the way Freud did. He just accepted them and enjoyed them:

> Do I contradict myself?
> Very well, then I contradict myself, I am large, I contain
>   multitudes.

Abraham Lincoln was arguably our greatest president, not in spite of his multiplicity of selves but because of them. Throughout his presidency, he drew on his statesman self, his compassionate self, his insightful self, his resilient self, and his folksy self. Like many human beings, he also had a depressed self which could drag him down, but he practiced holding it lightly.

There is a story about Lincoln going into a tavern one evening. He sat at a table by himself, looking as if he'd seen the end of the world. He was slumped and woeful. He looked hopeless. Then a group of people came in. A half hour later, Lincoln had joined them. He sat with his gangly legs sprawled out in front of him, his long arms animated, and everyone around him was completely charmed by his stories. Lincoln had an ability to work and play with his multiplicity of selves.

The poet Rumi says, "Be grateful for whoever comes because each has been sent as a guide from beyond." We can honor our many selves as they come up. We don't have to look for the real self or try to express only the good self, the accomplished self, or the calm self. Rumi says, "Half of any person is wrong and weak and off the path. The other half is dancing and swimming and flying in the invisible joy." With continuous practice, we can hold each of our selves with a light heart and appreciate the insight and knowledge they bring.

BODHICITTA: RETURNING TO OUR ORIGINAL NATURE

The fourth stage of continuous practice is returning. We are actually able to return to our original peaceful nature, what Suzuki called Big Mind, also referred to as *bodhicitta*. *Bodhi* means "awake," and *citta* means "thought." So bodhicitta means both "having thoughts of living wakefully," and "the mind that is already awake." These are referred to as relative bodhicitta and absolute bodhicitta.

Absolute bodhicitta is the mind that sees grasping but doesn't get caught by it, that sees anger but doesn't get caught by it. Sometimes there is a need to express our anger, but even then bodhicitta does not get caught by it. It is the mind that continuously senses our innate abundance, regardless of the multiplicity of inner beings that constantly vie for our attention. The three primary components of absolute bodhicitta are generosity, beauty, and love.

In 1964 when we had our sitting group in Palo Alto, Suzuki came every week to sit with us and give a talk afterward. We would always collect an offering, but he never wanted to take it.

"No, no," he would insist. "This belongs to you. You set this group up."

I was being supported by my father. I was driving a nice car that he paid for; I didn't have to worry about money. And here was Suzuki living off so little. Yet he had bodhicitta, an abiding feeling of inner abundance. He didn't need anything from us. But he did have much to give.

There is an African proverb that says, "It is the heart that gives; the fingers just let go." Suzuki gave from his heart, so his hands were always open.

The second aspect of bodhicitta is an appreciation for beauty. A few years ago, People Incorporated, the nonprofit I work with, purchased a beautiful turn-of-the-twentieth-century mansion to treat people who are struggling with mental illness and chemical dependency. It is located in the inner city of Minneapolis. We purchased it for next to nothing and renovated it. It has all the original hardwood floors and woodwork, and there's a palpable feeling of calm and spaciousness about it.

I toured the home with a psychiatrist. Walking from room to room, we discussed the programs we'd be offering. At one point he suddenly stopped and looked around.

"You know," he said, "I think what will help folks most is the beauty of this place. More than anything we offer them. Just the beauty."

He was right. When we really experience beauty, it stops us. Our agitation ceases, distractions of the mind drop away, and we rest unexpectedly for a moment.

The third component of bodhicitta is love, the kind of self-less, unconditioned love that bubbles up from the heart, needing nothing in return. When we were living on a farm in northern Minnesota, we used to call our four-year-old son "Jed-berry" because eating wild strawberries was one of his favorite things. At breakfast one morning, Linda spooned out strawberries for each of us. Jed-berry must have inhaled his. I looked up and saw that his bowl was already empty and he was finishing off the last of Linda's.

I said, "Linda, look! Jed ate all your strawberries."

"Yes," she said calmly.

"But you love strawberries," I protested.

Her face lit up. "And how good they tasted!"

FIFTEEN

Skin, Flesh, Bones, and Marrow

FROM THE BEGINNING, BUDDHISTS have spoken of two types of power that we can rely on to open us up to our true nature: self-power and other-power. Some Buddhist traditions rely on devotional practice, which is other-power (*tariki* in Japanese). In devotional practice, cosmic bodhisattvas are enlightened beings that exist in a spirit realm. Devotees pray to them or chant their names.

In Zen, however, we rely mostly on self-power, *jiriki*. We don't look to intermediaries such as saints, angels, or cosmic bodhisattvas to save us from the suffering caused by our ignorance. To Zen practitioners, the cosmic bodhisattvas are mythological archetypes that represent the qualities of an awakened being. They help us to visualize these qualities and quickly call them to mind.

Dreams, delusions, flowers of air;
foolish to try to grasp them.
Gain and loss, right and wrong;
away with them once and for all.
If the eye does not sleep,
all dreaming ceases naturally.
If the mind makes no discrimination,
the 10,000 things are as they are,
of single essence.
Within the deep mystery of things as they are,
we are released from our relationship to them.

This is a stanza from the seventh-century poem "Trust in Heart-mind" written by Seng-Ts'an. For me, these verses manifest the spirit of the four most popular bodhisattvas: Maitreya, the future Buddha; Manjusri, bodhisattva of wisdom; Avalokiteshvara, bodhisattva of compassion; and Samantabhadra, bodhisattva of great activity.

Maitreya. "Dreams, delusions, flowers of air" is a beautiful expression. As human beings that's what we are: deluded dreamers, flowers of air. In Zen we don't negate or try to transcend our humanness. It's wonderful that we are flowers of air. It suggests an ephemeral quality that allows for transformation. Because we're flowers of air, we can become whatever we envision.

When Shakyamuni Buddha told Maitreya that he, too, would become a buddha someday, Maitreya started envisioning himself as a buddha: calm, compassionate, and wise.

In Buddhist mythology, Maitreya is the icon of hope and of the intentionality to manifest something or express something.

He inspires us to stay on the path; as our practice matures, he expresses our deepest insights. When we get discouraged or feel despondent, Maitreya reminds us that in spite of, or possibly because of, our ephemeral flowers-of-air nature, we can reignite our dream anytime.

Maitreya was the first bodhisattva to enter into my life. He manifested as inspiration when I read *Teachings of the Mystics*. He manifested as the aspiration I felt when I was around Suzuki. And just when I needed it, he manifested as encouragement when I glanced down to see a little green sprout pushing up through the cement in midwinter.

Maitreya is always manifesting in our lives when we need him. We just have to be open to his multiplicity of forms. Maitreya is referred to as the future Buddha—but he is here for us right now.

Chino Sensei was young when he came over from Japan, and he really struggled with English. When Suzuki had to leave Tassajara unexpectedly during a practice period, it fell on Chino to give the daily talks. He had never given a talk in the United States before. He was terrified.

I was his attendant, so each day before the talk I went to his room to see if he needed anything. Every day he whipped up very strong Japanese ceremonial tea. It was bitter, frothy, and quite wonderful. But it had a lot of caffeine. He would sip his tea and say, "I am scared." I would nod knowingly and say, "I know you are. I'd be scared, too." This was our routine.

During each talk, Chino trembled; he was inarticulate and clumsy in his use of English, a stark contrast with the way he moved. I'm sure the ceremonial tea was partly responsible, because I sat in the audience with my head spinning from all the caffeine. I felt bad for him. But he didn't give up.

Years later, Chino Roshi became known as a great speaker. He was so relaxed giving talks that there's a story about him actually falling asleep for a few minutes in the middle of a talk. Is it a true story or a myth? I don't know, and it may not really matter.

We can let stories like these penetrate us, evoking the energy of Maitreya to support and steady our intentionality. If we waste our energy pondering their historical accuracy, they will not enrich us. It's better not to read Buddhist literature if we're going to get caught by it. Better just to do zazen.

Manjusri. The lines "Gain and loss, right and wrong; / away with them once and for all" point to the wisdom of Manjusri Bodhisattva. He is on the altar of most Zen centers throughout the world. Manjusri sits on a lion, which represents both courage and equanimity. He wields a sword in one hand and the Prajnaparamita text in the other. But the text is not present to teach us something new; it's about deconstructing our ideas and concepts. The only words Manjusri is interested in are turning words, words that penetrate and radically alter our consciousness.

Manjusri is the bodhisattva of beginner's mind because he is always cutting away old ideas, opinions, and patterns—down with his sword and away with them, once and for all! Such is the power of the bodhisattva of wisdom. He never develops new patterns, because he cuts away habituated thoughts before they have a chance to solidify into a pattern. His sword keeps coming down until the mind just stops; it goes completely silent, and there is only openness to just what is. With Manjusri's energy, it's possible to use our mental ability as a tool without becoming hypnotized by it.

Manjusri is youthful because we don't have to wait until we're old to realize our true nature. It's available to us right now.

Recently, I saw a bumper sticker that said DON'T BELIEVE WHAT YOU THINK. Because Manjusri doesn't believe what he thinks, he doesn't become rigid. Finally, Buddhist teachings are seeping into mainstream thought. People don't even know these are Buddhist teachings, but that's okay. Even better.

Avalokiteshvara. The lines "If the eye does not sleep, / all dreaming ceases naturally" evoke the spirit of Avalokiteshvara, the bodhisattva whose ten thousand eyes enable him to witness the suffering of the world with compassion. He sits on a lotus that grows in muddy water, its roots deep in the mud. The beauty of the lotus depends on the quality of the mud. Is the mud well composted? Does it really include all beings? If so, it will be a beautiful lotus, and Avalokiteshvara will do wonderful things.

Avalokiteshvara also changes gender because he isn't caught by anything. He sheds everything, continuously changing forms. He can have two arms or four or a thousand—as many as needed. He may have one head or ten, because he uses skillful means to accommodate himself to those who are suffering. He can do that because he has embodied the energy of Manjusri. If we haven't returned to the stillness of beginner's mind, we really can't give ourselves freely, because our own ego needs get in the way. After we've embodied the energy of Manjusri, we can manifest Avalokiteshvara with wisdom and sincerity. Frequently, in depictions of the Buddha, Manjusri stands on one side of Buddha, and Avalokiteshvara on the other. These two figures are representatives of wisdom and compassion.

Avalokiteshvara helps us deconstruct our thoughts and ideas about compassion so we can manifest true compassion. For most of us, compassion is caught up in our ideas about who we think we should be or is simply about being a good person. This is not the compassion that emanates naturally from the wisdom of Manjusri. With true compassion, we are wholeheartedly present wherever there is suffering. We're there personally and directly, without *trying* to be compassionate.

It takes skillfulness to cultivate true compassion. Chögyam Trungpa, a Tibetan Buddhist teacher, called compassion without skillful means *idiot compassion*. This is the energy of Avalokiteshvara without Manjusri. In recovery circles, it is called codependency because our own needs are feeding our desire to help others.

Codependent compassion usually includes anxiety and worry. It contains no Manjusri energy. Often we start off just being open. Then we start to worry. Is she okay? Did I show my compassion correctly? Maybe we stay awake all night worrying. This is not Avalokiteshvara; our own needs have gotten involved.

Avalokiteshvara involves forgetting the self so the self does not become an obstacle. It sounds mysterious, but it is our most authentic and natural state of being. If we feel that we are exceptional, then we've lost our beginner's mind. So we just recognize that that is happening and then step back from everything, go back to our cushion, and hang out with Manjusri.

My friends Jim and Sharon are in an intimate relationship. Sharon is quite needy, and Jim constantly indulges and excuses her behavior. I came to realize that Jim's codependence was getting under my skin. I found myself thinking, *Well, this is curious. What's going on here?* Recognizing my own reactivity was Manjusri's wisdom. Then I needed to evoke his energy to turn my eyes inward and look deeply at my own negative reactions—at my own shadow. I saw how deeply I was caught by Jim's situation.

Zen teachers are not immune to these conditioned reactions. If we can focus our kind attention on our shadow, there is the possibility of becoming enriched by it. When I saw my negative reactivity clearly, it dissolved—Manjusri's sword. My heart opened completely to both Jim and Sharon, and I felt deeply connected to both of them.

With Manjusri's courage, we draw the negativity toward us with an actual invitation. We charm our shadow into a relationship. After all, our shadow is just pent-up energy. Once it is free to flow out into the world, we are released, because the shadow is no longer a shadow. We return to our original compassionate nature, which is Avalokiteshvara, whose energy allowed me to be completely available to my two friends who were suffering.

Samantabhadra. The lines "If the mind makes no discrimination, / the 10,000 things are as they are, / of single essence" evoke the spirit of Samantabhadra, who represents "the deep mystery of things." He is introduced in the Flower Garland Sutra as the teacher of interconnectedness. There's a lot of drama with Samantabhadra Bodhisattva. He manifests in everything that exists, even in a blade of grass. Dignity, vibrancy, and light emanate from every pore of his body.

Samantabhadra is referred to as the ocean-mirror samadhi. When the ocean is still, it mirrors everything perfectly just as it is: the sky, the clouds, birds in flight, all are perfectly reflected in the ocean. Each thing is completely itself and also the whole ocean—individual and undivided.

Samantabhadra is also the ocean-seal samadhi. The ocean reflecting the sparrow seals the sparrow's existence, just as it is. The ocean seals its authenticity, so it doesn't need to be anything other than what it is. When our mind is still, we don't need to look anywhere else for validation, because we have Samantabhadra's ocean-seal samadhi. It comes from our interconnectedness with all life.

Samantabhadra rides an elephant. In Buddhist mythology, the elephant symbolizes calm, deliberateness, and unyielding action. If we're working with homeless people or in prison environments, calm and unyielding action are necessary. But we mustn't be unyielding in a rigid way; instead, we just continue, no matter what obstacles we encounter.

Samantabhadra is hard to see because he is the bodhisattva of great activity, which is the activity of buddha nature. When we are wholeheartedly engaged, we disappear into the activity. Every pore in Samantabhadra's body is the entire universe. So by helping one person, we help everyone. With the energy of Samantabhadra, we can transform the world.

Imagination, visualization, and imagery are powerful tools to help us access our inner power. The cosmic bodhisattvas illuminate our true nature. When we practice with them, one opens naturally into the next.

We start with Maitreya to help us set a clear and firm intention. He is both inspiration and aspiration. Manjusri keeps us steady, cutting away expectations, desires, worries, and anxieties. Next comes Avalokiteshvara to open our heart so we can radiate authentic compassion that arises from equanimity and includes all beings. And then Samantabhadra, inhabiting every pore of our body with vibrancy and light, manifesting great activity.

If we try to embody their energies in the reverse order, we risk making a mess of things. Activists who don't still their mind and let go of their personal agendas create a lot of problems, especially if their heart is not open. We need these wonderful cosmic bodhisattvas for guidance so we don't complicate things too much. The reason is that human beings are dreamers. We're flowers of air; it's our strength and our weakness.

IMAGINATION AND RITUAL IN ZEN PRACTICE

Whether we use the cosmic bodhisattvas in a devotional practice or whether we think of them as psychological archetypes, they can be powerful tools to help us imbibe the teachings. Buddhist teachings will not transform us unless we imbibe them—skin, flesh, bones, and marrow. Two other tools for imbibing the teachings are the powers of imagination and ritual.

Dogen believed that ritual has the capacity to activate our imagination—the energy of our inner world. In the developing consciousness of a child, imagination plays a powerful role.

When I was four years old, my family lived on a hill overlooking San Francisco Bay. There were no other kids around, so I was always lonely, until the character of Bobby Shafto from the old English folk song became my imaginary friend.

Bobby Shafto's gone to sea
He'll come back to marry me.
Bonny Bobby Shafto.
Bobby Shafto's bright and fair,
Combing down his yellow hair;
He's my love forevermore,
Bonny Bobby Shafto.

Bobby Shafto was my constant companion. When I got up in the morning and looked out on the bay, there he was, coming to marry me. My parents were tolerant—to a point. When I insisted that my mother and I go to Bobby's house for dinner, she played along for a while. But when I refused to eat dinner unless we went to Bobby's house, she lost her patience with the whole thing. I was hurt. I vowed not to talk to her about Bobby anymore.

Bobby Shafto changed my consciousness. I wasn't lonely anymore. I felt supported. I didn't feel so cut off. He connected me to the world at large, to the sea, and to the sky. He was always out there, always available, and all I had to do was call him in.

Imagination is also sparked through naming. Most religious traditions use the power of naming to evoke a spiritual longing. My Christian name is Timothy, which represents my grandmother's influence. It was my grandfather's, my great-grandfather's, and my great-great-grandfather's name. When I was nine or ten years old, she asked me if I knew what my name meant.

I said, "Yes, Grandma. Timothy means Timothy."

"Oh dear, didn't your mother tell you? It comes from Timotheus, and it means 'honor god.'"

I reminded my grandmother that my father was an atheist and my mother an agnostic.

She said, "That's all right, dear. Just honor the god in front of you."

Honor the god in front of me? What freedom! I didn't have to believe or not believe; I could just honor the god in front of me. The ocean, the birds, the trees, and the butterflies—those were the things in front of me. It was my name, so I was entitled to just honor whatever I saw.

Then, in 1978, I was given the name Zentetsu by my second teacher, Katagiri Roshi.

"Do you know what it means?" he asked. I didn't.

He said, "It means 'thoroughgoing Zen.'" Then, playfully, he added, "Not Zentatsu. Better!" (Zentatsu is the name Suzuki gave Richard Baker, who later became the abbot of San Francisco Zen Center, a position Katagiri had hoped would go to him.)

Katagiri carefully explained the important difference between Zentetsu and Zentatsu. Zentatsu means "attainment of Zen." Katagiri frowned as he stressed the word *attainment*.

"Not attainment!" he exclaimed. "You are Zentetsu: thoroughgoing Zen!" Then he roared with laughter.

Like imagination, rituals can help us imbibe the meaning of Buddhist teachings. During one long summer retreat at Tassajara,

I was having a difficult time. I had pain in my legs and a sense that what I was trying to do was impossible.

I went to see Suzuki in dokusan. He took one look at me and said, "You have been swimming in the ocean."

"Yes," I replied, wiping the perspiration from my forehead and the back of my neck and noticing that my shirt was dripping wet.

"Since you are having a difficult time, please repeat to yourself the mantra in the Heart Sutra. It will help you."

I was surprised by this, because back then I didn't associate mantra practice with Zen. "Should I repeat the *whole* mantra, or just part of it?"

"The whole thing," he replied, and then he added, "but it's all the same."

I had probably heard him say "It's all the same" a hundred times, but this time I experienced a sense of space surrounding his words.

I went back to my cushion and began repeating the mantra: GATÉ GATÉ PARAGATÉ PARASAMGATÉ BODHI SVAHA! Loosely translated, it means: Gone, gone, gone beyond, gone utterly beyond. Enlightenment yippee!

After three or four hours, I was suddenly overcome by a sense of openness and space. I leaped off the cushion and ran out of the zendo. I ran into the woods with tears flowing down my face. I was laughing and crying at the same time, but they were tears of joy.

I vividly remembered the experience of boundlessness I had encountered years before in Utah. This was just like Utah! Totally different from Utah! Not Utah at all/completely Utah! Sameness/difference. Difference/sameness.

I felt immense relief. From what, I don't know. From separation, I suppose, and from the isolation and anxiety of being a discrete being alone in a hostile world. Everything seen, heard, felt, and thought was timeless, spacious, and teeming with life. In all this fullness, how could I have ever felt alone?

That night I had an interesting dream. I was sitting across from Suzuki as he drank a cup of tea. He said, "You have had a wonderful experience. Not everyone will be able to have that experience, so please do not talk about it with others."

The next day I went to see him in dokusan. He was holding the same cup as in the dream. When I sat down, he leaned in and said, "You have had a wonderful experience. Everyone will not be able to have that experience, so please do not talk about it with others."

It felt a little bit surreal, as if maybe I were still dreaming. I said, "Well, I know that, you told me last night."

He made no comment.

"But it's too late," I said. "I already told someone." I had mentioned it to my wife and one of our close friends. But I honored his request for the next decade.

I was involved in another ritual when my father died. My wife and I flew back to San Francisco to make all the arrangements. After the funeral was over, there remained the question of my father's ashes. They were in a cardboard box, and it was up to my sister and me to decide what to do with them.

First we decided to split them up. She took her half and just spread them out over her flower bed in her backyard. She and our father were always close, so she was relaxed about the whole thing.

But that wasn't the case with my father and me. I wanted to do something to connect with him and honor him. I also wanted to help him pass on into stillness. But I didn't know what to do. For a while his ashes sat in their cardboard box in the backseat of my car. A friend said, "Well, take the ashes back to the Minnesota Zen Meditation Center and put them on the altar for forty-nine days. That's the ritual we have in Zen."

But that didn't feel quite right. My dad was an atheist. He hated this Zen stuff, especially the fact that I did it. He never really got over that. It seemed like a rude thing to do. So I continued to drive around with the ashes in the backseat of my car.

My cousin said, "Tim, you should put his ashes in the family mausoleum. That is where Grandmother is." He went on to name several other relatives who were also there. So that sounded okay.

I got my wife and son and we drove to the mausoleum. We got there and I took the ashes out of the car. That's when I realized: *This is Christian!* My dad hated the hypocrisy he saw in much of Christianity almost as much as he hated my Buddhism. So I put the ashes back on the backseat.

My family was starting to get impatient. They probably thought I was being disrespectful.

Finally, we were scheduled to fly back to Minnesota in a day and his ashes were still in my car. We couldn't take his ashes to Minnesota, because he'd hated that I moved to Minnesota. He took it personally when I moved away.

I decided to go to the area in San Francisco where my father grew up and just drive around. I have a very poor sense of direction, but I had some idea of where he used to live. Finally, we came to his childhood house. I remembered the embankment in front of the house that led to the sea—the same sea that Bobby Shafto hung out in. As a child, I always wanted to climb down the embankment, but my grandmother would say, "Oh, Tim, you can't go down to the ocean. It's too steep."

I parked on the street. We didn't want to freak the owners out, so we left the ashes in the car when we went to ring the doorbell of my father's old home. When the couple who lived there answered the door, we introduced ourselves, and I told them that my father had grown up there and that I had spent time there as a boy. They were very friendly and invited us in. I told my story, and then asked whether we could take my father's ashes down the embankment to the sea. The woman said, "Oh, no, you can't go down the embankment. It's too steep."

So we left. Down the road we pulled over and went looking for another way down to the sea. We found one, and after scrambling down it, I dumped the ashes into the ocean right below the house where my father was raised. There was a great release, and I felt a wonderful connection with him.

DREAM BUDDHA

Last night I dreamed I was a butterfly flitting from flower to
flower,
flitting from plant to plant.
Or is it now that I am a butterfly dreaming I am
Chuang-tzu,
flitting from sentence to sentence,
flitting from word to word?

—CHUANG-TZU, TAOIST PHILOSOPHER AND POET,
FOURTH CENTURY B.C.E.

We don't talk much about dreams in Zen. But even Buddha believed in the power of dreams to move us toward awakening.

I once had a dream that I was underwater. I'm struggling, I can't reach the surface, and I drown. Other times, I dream I'm buried alive. After death, I always feel wonderful and completely free of all my worries and concerns.

There is a certain type of dream that can cut us free of our obsessive thoughts. In dream time, an archetypal guide may appear to offer help. We don't know where the guide comes from, whether it's real or imagined. If it's helpful, why do we need to know any more than that? Our interconnectivity is alive; it is active, and we are always in contact with it. It works in mysterious ways. We don't need to understand it.

In the sixties I often visited a Chinese Zen teacher named To-Lun, the only Zen master in San Francisco other than Suzuki. To-Lun lived about three blocks from the Zen center. Betty Wong, the concert pianist that Suzuki played tennis with, and her sister, Shirley, were quite close to To-Lun. For a while I went once a week to his tiny zendo in the living room of his home. There were three or four Chinese practitioners and me. To-Lun spoke only Mandarin, so someone translated for me.

He was very warm but kind of trippy. He showed us his scars from burning incense on his body. In China he had lived in a cave and had gone long periods without food. He often told stories about wolves, which seemed to be his archetypal guide. In a dream-time experience that happened to To-Lun during meditation, a wolf spoke to him and showed him images about coming to America. The wolf told him there were people in the United States who were interested in learning about Chan Buddhism (Zen). To-Lun didn't know anything about America, but the wolf told him about it. And he came here.

On several occasions since Suzuki's death, he has appeared to me and offered guidance, sometimes in night dreams, other times when I am fully awake.

Once it happened at the end of a *sesshin* (traditional retreat) led by Katagiri in Minneapolis. Everyone had left, and I planned to spend the night in the zendo before going home to Two Harbors the next day. I happened to glance at one of Suzuki's books, which had his picture on the cover. He came out of the picture. His body was not clearly visible, but it was so clearly him. As I looked at him in wonder, he indicated that I should move down to Minneapolis and work with Katagiri.

The next day in Two Harbors, as I told a friend about my experience, I fell into a great and joyous spaciousness in which the small egoic Tim was again completely gone. It was pure ecstasy that lasted for several days.

Another time in a night dream, I found myself watching Suzuki build a wall of stones. He told me he needed my help. I said, "But you have lots of people to help you." He seemed to gesture toward all the different stones that he was using to build the wall. They were different sizes and colors. And he said, "Yes, but I also need you." This dream led to the second time that I returned to formal Zen practice after being away.

And then there have been dreams that I have had over the past dozen years, probably six to eight times, in which Suzuki suddenly appears. I say, "Sensei, I thought you were dead!" and he laughs uproariously. That's all he ever does.

Zen teacher Jiyu Kennett Roshi frequently talked about various bodhisattvas appearing and speaking to her. Dream-time practice is a regular practice, just like zazen. But I don't recommend mixing it up with zazen. If it comes up on its own, that's okay. But I wouldn't recommend trying to evoke it, because we can get tangled up in trying to figure out its meaning or significance and it can turn into just another infatuation or ego entanglement.

LETTERS FROM BUDDHA'S WORLD

The first few years of my Zen practice were mostly about penetrating my bodily veils. My mind was always easier to deal with than my body. Whenever my concentration became focused, my body would shake. If I quit focusing and just spaced out, my body was still. It was a difficult time for me. I wanted to do this practice with some grace, but it seemed impossible. Others appeared to have no problems. It looked effortless for them. Some almost floated across the zendo and sat as still and tall as a mountain through an entire retreat. My body just wouldn't cooperate, and it was very discouraging.

Then I had a big dream. In the dream I was standing at the entrance to the zendo. I was supposed to go in, but I couldn't. Two guys were sitting like great mountains and taking up the whole zendo. They were very tall, very erect, totally still, and gigantic. I knew I should go in and sit the way they were sitting, but I couldn't. I said, "Oh, no. I could never do that. I'm not tall enough."

Then, out of the corner of my eye, I saw Suzuki Sensei come *rolling* into the zendo, actually doing somersaults. He was tiny compared with the two guys. They didn't even notice him. He somersaulted all around and between them, smiling joyfully, having a wonderful time. He beckoned me to come in and join him, not by gesturing or saying anything. It was joy itself that beckoned me.

We don't have to be special or graceful or beautiful. Those guys in the zendo didn't even see Suzuki. They missed his presence because they were too good. They were like beautiful butterflies pinned down in a butterfly collection.

In our desire to be good, we become frozen trying to be correct. We will never be that perfect person we want to be. Let's just give ourselves to this messy, hurly-burly life, whatever it brings.

Perhaps archetypal guides, transformative rituals, and dreams are merely psychological rather than mystical. But if they help us to be kind to ourselves and others, if they help us to cultivate gentleness, generosity, and compassion, then what more do we need? Profound experiences, whether we label them mystical or psychological, may support us on the path to awakening. According to Suzuki Roshi, they are letters from Buddha's world, reminding us who we are.

Suzuki Roshi said, "When you see a plum blossom or hear the sound of a small stone hitting bamboo, that is a letter from the world of emptiness." When we empty ourselves of any thought of an isolated self, we experience the universe as a single entity extending itself.

The final part of this book focuses on the world of emptiness—Buddha's world. It discusses how contact with that world informs and nurtures a mature Zen practice.

PART FIVE

Time Dissolving into Timelessness

SIXTEEN

Turtle Mountain
Has Finally Awakened

AN OUTSIDER JOURNEYED TO Buddha's camp to ask for guidance. He wanted to stop the mind road that was always taking him off in different directions. When he approached Buddha, he said, "I do not ask for the spoken; I do not ask for the unspoken." Buddha's response was to sit in stillness. The outsider understood. He praised Buddha, proclaiming that Buddha had opened the clouds of delusion and enabled him to find the way.

When the outsider left, Ananda stepped forward and asked what the outsider had seen. Why did he offer such praises to the Buddha? Buddha said, "He is like the horse that runs at the shadow of the whip."

The outsider was not habituated to Buddha's way of expressing the dharma. The insider, Ananda, was used to Buddha. His moods, his manner of speaking, all had become stale over time. Poor Ananda had zoned out, as we all do when things become too familiar. He was not resting in the fresh reservoir of stillness that's our true mind. It's more comfortable to be an insider, but in terms of being present, awake, and alive, it may be best to remain an outsider—a refugee.

When Ananda said, "What did the outsider realize to make him praise you?" he was probably feeling a little agitated. He was Buddha's right-hand man, his constant companion, memorizing his teachings and serving him, but Ananda had not yet experienced enlightenment. His mind was very busy because it was fixated on Buddha's words, his moods, and his needs. The mind that is not fixed on anything (that is, an empty mind) eluded Ananda until after Buddha's death.

AN EMPTY MIND

My friend Phil used to drive Suzuki Sensei to and from our Palo Alto sitting group every week. The morning sittings ended at rush hour, so the drive to San Francisco meant sitting in heavy traffic. Every week, Suzuki fell asleep during the trip. Through all the starts and stops, the horn-blowing and hollering out windows, Suzuki just slept. Once, Phil was telling Suzuki about an interesting dream he'd had. When he glanced over, he saw that Suzuki was sound asleep.

As Phil told me this, I felt bad for him. I said, "You know, I don't have any classes this early. I could drive him back to San Francisco some mornings."

Phil shook his head. "No," he sighed. "The traffic is my koan." It was the same tone of resignation my grandmother always used when she said, *Oh, it's my cross to bear.*

But then Phil lit up and added, "But he *is* teaching me something. He's teaching me how to rest where I am."

I was touched by Phil's tenderness and willingness. His mind was fresh, open, and oriented toward the teachings. It was beginner's mind, an empty mind, the mind of an outsider.

When Katagiri Roshi was abbot of Minnesota Zen Mediation Center, the scholar Robert Thurman came to speak. Robert seemed delighted with Katagiri. He appreciated him for the great teacher that he was. When Robert returned to his own center in Massachusetts, he invited Katagiri to come and give some talks. I went along as his attendant. We were both outsiders there—and Katagiri Roshi amazed me. I thought, *Just look at this guy! He's wonderful.*

I had listened to Katagiri day after day, year after year—but that week he amazed me. Was it my mind? Was I no longer anticipating his every move? I had been so close to him for so long. I'd forgotten how to appreciate him. I had to become an outsider to see him with fresh eyes.

And of course the people in Massachusetts were so attentive and open to him. They appreciated the stillness he manifested because they were not accustomed to him.

On the way back to Minnesota, I talked with Katagiri about how good he was and about how much everyone loved him. "I bet you wish you could have stayed there," I said.

"Oh," he sighed, "they would just get used to me, too."

This is what we do as human beings. But it's all in our own head. So after we got back, I tried to do a better job of keeping my mind fresh and appreciative of Katagiri's gifts. It worked for a while, but then I settled back into my critical way of thinking. I regret that. I'm sorry I wasn't more supportive and attentive to Katagiri Roshi.

Seppo and Ganto were dharma brothers, about six years apart in age. They lived in China near the end of the Tang Dynasty.

Seppo practiced with great diligence. In the monastery he was a cook and a manual laborer, and he played many other roles where he supported other people. But he'd had no awakening experience.

Once they were snowed in on Turtle Mountain for three days. Ganto mostly slept, while Seppo sat zazen. After three days, Ganto woke up from a nap, sat straight up, and yelled at Seppo, "Get some sleep! What do you think you are—a roadside shrine?"

A roadside shrine looks very upright and beautiful. Maybe we bow to it as we pass by. But then we forget all about it. It's not very deep. It doesn't emanate stillness. Ganto was making fun of Seppo as he sat there trying to be someone special through his zazen.

Seppo touched his chest and said, sadly, "My heart is not at peace. I can't fool myself."

Ganto shouted, "Don't you know the family treasure doesn't come in through the gate! Let it flow out from your own breast to cover the sky and the earth."

With that, Seppo had a great awakening. "Turtle Mountain has finally awakened!" he exclaimed.

Seppo didn't say that *he* had finally awakened—he, the person who traveled the mind road, looking to become someone special. Seppo had gone beyond the mind road. He had tapped in to the great awakening that includes everything.

Later Seppo became a respected teacher with thousands of followers. When they praised him, he said, "It has nothing to do with me." He was not just being humble; he was revealing a deep truth about reality, a truth Bodhidharma referred to in his statement "a vast emptiness with nothing holy about it."

In the stories of the outsider and the roadside shrine, Buddha and Ganto are depicted as teachers in the role of a wise friend. A wise friend doesn't do very much. A friend that is not so wise is always doing, doing, doing. But a wise friend offers just enough support to help us open up to our own treasure.

I told these two stories in a talk once, and afterward someone asked, "Are you suggesting that Ananda and Seppo no longer had a busy mind after their awakening?" I am not suggesting that at all. Research today suggests that in some people a busy mind is innate, just like eye color or height. We shouldn't judge and compare. A busy mind can learn to rest where it is, allowing thoughts to pass through without fixating on them. Even with a busy mind, we can fully engage in our activity. Ananda is credited with memorizing all of Buddha's teachings. Without a busy mind, I don't think he could have done that. It took a lot of mental energy. And what a service to the dharma.

In an interconnected universe, nothing gets left out. It's not about one or the other, a busy mind or a still mind. It's about relationships. "Turtle Mountain has finally awakened" expresses a deep understanding of interdependence.

LIVING AN INTERDEPENDENT LIFE: THE FOUR IMMEASURABLES

I said to the wanting creature inside me:
What is this river you want to cross?
There are no travelers on the river-road and no road.
Do you see anyone moving about on that bank, or nesting?
There is no river at all, and no boat, and no boatman
There is no tow rope either, and no one to pull it
There is no ground, no sky, no time, no bank, no ford!
And there is no body and no mind!
Do you believe there is some place that will make the
soul less thirsty?

In that great absence you will find nothing.
Be strong then, and enter into your own body;
There you have a solid place for your feet.
Think about it carefully!
Don't go off somewhere else!
Kabir says this: Just throw away all thoughts
of imaginary things,
And stand firm in that which you are.

—KABIR, FIFTEENTH-CENTURY INDIAN POET

Siddhartha Gautama's enlightenment experience is surrounded by mythology. Its historical accuracy really doesn't matter, because it is an archetype. After six years of trying different meditative approaches and purifications, Siddhartha sat down under the Bodhi Tree to meditate.

Six days later, in the dark of night, he had a vision of the interdependent nature of all life, empty of a fixed ego. He saw that all things are interconnected, influencing each other, conditioning each other, relating to each other constantly. Everything is the cause of everything else, and everything is the effect of everything else. The thoughts and actions of each one of us affect us all. We support each other and all beings by cultivating wholesome attributes.

Buddha's teachings focus on healthy emotional development because our emotions reverberate throughout the universe. Healthy emotions promote spiritual maturity and the capacity to live happily in an interconnected universe, letting go of a solid, separate self.

The cornerstones on which emptiness and interdependence are based are equanimity, loving-kindness, compassion, and noncontingent joy. They are called the Four Immeasurables. The measuring mind cannot come close to them. Each is based on deep and abiding love—not adolescent, romantic love. Abiding love doesn't involve attachment or grasping. It doesn't need anything beyond itself.

Equanimity. In Zen we stress equanimity. It stills our judgments, prejudices, and preferences. It allows us to accept the ups and downs of life, and it is the underpinning of steadiness and resilience. Equanimity is a key to deep and abiding love.

In the eighteenth century in Japan, a village girl became pregnant. When her parents asked who the father was, she named Hakuin, the Zen priest in the temple.

When the child was born, the parents took the baby to Hakuin and said, "Our daughter says you're the father of this baby. We can't afford to take care of it. It's your baby, so you keep it."

"Oh, is that so?" Hakuin replied. He took the baby in. He loved and cared for the child for a year.

But all the while, the young woman was feeling guilty. She went to her parents and confessed that she had told a lie. The parents returned to the temple and said, "Our daughter said you are not the father of the baby."

Hakuin said, "Oh, is that so?"

They took the baby back. By then, however, Hakuin's reputation had been ruined. But Hakuin wasn't caught by ideas of fame and ill repute. Equanimity allowed him just to be with whatever life brought. The most important thing was to be open and available.

Loving-kindness. Loving-kindness is a warmth that fills the heart and radiates outward toward everyone. It doesn't discriminate between those who are nice and those who aren't. The warmth just radiates, and it can have a powerful effect on people.

I happened to meet someone once at the Minneapolis/Saint Paul airport who radiated loving-kindness. The memory stuck with me.

I had missed my plane. Some friends were waiting for me in Milwaukee, but I was stuck in Minneapolis. I tried calling, but all I got was an answering machine. In Milwaukee a whole group of people were holding dinner for me and I couldn't even contact them. I felt awful and helpless, waiting in line at the airport to try to make other arrangements.

When I finally got to the front of the line, the woman behind the counter was really attentive and present. She seemed to genuinely care about my plight and wanted to help however she could. It wasn't just courtesy or good manners. She radiated warmth. I was with her for only three minutes, yet my mood completely changed—and not just for a few minutes, but for the rest of the day.

According to Buddha, the powerful effect of loving-kindness happens only when it is received and acknowledged as a gift. This woman gave me a gift. She didn't know me from Adam. She had no motivation, no agenda. It wasn't even *her* loving-kindness; it was bigger than that. She manifested it, and I received it. I felt it in my heart immediately. But it wasn't until afterward that I realized what an impact she had on me.

Often, when we receive a genuine exchange of caring, consideration, and support, we shut down a little because we're embarrassed or self-conscious, or we think there may be strings attached. Or maybe we feel too vulnerable to take it in and acknowledge it as a gift. Sometimes we can't appreciate it because we think we're not worthy of it. We feel guilty. If so, we have worthiness issues that need our kind attention. Or maybe we think it exposes us too much: *I'm supposed to be a Zen teacher, and here I am running around the airport trying to catch the next plane—then a woman says something nice to me and I melt.*

However, as with anything, there are caveats—even with loving-kindness. One is that the person on the other side of the exchange may actually have expectations attached. If so, it's important that we pick up on these—that we practice big, broad seeing rather than narrow or cloudy seeing, as I explained in the discussion about vidya in chapter 2. There is an ancient Tibetan saying: "Think of all beings as buddha, but keep your hand on your wallet."

A second caveat involves dependency. Because loving-kindness can have a powerful and lasting effect, there is the possibility of becoming dependent on it. Warmth fills our heart, and we become addicted to the feeling. We start craving it. Then when the person radiating the warmth is no longer around, the craving intensifies. Any time we cling to something—even to loving-kindness—it becomes a source of suffering.

A third caveat involves fear. If we harbor a fear of rejection, we may withhold the warmth in our heart. If so, we need to return to our meditation, the birthplace of equanimity, until the warmth we feel can blossom into true loving-kindness that radiates indiscriminately and creates a context for compassion.

Compassion. For true compassion to bloom, loving-kindness has to come first to create the context. Then there must be a willingness to experience the suffering of others. Authentic compassion has nothing to do with sentimentality, politeness, or being nice. Compassion allows us to be present with people in their pain regardless of how severe it is. If you're not in a good space to do that, it's important to recognize that fact and return to your practice of equanimity and loving-kindness. Return to stilling your mind, even if it doesn't seem possible. At base level, it's always still. Stay with it until compassion wells up naturally.

During the news coverage of the terrible aftermath of Hurricane Katrina, I turned off the television. I didn't want to think about it. But if I'm not willing to expose myself, if I guard myself from the suffering of others, I'm not going to feel compassion.

I have to be willing to see suffering, to hear others' cries, to feel their pain, and to be vulnerable.

Then it's important that we observe our reactions. We'll have all kinds of reactions. Compassion isn't something distant. It's easy to talk about Avalokiteshvara, the bodhisattva of compassion, but to actually experience the excruciating suffering of someone else means seeing your own fear, feeling your own sense of powerlessness, and at times enduring your own exhaustion from trying to keep your heart open.

In Tolstoy's short story "Master and Man," the landowner Vasili Brekhunov leaves his servant Nikita in the snow to die. Then he has a change of heart and rushes back. He covers Nikita with the warmth of his own body and brings him back to life. But Vasili himself dies in the process. Tolstoy describes it this way:

Yes, he awoke. But awoke a very different man to what he had been when he fell asleep. He tried to rise and could not. He tried to move his hand and could not. He tried to move his leg and could not. Then he tried to turn his head but that also he could not do. Nikita was lying beneath him and Nikita was growing warm and was coming back to life. It seemed to him that he was Nikita and Nikita he and that his life was no longer within himself but within Nikita. He strained his ears till he caught the sound of breathing. Yes, the faint deep breathing of Nikita. Nikita is alive, he cried to himself in triumph. And therefore so also am I.

This kind of compassion comes from the deep sense of oneness we can experience when we penetrate the core of suffering. If we're willing to be with suffering and penetrate it, the joy that bubbles up is not conditioned by circumstances. When Vasili embraces the suffering of Nikita, the possibility arises for Vasili to realize that nothing is separate; therefore nothing is ever born and nothing dies.

Here are four behaviors that are often confused with compassion:

1. Going along to get along
2. Giving unsolicited advice
3. Losing ourselves in another's suffering
4. Codependency

In Buddhism these are called "near enemies of compassion" because we often substitute them for the genuine thing. We may feel compassionate and look compassionate, but our actions are not coming from equanimity and loving-kindness. When there's self-involvement, control issues and suffering will be associated with the outcome. We want to control the situation, the way we feel in our own heart, or the way others feel about us. Often we're left feeling helpless and exhausted.

Noncontingent joy. Sometimes I have a good day, sometimes I have a bad day. Sometimes I tell my wife I'm happy, sometimes I say I'm not happy. But noncontingent joy isn't like that. This is the joy that is here all the time. It's an aspect of our true nature, of life itself.

As I mentioned before, Ananda, whose name actually means "joy" in Sanskrit, was Buddha's constant companion and his attendant. It was his warm and compassionate influence that ultimately persuaded Buddha to allow women into the sangha. But noncontingent joy is not something we can practice. We can't elicit it directly. It arises naturally from the other three immeasurables after we've practiced them for some time.

Ananda's focus was not on his own meditation practice. He focused on taking care of Buddha. But after Buddha's death, he sat down and went into a deep meditative state. He sat for twenty-four hours. Then, exhausted, he went to bed. The moment he lay his head on the pillow, he had a big opening. He finally experienced the joy that is neither conditioned by anything nor dependent on anything.

Another person who exuded noncontingent joy was Nyogen Senzaki, one of the first teachers to bring Zen to America. He came here in 1905 as an attendant to his teacher, Soyen Shaku. When Shaku was ready to return to Japan, he gave Senzaki permission to stay. Senzaki supported himself by taking odd jobs and spent hours in the public library learning English. In 1919 he compiled the well-known *101 Zen Stories*.

One of Sensaki's most famous sayings is, "My gladness is your gladness. I have no other gladness than this." We can extend the idea to include, "My sadness is your sadness" and "My anger is your anger." When we come from this place in our heart, there is a deep joy that resonates through our shared gladness, our shared sadness, and our shared anger. Through our wholehearted practice of the Four Immeasurables, our biochemistry actually changes as we change our cognitions, beliefs, and attitudes about who we are and how we fit into the world.

NOTHING TO ATTAIN

"I have heard how the teachings say the great sea doesn't harbor a corpse. What is the sea?" the monk asked his teacher.

"It includes the whole universe," the teacher replied.

"Then why doesn't it harbor a corpse?"

"It doesn't let one whose breath has been cut off stay."

"Well, since it includes the whole universe, why doesn't it let one whose breath has been cut off stay?"

The teacher replied, "In the whole universe there is no virtue.
If the breath is cut off, there is virtue."
   "Is there anything more?"
   "You may say there is or there isn't. But what are you going to
do about the dragon king who holds the sword?"

—ZEN KOAN

As human beings, we feel adrift. We always want a harbor, a safe place, a group we can belong to. We want support. We have a deep need to feel protected. But the great sea that includes the whole universe does not see dividedness. This lack of division is what we experience in deep samadhi, where there is no I. We think we want to experience deep samadhi, but sometimes we pull back from the edge. Feeling ourselves dissolve doesn't feel very secure. But everything is included in this sea of interdependent life. What could be more secure than that?

In the koan, the monk is referring to a passage in the Nirvana Sutra. If this wonderful sea includes everything, even our fear and anxiety, then why doesn't it harbor a corpse? "Because it doesn't let one whose breath has been cut off stay." When we stop making wholehearted effort, our breath becomes shallow. (This actually happens; you may have noticed it sometime.) Trying to attain something for ourselves, worrying about things, or comparing and criticizing closes our heart and cuts off our breath. Our lives become shallow and easily overwhelmed by anxiety and discouragement.

When we are wholeheartedly engaged in our activity, we do not worry about a destination or accomplishment. Our breath naturally sinks all the way down into the abdomen. One wholehearted breath opens us up to wholehearted energy. The energy is always available, not a breath away or even an inhalation away.

The energy of the whole ocean rests in our own *hara,* our own abdomen. It is the energy of interdependence, so how could it possibly run out? There's no need to try to get to it or to try to change our consciousness. We are perfect just as we are.

The teacher in the koan goes on to say, "In the whole universe there is no virtue. If the breath is cut off there is virtue." If our breath is cut off, virtue becomes just another thing that we seek to manifest. If virtue arises naturally, it is not a thing that is separate from the great sea. In the whole universe, there is no separate thing called virtue. If our breath is cut off, there is a thing called virtue, and we seek to manifest it.

"Is there anything more?" the student asks. He is still seeking, still trying to get something from the teacher.

The teacher replies, "You may say there is or there isn't. But what are you going to do about the dragon king who holds the sword?" The teacher is saying, *I could teach you more. Or you could just shed all the dead corpses as a serpent-dragon sheds its skin, going freely wherever you want to go.*

Dragons can move through the air, through water, or through the earth. They are always moving, changing, and living wakefully.

If we seek a destination, when we arrive we will find only the dead skin of corpses. It will not bring us true joy. To constantly shed the dead skin of the past is our natural activity. It is enlightened activity. But when we view our moments as a means to an end, we are just piling up the corpses.

Once while participating in a long retreat at Tassajara, I had a wonderful opening experience. On my way home, I couldn't wait to show my mother how much I had changed.

But when I walked into the house, she was shocked. She glared at me. "Don't they feed you at that place?" she demanded.

Where did my mind go then? *You skinny boy! Skinny boy who dropped out of Stanford. Who wouldn't go to law school like your father!*

I'd had a wonderful enlightenment experience, but what did I do? I grabbed hold of it and went running off to show my mom. When she glared at me, my mind immediately reacted: *Mom, can't you see that I'm transformed? Goddamnit, I'm transformed!* But I was carrying a dead corpse.

We all do this. We all breathe shallowly sometimes. But one deep breath is all that's needed to return.

SEVENTEEN

Delusion and Enlightenment Have No Fixed Nature

I F BUDDHISM IS ABOUT ANYTHING, it is about enlightenment. Historically, there are three ways of thinking about enlightenment. All three have merit and can be helpful at different stages of our practice.

The first approach, which I refer to as the Bright Mirror approach, comes from the Theravada tradition, the oldest surviving school of Buddhism. *Theravada* translates to "teachings of the elders" or "ancient teachings." It relies on the scriptures of the Pali canon, the earliest collection of Buddhist literature. The Bright Mirror approach focuses on the duality of delusion and enlightenment.

The second attitude toward enlightenment, which I refer to as the No Mirror approach, deconstructs all of our beliefs. It comes from the Madhyamika school, founded in the second century C.E. by the famous Buddhist deconstructionist Nagarjuna. He deconstructed in order to illuminate Buddha's most profound insights.

In Zen we focus mostly on Shattered Mirror, a later approach that follows Dogen's view on enlightenment. Dogen didn't merely deconstruct the teachings in the way that Nagarjuna did. His way of keeping the dharma alive was to shatter it completely, then put the different facets back together in a fresh way.

BRIGHT MIRROR: THE EIGHTFOLD PATH

If the doors of perception were cleansed every thing would appear to man as it is, infinite.

—WILLIAM BLAKE

The metaphor of a bright mirror suggests that our natural state of mind is mirror-like in that it reflects everything within it. The Bright Mirror approach likens the path from delusion to enlightenment to polishing a mirror. We keep it polished so that it reflects accurately and its luminosity penetrates everything. It is a long, gradual, arduous process. Bright Mirror embraces the spirit of repetition and commitment. An advantage of this approach is that it's straightforward. It is arduous and tedious, but at least we have a goal and a clear direction.

This approach calls for the practice of sitting in meditation and wiping the mirror clean of all the dust and residue. Dust is always accumulating: our concepts, ideas, worries, and anxieties are always arising and darkening our vision. I don't know whether the poet William Blake knew anything about Buddhism, but his famous saying about "the doors of perception" corresponds to the Bright Mirror view of enlightenment.

Buddha offered very clear instructions on how to keep the doors of perception cleansed. His Eightfold Path describes eight elements or aspects of an awakened life. It begins with an understanding and acceptance of interdependence. As we clarify our understanding of Buddhist principles, we open up naturally into the second aspect, which is an intention to apply our understanding to our daily lives. These first two elements involve faith—not faith in anything in particular, not a faith that we can cling to, just moment-to-moment faith in an interconnected universe.

The next three aspects of the path involve ethical behavior. The third focuses on speech, which refers to expression of all kinds, including the Chatterbox Café in our heads. Appropriate speech requires insight. In dealing with others, what is the intent behind our words? Are we seeking to illuminate or conceal? Are we using skillful means or just venting? Are we being upright and honest in our expression? These questions require honest inquiry. Appropriate speech also demands a degree of foresight. What will the impact of our words be? Will they create suffering or harmony?

The same kind of inquiry is applied to the fourth element of the path, appropriate action, and also the fifth, which involves our livelihood. Are we engaging in activities and jobs that support Buddhist values and ethics? In his book *Each Moment Is the Universe*, Katagiri Roshi said, "When you understand how the various aspects of human life unfold in a moment, you can live freely in the realm of time. You can face the moment and know what to do. Then, through conscious action, you can create your life, and your life really works."

The last three steps on the path concern meditation. The sixth is effort. It takes relentless and diligent effort to maintain a sincere meditation practice. The seventh, mindfulness, is the energy that keeps bringing us back to the present moment. It brings greater awareness and supports the other seven disciplines on the path. The eighth is concentration, which brings one-pointed focus into our meditation and builds inner strength.

Sometimes we get stuck on the path and lose our aspiration. If you have trouble bringing your aspiration back to life, go back to the first step of the Eightfold Path. Focus on your understanding of the teaching that everything is interdependent until your commitment to manifest that interdependence is reaffirmed. It doesn't matter how many times you return to the first aspect of the path. There's a saying in Buddhism that if we pull a single thread, the entire universe comes along. When you imbibe completely any one aspect of the Eightfold Path, the other seven are equally present.

In a Zen community, the teacher is the model of someone who's been on the path for years and manifests clarity and joyfulness. Certainly I felt that way about my two teachers, Suzuki Roshi and Katagiri Roshi. They sat zazen every morning and every evening, day after day, year after year. They led retreat after retreat with a quiet joy that was unending.

In a way, the Bright Mirror approach is similar to learning to play a musical instrument or learning a foreign language. We began sending our daughter, Erin, to a little French language camp when she was eight years old. She didn't seem to be learning much, but she loved it, so we kept sending her every year. Then she took French in high school, but she didn't seem to be very good at it. Every morning she practiced her vocabulary. My wife, who is fluent in French, cringed when she heard her, but we just kept encouraging her.

After college Erin joined the Peace Corps, hoping to go to a French-speaking country. Instead, she was sent to an English-speaking part of Africa. But she became friends with someone who spoke French. She practiced regularly when living out in the bush. Now Erin lives in France, and she speaks beautifully fluent French. But after how many years, how much repetitive practice, how much boredom, how much frustration?

There is a famous story set in northern China during the eighth century. At Hung Jen's monastery, it was time to appoint a successor. Hung Jen announced a verse-writing contest. The monk whose poem revealed the deepest understanding of the dharma would be his successor. None of the monks dared submit a poem, feeling that the senior monk, Shen Hsiu, was the most worthy. But even Shen Hsiu was intimidated by the contest. Fearful of falling short of his teacher's expectations, he wrote his poem anonymously on a wall. Today this verse is quite famous. It exemplifies the Bright Mirror approach to enlightenment:

> The body is the awakening tree,
> The mind the mirror bright.
> Take care to keep it clean
> And let no dust alight.

NO MIRROR

Shen Hsiu's poem is not the end of the story. It continues with the story of another famous Zen teacher, Hui Neng, who was born in southern China. His father, an exiled administrator, died when he was only three years old. Eventually, his death plunged the family into poverty. To earn a living, Hui Neng became a woodcutter.

Hui Neng was at the market one day selling wood when he heard a sutra being chanted. He was deeply affected. He inquired into it. He discovered it was the Diamond Sutra, and he learned that he could study it at Hung Jen's monastery in northern China.

He immediately set out on the long journey. Upon arrival, Master Hung Jen recognized the great potential of this young illiterate and allowed him to stay. Hui Neng was assigned to the rice-hulling shed.

Hui Neng knew nothing of the verse-writing contest to find Hung Jen's successor until he heard a monk chanting Shen Hsiu's verse. He quickly realized that the verse did not express the central meaning of Zen and asked to be taken to the wall where the verse was inscribed. Being illiterate, Hui Neng asked another monk to inscribe his own verse on the wall:

> The body is not the enlightening tree
> Nor the mind a mirror bright.
> Since from the first no thing exists,
> Where can dust alight?

Hui Neng's verse exemplifies the No Mirror approach. It denounces the idea of a path leading us somewhere other than where we are right now. This view says that enlightenment is always present and available. All we have to do is stop discriminating.

The No Mirror approach is not about traveling from here to there. It's not about working hard and checking our investment each day: *Was my zazen sincere, or was I just spaced out the whole time? Am I working hard enough? Shouldn't I be better by now?* In the No Mirror approach, enlightenment is always right here. All we have to do is stop dividing things up through our thinking.

In this approach, enlightenment is not something you discover through arduous practice. It doesn't require years of sitting. As a matter of fact, it doesn't require any sitting at all. All we need to do is see clearly that our divisions, categories, and judgments are mere fabrications. It doesn't matter how much sitting meditation you do or what posture you take; you could stand on your head or take up calypso dancing and still see through this fictional creation. Enlightenment is the simple realization that all of our constructs about the world are fictional.

Hui Neng became the hero of Chinese Zen. He is portrayed as illiterate because you don't have to know anything to experience this radical awakening. His approach offers a radical freedom from attachment to images, opinions, or even meditation. He woke up to reality by simply paying attention, by stopping, looking, and listening. The idea has become so familiar that it is almost a cliché, but how often do we actually do it in a deep and sincere way? When we do, we discover undividedness.

In No Mirror, enlightenment takes no effort at all because it was here before Adam and Eve ate the apple from the tree of good and evil—before consciousness divided things up. All we have to do is come back to our original beginner's mind, as Suzuki Roshi would say. Or come back to our original innocence, as the Bible would say.

Both the Bright Mirror and the No Mirror approaches say that we can empty ourselves of greed, anger, and delusion, and then we can be immersed in delusion and completely free of it. Bright Mirror says there's a path from delusion to enlightenment. No Mirror denies the path. Instead, it says, *Just let go of all the ideas you've accumulated and come back to* just this.

These two approaches have several limitations. The first approach supposes a major division between things as they appear to be in conventional reality, which is the world we live in, and things as they truly are in ultimate reality. The limitation is that it can lead us to discount the world as it appears to be, to disparage conventional reality as if it were inferior. But our opportunity to cultivate compassion and wisdom is right now, right here. Ultimate reality permeates everything. If we dismiss the value and beauty of what's in front of us, we won't truly appreciate anything.

A second and related limitation is that both approaches emphasize and value the nondiscriminating mind at the expense of the discriminating mind. Bright Mirror implies that through zazen you'll attain a permanent state of enlightenment. No Mirror suggests zazen is not even needed to see things as they truly are. All you have to do is to stop believing in anything—including this statement. Both views espouse the possibility of cutting off all dualistic thinking at its root.

The third limitation in both Bright Mirror and No Mirror is that knowledge, reasoning, thinking, logic, and scientific pursuit are not valued. In both approaches, the act of discrimination and activities that support it are not important, because our aim is to transcend them. Yet the world needs discriminating activities. Science, reason, and logic are important. After all, we are thinking, reasoning, logic-making beings. Where would we be without these capacities?

The fourth limitation, which applies only to the Bright Mirror approach, is a matter of divisiveness. There's a division between the empowered and disempowered, between those who succeed at wiping their mirrors clean and the rest of us. This differentiation puts the power in a few great teachers. As a young Zen student, I was enamored with my teacher. But the more empowered Suzuki became in my mind, the more disempowered I became.

When I first knew Suzuki Roshi, he was just a regular guy. Look at him now. He has become a superstar of Zen. Over the years, he has gotten bigger and bigger. When Thich Nhat Hanh came to the Minnesota Zen Meditation Center in the eighties, he was just a teacher. Katagiri said, "Pay attention to this teacher, Tim. He is deep." But he was just a teacher. Look at him now. And how about the Dalai Lama? He is perhaps the biggest of them all.

We've made these teachers into deities. When we create deities, we disempower ourselves.

A final limitation to the No Mirror approach is the implication that it takes no effort to return to our original enlightened state—just stop discriminating. It's too simplistic and possibly even dangerous, because we need our ability to discriminate and analyze. Any time we go too far in one direction at the expense of the other, our view of reality becomes distorted. Wholeness is lost.

SHATTERED MIRROR

A greatly enlightened person is nevertheless deluded—
to understand that is the quintessence of practice.

—DOGEN

When Buddha was alive in the fifth century B.C.E., he prophesied that in the first age after his death, which would last five hundred years, people would wholeheartedly embrace the dharma. During the second age, things would fall into decay: people would listen to the dharma, but they wouldn't really imbibe it. By the third age, Buddha prophesied, the dharma would be in total disarray.

Dogen was born in the year 1200 C.E., around five hundred years after Shen Hsiu and Hui Neng. He lived in Japan during the Kamakura period, a time of great chaos. The emperor was weak. Civil wars broke out. Monks were fighting each other. It was a dark time in the history of Buddhism.

Many teachers believed this was the third age that Buddha predicted. There was much suffering, and people didn't seem to care about one another. Many believed an awakening experience would have no lasting effect because this was the fallen time.

But Dogen rejected that idea. He considered this view a negative fantasy that arose from the pessimism of the times. It became apparent to Dogen that enlightenment is not the absence of delusion and delusion is not the absence of enlightenment. He stated that delusion and enlightenment have no fixed nature. They are separate yet indivisible, like two sides of the same coin.

Consequently, delusion doesn't disappear in an awakened life. On the contrary. Great enlightenment is ever intimate with delusion. For Dogen, Zen practice provides us with the opportunity to shine an unwavering light on each of our delusions. The ability to shine our light of awareness on our delusion is enlightenment itself.

Think of your psyche as a cave and bare awareness as a flashlight that enlightens the cave. But the cave extends forever. There are always undiscovered nooks of anxiety and crannies of fear and doubt. Zen practice is the simple process of aiming your steady, calm flashlight inward and penetrating to the depths of the cave. Even when you have a strong desire to flee, you honor your commitment to stay and explore—not with your head but with your entire being, with focused and gentle awareness. Anxieties begin to dissolve. They never disappear entirely, because there's always another cranny you haven't seen yet. But luckily, your flashlight never runs out of batteries. Bare awareness is your original nature.

Years ago I had a student whom I'll call Dan. He had been practicing zazen wholeheartedly for about five years when he came to see me in dokusan and said, "Before I started practicing, my relationships with women were always difficult." He would have intense relationships, then things would get all tangled up. So he would back off. Then she would back off. Then he needed her to be close. She'd come back. And then he needed more space.

But once Dan started practicing, things began getting better. In his current relationship, he didn't feel so tied up in knots. "The problem is," Dan said, "I don't know how much is due to zazen and how much is that I am still distancing myself for protection."

This is a common question in Zen. Distancing is associated with suppressing, repressing, or denying. People confuse distancing with detachment. But detachment is actually the path to intimacy. What we detach from is the drama, which is just a means of distancing ourselves from the difficult emotion. We even create drama around our positive emotions, so we don't truly experience them in a deep way either. That is why life often feels dull and unsatisfying, even when things are going well. When we are practicing detachment, we have the ability to move in very close to our emotions—but without the drama.

Even in Dogen's time, people confused distancing with detachment. So Dogen talked primarily about intimacy. He stressed the intimacy between the light and the darkness, as his predecessor Sekito had before him. The two exist as interplay—not cohesion, not unity, not oneness, but interplay. Enlightenment sensitizes us to the complexities and problems of our human existence. Instead of trying to get away from them or overcome them, we're just *with* them, with compassion and kindness.

Dogen wrote, "When the dharma does not yet completely fill your body and mind, you think that it is already sufficient. When the dharma fills your body and mind, you think that something is missing." As you become more aware of your frailties, you see that enlightenment is ever intimate with delusion. Often people feel as if they have more problems after starting a meditation practice than they did before. Actually, they are just seeing more clearly, with less suppression and distancing.

You may need to distance yourself sometimes, and that's okay, but please don't confuse it with genuine detachment. The detachment in which we disidentify allows us to stay with our pain until it dissolves on its own. But if fear is involved, it is not detachment, it is distancing.

When Dan talked about his confusion between distancing and detachment, I said, "Just look into it. In zazen, invite the feelings in. The feeling of being abandoned when she moves away. The feeling of being overwhelmed when she gets close. Shine your light of awareness on these emotions and keep looking until you feel them start to dissolve. Do you sense an undercurrent of fear? Or a dropping away of anxiety? Or something else?"

Light is always mediated by darkness. There's no universal light that we just melt into, where there's no trace of ego left for the rest of our lives. For Dogen, meditation was not about finding some blissed-out state. Shattered Mirror is about settling into the interplay. We don't have to conquer the darkness or struggle against it. When we learn to just settle in, we will have authentic experiences of well-being, experiences that come from the ground of our being rather than the shallow ego experiences that are merely mental constructs.

A limitation of Shattered Mirror is that it overlooks Bright Mirror's stress on the importance of progress in meditation. Most of us need to engage in activities where we feel we can and will make progress. Dogen's approach also tends to de-emphasize our capacity to completely and effortlessly unburden our mind of thought, moment by moment, a capacity deeply valued by the No Mirror approach.

DIZZY KARMIC CONSCIOUSNESS, FLOWERS IN THE SKY, AND SKILLFUL SILENCE

To what shall I liken the world?
Moonlight, reflected in dewdrops,
Shaken from a crane's bill.

—DOGEN

Karmic consciousness. The way we live inside our memories and repeat the same habits, over and over, is known as karmic consciousness. Early Buddhist texts say that karmic consciousness is vast and crazed. Another translation uses the word *dizzy* instead of *crazed*. We become dizzy because we're so caught by our past and unable to be present with whatever is going on right now.

For twenty years Dan was entangled in his dizzy karmic consciousness. He tried to rid himself of his painful habit patterns so he could have a lasting, intimate relationship. But he couldn't seem to free himself from the past.

In Shen Hsiu's Bright Mirror approach, as we go from delusion to enlightenment, we are eradicating karmic consciousness. Little by little, practice on the Eightfold Path dissolves our karma over twenty or thirty years or, according to some Buddhist traditions, twenty or thirty lifetimes.

Hui Neng's No Mirror approach says that karmic consciousness is just a shell that covers over enlightenment, which is always here. In both cases, karmic consciousness is something we try to rid ourselves of.

Dogen, however, said that karmic consciousness is the *essence* of Zen practice and we should totally embrace it, because only then can we shine our light of awareness on it. Through the interplay of darkness and light, transformation happens. Dogen doesn't say that dark and light are the same. Darkness is just darkness, and light is just light. But the interplay makes them one interpenetrating whole. Interplay is what makes transformation possible.

Dogen stressed that regardless of how strongly your light shines on the darkness, the darkness is still there—your dizzy karmic consciousness is still present. So along with our practice on the Eightfold Path, we must include our dizzy karmic consciousness, because it will always be with us.

Eventually, my friend Dan moved out of state, and we lost contact for several years. Then I got a phone call from him. He was happy to report that his current relationship had lasted longer than any other—about five years.

"Things are really good," he said. "Stuff still comes up, but I'm able to just see it so much more often now."

Then he added, "But I better be careful. As soon as I get off the phone, she may say something that drives me right over the edge."

Flowers in the sky. Seng-Ts'an points out that both our dreams for the future and our reveries about what might have been in the past are just flowers in the sky. We are hypnotized by them. We waste our precious time gazing at them, reaching out to them, smelling their wonderful aromas, trying to draw them down and make them real. But the minute we do, they wilt. We need to see that they are just made up and let them go so we can be present to what is actually happening.

According to Seng-Ts'an and others before him, flowers in the sky are due to dim-sightedness, which is likened to cataracts. They arise from our worries, fears, concepts, and ideals. For example, when I see you, I remember you from before, so I don't really see you as you are now. I remember my reaction to you and your reaction to me. I can't be present with you as you are because of my cataracts—so practice is about getting rid of them.

But Dogen turns that metaphor on its head. He says that flowers in the sky are the flowers of both emptiness and joy. Flowers in the sky are what *is*. Are we going to fight that? It's the human condition to have cataracts. We can't get away from our dim-sightedness. It isn't a defect that needs to be removed. Just see it and be intimate with it.

Instead of getting rid of the wonderful sky flowers, we can enter into them completely. We move into that great spaciousness that is not separate from the flowers. Dan never gave up on his dream to enter into an intimate relationship. His difficulty with relationships was a dharma gate, and he kept moving toward it.

Skillful silence. In traditional Buddhism, knowing how to be with someone in silence is important. Often, particularly when we are with someone who is suffering, we think we have to say something so the person feels supported. We're afraid that if we're silent, it will be interpreted as indifference. But in Buddhism, silence is a manifestation of compassion. Silence that arises from stillness is very attentive and nourishing.

If you want to be intimate with Zen, you have to be intimate with silence. The only way to do that is to *be* silent, to steep yourself in silence. But here again, Dogen cautions us against putting too much emphasis on one thing at the expense of another. Enlightenment has no fixed nature.

For Dogen, there's no difference between silence and sound. Any time we speak sincerely, great silence is always included. Therefore, there's no need to deify silence at the expense of sharing, creating, and expression. Furthermore, silence that is not skillful can be misinterpreted and create distance. Zen practice is not about distancing.

When Dan called me that day, he said, "Now when the stuff comes up, I talk with my partner. But not until I've cooled off enough that I can be honest and compassionate—even if I'm saying that I need to distance myself for a while."

EIGHTEEN

Buddha's World

WHAT A WONDROUS
COUNTERCULTURE!

TWENTY-FIVE HUNDRED YEARS AGO, Buddha lived in an Indian society that was dominated by the caste system. (That system survived until the twentieth century and still has an impact on Indian culture today.) Buddha created a counterculture based on the view that everyone can become enlightened. In this view, the caste system was totally irrelevant, because all people are interconnected. This was a radical idea that challenged the authority of the Brahmans, the members of the ruling caste.

Five hundred years later in Palestine, Jesus of Nazareth created an equally challenging counterculture based on the principle "Do unto others as you would have them do unto you." The main difference is that in Buddha's counterculture, there are no "others."

Another difference is that Buddha's counterculture does not emphasize religious ideals. His teachings are about learning to stay upright, composed, and resilient amid the flux and flow of an ever-changing universe that is marked by three fundamental characteristics: nonself, suffering, and impermanence. He called these the Three Marks of Existence.

We have talked a lot about the first two of these marks. Now let's look at the third: impermanence.

This concept sounds threatening. Everything we love is going away. Where is the security in a world where nothing stays still, even for a moment? But remember, "In darkness there is light": the gift of impermanence is resiliency.

My youngest grandson, Logan, doesn't like change. He has temper tantrums when he has to stop what he's doing and do something else. His mother works diligently to help him be more flexible.

When we took Logan to the playground one day, Erin told him, "When the shadow falls across the slide, we will leave the playground." Every five minutes, she reminded him, "Remember, Logan. See where the shadow is now?" She knows that everything is constantly changing and that, to find contentment, Logan will have to learn to be resilient.

In Buddha's world, the shadow is always falling across the slide. There is always something else happening. Buddha's teachings are about settling in to this ephemeral life where nothing is static and everything is transforming into something else.

When you really think about it, impermanence is a strange phenomenon. How is it that we transform, from one moment to the next, into another human being, while the world around us is also transforming, completely disappearing, then reappearing in the next moment? It's very mysterious. But little by little, zazen prepares us to experience the world as it truly is.

When we truly experience impermanence, we feel our own death and rebirth and the death and rebirth of all things in each moment. It's easy to understand why we create barriers between ourselves and this unstable world. We distract ourselves with thoughts about what we want and what we don't want. We attach to things and push other things away by denying or repressing. To just live our life and experience it fully is the hardest thing for human beings. So we create delusion.

The dominant religions of our time seek to shield us from the ever-changing nature of things. Buddha's counterculture is about dissolving the shield.

CHAN: A CHINESE COUNTERCULTURE

A special transmission outside the scriptures
Not based on words or letters;
Directly pointing to the heartmind

This was how Bodhidharma described Chan (Zen). It's one of the most famous quotations in all of Zen literature. It says that insight, which allows us to see into our true nature, is passed down directly, mind to mind. This idea is central to Bodhidharma's teachings, and it marks the beginning of Zen.

According to legend, Bodhidharma, referred to as the first patriarch of Zen, ventured from India to China in 475 C.E. A large audience awaited his arrival, hoping that he would teach them the dharma. When he arrived, he sat down and started meditating. Afterward he got up and walked away without saying a word.

That may seem like an inauspicious beginning. But in time, Buddha's counterculture based on sitting quietly in meditation became the accepted way in China. During the Tang Dynasty, from 618 to 907, Buddhism flourished and became the dominant culture. Temples were built by the emperor and land was appropriated for Buddhist monasteries.

As history has demonstrated over and over, when a worldview is solidified and an institution develops around that worldview, something is genuinely lost. Neither Christ nor Buddha advocated building temples or churches and creating walls around their teachings.

As institutionalized Buddhism flourished, the harmony and openness of the Buddhist counterculture was replaced by self-importance and political maneuvering. Hanshan was a hermit poet who lived in southern China at this time. He recognized the decline from the Zen ideal and spent his life pointing it out in a characteristically Zen manner, joyfully and with humor.

Historically, little is known about Hanshan. What we do know is mostly deduced from his poems. These have given rise to so many folk legends around Hanshan that it's impossible to distinguish fact from fiction. It's generally agreed that he was born into the privileged civil servant class, and he was handicapped, which made walking difficult. In one of his poems, he wrote about wearing heavy wooden clogs, which perhaps helped him to get around. When he was about thirty years old, he left his life of wealth and privilege to take up the life of a hermit poet. He moved into a cave beneath a rocky overhang, took the name Hanshan, which means "cold mountain," and began inscribing poems on stones and trees.

Hanshan had two companions, Feng-kan (Big Stick) and Shih-te (Pickup). All sorts of folktales have grown up about these three because of their foolish antics. They poked fun at the self-importance of the monks living in monasteries. The stories of Cold Mountain, Big Stick, and Pickup reveal that there were still a few enclaves where the true counterculture was kept alive.

Hanshan lived to be 120 years old. There's an interesting legend around his death. An official recognized him as a great spiritual teacher and sent several men to his cave to bring him out. But when Hanshan heard them coming, he yelled, "Thieves,

thieves!" He wedged into a crack in the rocky cliff outside his cave, and then the cliff closed up around him. The fissure, still visible today, marks the spot where he vanished.

Hanshan's poetry has influenced poets and writers around the world. He was an important figure for Beat generation writers like Gary Snyder and Jack Kerouac. But perhaps the best-known English-language source of Hanshan's poems is the book *The Collected Songs of Cold Mountain* by the American translator and scholar Red Pine. Here is a stanza from one of Hanshan's best-known poems:

> to learn where the wild ducks fly
> follow the white-hare banner
> find a magic melon in your dreams
> steal a sacred orange from the palace
> far away from your native land
> swim with fish in a stream

DOGEN'S COUNTERCULTURE

Buddhism moved into Japan in the mid-sixth century. Shortly thereafter, Prince Shotoku declared Buddhism the official religion and ordered the construction of Buddhist temples and monasteries throughout Japan.

Over time, as Buddha had predicted, his counterculture began to fade, first in India, then in China, then in Japan. This happened as Buddhism became the dominant culture in each of these countries. As all dominant cultures seem to do, Buddhism took on the fear body as its corpus.

When Dogen came along in the thirteenth century, the corpus of Buddhism—the fear body—was so dense and heavy it seemed impenetrable. Dogen saw that people had not imbibed

Buddha's true teachings. So he left Japan and went to China, hoping to find some remnant of the original counterculture. After searching for a year and a half, discouraged and exhausted, he was ready to give up. Then his luck turned around.

In 1224 C.E., Dogen heard about old Master Rujing, who had a monastery in the mountains, and so he decided to visit him before heading home. Rujing welcomed Dogen warmly and invited him to practice with his fellow monks. The two of them developed an immediate bond.

One morning Dogen was sitting zazen with other monks at the monastery. Rujing was making his routine morning rounds, walking slowly behind the meditating monks, when suddenly he stopped. The monk next to Dogen had fallen asleep.

"The practice of zazen is the dropping away of body and mind!" Rujing shouted. "What do you expect to accomplish by dozing?"

At the words "dropping away of body and mind," Dogen experienced a deep letting go of all concepts, including those of "body" and "mind." Finally Dogen had met a teacher who seemed to exude the stillness of Buddha's original counterculture, and furthermore someone who helped Dogen tap into this deep stillness himself.

Dogen stayed at Rujing's monastery for two years. At the end of his stay there Rujing gave him a certificate of transmission. His return to Japan in 1227 C.E. marks the beginning of Soto Zen as we know it. Later he would use the phrase "dropping away of body and mind" frequently in his own teaching.

EXPRESS A DREAM WITHIN THE DREAM

Without expressing dreams there are no buddhas.

—DOGEN

Buddhism has always been about waking from the dream of ego-centric separation from all life. Dogen's counterculture took this one step further. He taught about "expressing a dream within the dream." For Dogen, Zen practice was about being fully engaged in the dream we're in, since the ordinary conventional world and the timeless world of quiescence are one and the same. Rather than trying to awaken from the dream of separation, he talked about becoming completely engaged in our dream. When we think of the world as a dream, we can be intimate with each component without being caught by it.

In many ways, Dogen's view seems to align with the teachings of Chuang-tzu, the Taoist poet who, after dreaming about being a butterfly, pondered the question: Am I a man who dreamed he was a butterfly? Or am I a butterfly, dreaming now that I am a man?

Chuang-tzu didn't talk about waking from the dream. The dream is what we have; it's what is. Are we going to deny it or ignore it? We can try to do that—or we can just fully express the dream that we are in without being captured by it.

This is what my friend Alice has learned to do. Without any warning at all, Alice's ordinary world ended when she suffered a psychotic break. She was hospitalized. Then she got the diagnosis: schizophrenia. She felt it meant a lifetime of disability, sense-dulling medication, and stigma. "I've had bad dreams all my life," Alice said, "but I never thought I could have this bad a dream."

Alice struggled and bemoaned her dream. She wanted out of it. But there was no out. It was her dream, and all she could do was engage it.

After about a year, Alice was able to fully accept and even embrace her situation. She learned to stay on her meds. She completed the Mindfulness-Based Stress Reduction program developed by the medical professor Jon Kabat-Zinn, which uses meditative techniques from both Zen and Vipassana traditions. Because it's taught in a hospital milieu, Alice was in a safe environment, surrounded by others living with a grave diagnosis. She was taught to stay in her body and to be with the pain she was experiencing, to open up to it, and breathe into it.

"Without expressing dreams there are no buddhas." Alice steeped herself in meditation, and after a while she found peace. It was somewhat limited. But she made up for the limitations by the depth of perception. She went back to college and finished her degree. She is now very happy, fully expressing her dream as a professional counselor for others who have mental illness.

Dogen didn't attract many followers in his lifetime. People thought his way of practicing was too demanding. His dream was to express harmony and interdependence right in the midst of the dark dream of corrupt thirteenth-century feudal Japan. He expressed his dream completely, even though few were listening. It wasn't until several hundred years after his death that many people started paying attention to his life's work. And in the last hundred and fifty years, his popularity has soared.

There's no need to wait until you have the perfect dream. Express your dream as it is. It is perfect right now, because it perfectly reflects where you are right now. It grows and transforms because you yourself are growing and transforming. The possibility of transformation is a gift of impermanence.

SUZUKI ROSHI'S COUNTERCULTURE

Eight hundred years after Dogen, Suzuki Roshi breathed new life into Buddha's original counterculture. He made it come alive again. Everything he did seemed to arise from the ground of his being, the same ground as Buddha in India, Bodhidharma and Hanshan in China, and Dogen in Japan.

Like Dogen, Suzuki felt that Buddhism in Japan had taken on a corpus of fear. He came to America seeking an enclave of fresh ground to cultivate. He discovered a wellspring—but it was unlike anything he could have imagined.

On November 13, 1967, to raise money to buy Tassajara, we organized a "Zenefit" held in the Avalon Ballroom in San Francisco. The concert featured performances by the Grateful Dead, Quicksilver Messenger Service, Big Brother and the Holding Company, and Janis Joplin—artists who have since become legendary.

I didn't usually go to the Haight-Ashbury district because it wasn't my scene, but I went to the Zenefit. The auditorium was full. Light effects emanated from strobe lights and lasers mounted throughout the theater. Pungent odors filled the air. People were dressed—or undressed—in an amazing variety of regalia. And the huge sounds of 1960s rock boomed from the stage.

Katagiri Sensei had been in the United States for only two years at the time. He was reserved, quiet, and a very gentle presence. I remember seeing him standing anxiously in the shadows, half-hidden, and looking quite out of sorts and unsettled in that crazy environment. He looked as if he wanted to run away. I'm sure he did.

Suzuki was older and had been doing resiliency practice for years and years. He sat in the front row of the theater, with lights flashing on him from all directions. What a memorable sight. Surrounded by utter chaos, he was completely relaxed and seemed totally in his element. He was looking around, smiling, taking it all in—I think he was grooving on the whole thing.

Finally, the last performer, the amazing blues singer Janis Joplin, took the stage. She gave it her all—talk about shedding the fear body. In front of a thousand people, she bared her heart and soul in a classic Janis performance.

Then it was time for Suzuki to say something to the crowd. The auditorium grew silent as he crossed to the microphone. When he spoke, his voice was calm and warm. "At first," he said, "I think your way *very* different from ours. But now I see, not so different! Not so different!"

The crowd roared.

Suzuki was touched by Janis's ability to shed her fear body and give her whole heart to others. People responded to her in a visceral way. Janis imbibed the music. It seemed to come from the ground of her being. But she didn't have a practice that cultivated resiliency. She could bare her soul onstage in front of people, but privately, her life was tragic. Less than three years after the Zenefit, she was dead.

Zen is a "special transmission, outside of scriptures." From the time of the Buddha, insight into our true nature has been transmitted from one teacher to one student. As long as this is the accepted path, Zen will never become stale food from the refrigerator. As our capacity for realization deepens, the path itself deepens. It will always be fresh, because realization is transmitted through relationship.

Zen literature is filled with stories and exchanges between teacher and student that end with words like "Then he had an awakening" or "Then he attained enlightenment." Although Suzuki never talked about satori, he didn't deny the importance of direct transmission.

Suzuki's own enlightenment experience came through a teacher whom Suzuki referred to only as "Tanker." It is a story he told only once, as far as I know.

In early 1967 Suzuki made a trip to the East Coast and gave a talk to a group of people who were curious to hear a Zen master. After his talk, someone asked him about his satori experience.

Suzuki recalled having been a young Zen student participating in a retreat. The leader was a teacher called Tanker because he was the size of a sumo wrestler. Several days into the retreat, Suzuki was in a deep concentrative state. When his turn came for dokusan, he walked slowly toward the tiny meeting room.

Suzuki stopped at the entrance and bowed. Tanker, sitting on his cushion, seemed to be taking up the whole room. The young Suzuki stepped into the room. In that moment, Suzuki said, "I saw that I am Tanker."

Suzuki and Tanker could not have been more different. And yet they were exactly the same.

Soon word got back to us in San Francisco that Suzuki had finally shared his enlightenment experience. Since he never talked about it with his students, none of us had ever had the audacity to ask. We assumed this type of probing was off-limits, although we frequently wondered about the topic, both silently and among each other. But after hearing about it, I brought it up with Suzuki at the first opportunity.

"You should focus on living your own life," he said. This was typical of him. Over and over, Suzuki turned my focus back on taking care of my daily life with nonjudgmental attention.

In the sixties, we put a lot of emphasis on satori experiences, partly because many of us were enamored with our LSD trips, where attachment to dualistic concepts like "body" and "mind" dropped away. But Zen is not about having some big experience to hold on to or brag about. That sort of focus can easily turn into spiritual materialism.

In one of his talks, Suzuki quoted Bodhidharma's famous description of Zen: "A transmission outside of scriptures, no reliance on word and letters, directly pointing to the heartmind." Then he paused and turned to Katagiri. In a barely audible voice, Suzuki said, "I wonder if Americans will ever understand transmission."

Katagiri didn't reply. He just looked straight ahead, stone faced and appearing doubtful. I can't say that I understand what transmission is, even though I have now given transmission to several individuals myself. But I do have a feeling of Suzuki's continual presence, whether I am healthy or sick, mad, happy, or sad. I don't mean that I think about him—I rarely do—or that I hear him or see him, although he does appear in my dreams once or twice a year. It's more like he is in my cells and bloodstream.

Maybe that is what transmission is all about—but I am not at all sure.

LIVING VIBRANTLY IN THE GREAT UNKNOWN

When Buddha's world has penetrated our entire being, we uncover a core flexibility about how we think and how we view things. We understand that our ideas are just our ideas—projections—and not an integral part of the world as it is. The word *water* and all our thoughts about water have nothing at all to do with water itself. If we have a childhood memory of nearly drowning, a large body of water is dangerous—we associate water with dread. But water is just water, and we can live and experience water as water without even needing to label it.

Suzuki Roshi said, "With various scales in our mind, we experience things. Still the thing itself has no scale." Our mind necessarily projects scales, ideas, and categories onto our experience; we can't get away from this, and it's not a problem. It's just how we are. The problem comes when we don't distinguish between our projections and actual reality. We may know the difference in a heady philosophical way. But that isn't enough to penetrate our way of being.

If we have a dreadful feeling when we see a beautiful, serene lake because of a negative memory about water, this is obviously not deep knowing, which arises from the timeless ground of our being. Deep knowing is always fluid and can be experienced only in the moment. It's not something we can grasp. We can embody it, but we cannot *hold* it, even within our body.

Deep knowing comes from practice, from zazen, *not* from books or lectures. Without a deep understanding of the world as it is, we complicate things with our projections and then get caught by them. Actual reality is quite simple and beautiful. There's nothing there to get caught by. Our projections will always be there, but it's possible to see through them . . . to bare reality itself.

By coming back to our cushion over and over again, we learn to accept the ephemeral quality of all of our thoughts. Then we get up and go about our lives. There are things to do. Being alive is doing things, acting fully in the world. We never have the complete picture. But if we go about doing things without a reference to emptiness and interdependence, we get caught by the ten thousand small things in our lives. We become enmeshed with the unintended consequences of our limited views. We have to keep coming back to this bigger, wider view of an interdependent world, which functions completely just as it is.

Accepting this wider view doesn't mean that the world is inert and we should be passive. It means that as we practice, creativity springs up and things extend themselves on their own, blooming in whatever way they may. Whether this creativity is due to a dream or a dim vision, we discover avenues and portals that we were never aware of, leading to a life that's not limited by preconceptions and self-centered involvement.

Nevertheless, selfishness is the human condition. Desires are endless, and therefore suffering is endless. So when we have a desire or we're seeking something, there's always some distortion caused by our self-involvement. But this is not a problem if we manage it skillfully. In Zen, there is the idea of effortless effort—a very simple letting go.

Instead of making an effort to do something or get something, our effort in meditation is toward letting go, and in that way we purify our experience. When we sit and concentrate the mind, we're not really trying to *do* something. We're undoing the mental patterns that keep us constantly creating thoughts, feelings, and ideas that extend themselves in all directions because we get so attached to them.

The idea of effortless effort may be confusing at first. Our effort may be toward a very specific cultivation that is involved in zazen. When we feel our mind drifting, we know we've wandered off the cushion, away from zazen. Our effort is to remain in that gentle awareness of whatever comes up. Our effort is to open into the feeling of unbounded space—and then allow it to expand.

Behind the idea of effortless effort is the necessity of undoing our mind's patterned activity. When patterned activity stops, we sit in a space of emptiness. If we can stay there, mindful of the subtle energy of effortless effort, a settling-in happens. We get a taste of boundlessness. There is nothing more to do or to know. Just sitting still and doing nothing is it.

A LETTER FROM HOME

*If you want to read a letter from Buddha's world,
it is necessary to understand Buddha's world.*

—SUZUKI ROSHI

From my first meeting with Suzuki Sensei, I knew I wanted to do this practice. For weeks I was on a cloud. *Wow! This Zen med-*

itation practice is something novel. It's brand-new to the Western world. It is unparalleled. And I am a part of it!

At the same time, I was taking an art history class at Stanford. One afternoon we spent the entire class on cave paintings in France. When we came to a figure sitting in a cross-legged position, the professor pointed out that he was in a posture of meditation—this in an image painted fifteen thousand years ago.

These cave paintings are evidence that we humans *evolved* with this capacity to meditate, to sit right in the middle of our hurly-burly lives and situate ourselves at a deeper and more fundamental level than our capacity to think or even feel. When we're there, we know we are touching our true source, because this place is more real than anything else we experience.

There is something warm and familiar about it, like a letter from home, connecting us to the whole universe. It's always reaching out to us. Everywhere we look, from cave images to the stars, the universe is sending us a letter from home.

When early humans looked up at stars, they identified with them. They saw their own image mirrored across the night sky. One image in the Lascaux Caves in France is a magnificent painting of a bull. Hanging over its shoulder is what appears to be a map of the Pleiades, the Seven Sisters prominent in the night sky in the winter. We thought the Greeks and Romans created the heroic stories of Taurus and Orion, but maybe they were just passing down the lore of their ancestors. No wonder our eyes are drawn to the night sky.

As human beings, we're always reaching out, trying to connect—with the stars, with each other, with the future, with our past.

When I lived on the Iron Range of northern Minnesota, I reached out to connect with my old teacher, whom I missed deeply. I never expected Suzuki to write back. He was not good at returning letters. But he did. I checked the mail one morning and there it was. I recognized the handwriting immediately. How wonderful!

It was just a short note, and I don't remember much of what it said. Suzuki mentioned the book that Trudy had edited, *Zen Mind, Beginner's Mind,* of which he was very proud. What I remember most is how he signed it. Suzuki was absentminded his whole life, even more so than I am, and he could never remember names. So at the end of his letter, he wrote, "I may not remember your name, but I will always remember you."

We need spiritual friends on this path. I was fortunate to have Suzuki as one of mine. Spiritual friends come in all forms. If you're looking for one, don't impose limits. The universe doesn't recognize limits and boundaries.

The Taoist poet Chuang-tzu had a spiritual friend in the form of a butterfly. It asked him, "Am I you, or are you me?" Spiritual friends point to our togetherness.

The Zen poet Basho had a spiritual friend in human form named Doi. One time when the two had been physically separate for a long time, Basho reached out to Doi through a letter. We don't know if Doi ever received it; probably not. But he didn't have to receive it; the words were symbols of their togetherness. In his letter to Doi, Basho wrote: "You are the butterfly and I the dreaming heart of Chuang-tzu."

Suzuki Roshi said once, "When my mother died, I did not cry. When my father died, I did not cry. But when my teacher died, I cried and cried."

When Suzuki's own death was imminent, he told his students that his death was no problem: "If my death is a problem for you, then you are not a Zen student."

Suzuki wasn't asking his students not to be sad. It is natural and appropriate to feel sadness when we lose someone we love. He was reminding us to penetrate our sadness. Then we see that being sad is not a problem. Death itself is not a problem. Beyond sadness and death is our togetherness.

Death is just a rebirth into a different form. I'm not talking about reincarnation. I have no views on that. But contained within every moment there is birth/death, death/birth. The great matter of Zen is to realize that death is just a momentary transition. We don't know what we're transitioning into. We don't need to know. That's a part of the great mystery.

Shunryu Suzuki's dream came to full bloom on December 4, 1971. We never know when our dream will come to full bloom. For now, my dream continues, and Suzuki Roshi is part of it. He has been since I was twenty years old.

I didn't cry when Suzuki died. I didn't feel a loss, because he lives so vividly in my heart. I'm old now. Many of my memories have faded. But even if I forgot everything, he's still here.

We think we need him in a body that we can see with our eyes and hear with our ears. But heartmind doesn't need a body. Suzuki's heartmind is not separate from my heartmind.

Perhaps that is what transmission is.

I think so.

To Forget the Self Is to Become Intimate with All Life

N OT LONG AFTER I HAD MY satori experience at Tassajara, I went in for dokusan with Suzuki. He looked at my shoes strewn by the door where I had kicked them off. They were dirty and disheveled. His were tidy and placed carefully, side by side. I had never noticed that before.

"Now that you are *so-called enlightened,* it's time to take care of those," he said as he glanced at my shoes.

I wasn't interested in my shoes. Zen was an opportunity to transcend the physical, to experience something beyond ordinary. I was often frustrated by Suzuki's reluctance to give us the *real* stuff. What did my shoes have to do with emptiness?

What I wanted was to understand the profound teachings of the Heart Sutra. We chanted it every day after zazen. It contains phrases such as "form is emptiness; emptiness is form," and it negates everything that exists in the ordinary world: "no eyes, no nose, no object of sight, no object of mind." We chanted it in

Sino-Japanese. Below some of the phrases, Suzuki wrote in his own translations. For *inverted world,* the translation we use at the Minnesota Zen Meditation Center, he scribbled in "topsy-turvy."

I told him once that I had some college buddies who were interested in meditation. I invited them to join us for zazen, and they were planning to come. My concern was the Heart Sutra. I didn't want my friends to think I belonged to some crazy cult. Would he explain it to me so I could answer the questions my friends were sure to ask?

"Yes," he said, "But let's do it later. Look at all the sweeping we have to do. Help me with the sweeping first."

We did the sweeping. Then he was off doing something else. It seemed he'd forgotten.

Later I again invited some friends over. At breakfast I said to Suzuki, "This would be a good time to tell me about the Heart Sutra, so I can answer my friends' questions."

"Yes, I'll do it, but I need to clean up the dishes first. Okusan is gone, and we have people coming later. So help me clean the kitchen."

We finished up the dishes and then he rushed off.

The last time I asked was in Palo Alto at the sitting group. This time was different. My buddies were actually there. "Well, can we talk a little bit about the sutra we just chanted?" I suggested eagerly.

"Oh, I promised Darlene we would work on the trees in her yard. They need pruning, and I was hoping you boys would help me prune them." So we all went to Darlene's house and pruned the trees.

Back then, I had no interest in sweeping, washing dishes, or pruning trees. I wanted to understand Zen well enough intellectually so I could talk intelligently about my practice. I thought we chanted the Heart Sutra every day in order to understand it.

Ego always wants to measure and analyze and present itself well, as I wanted to do with my Stanford buddies. In its deepest sense, the Heart Sutra is a sword that cuts through all that so we can experience the world directly, with no self-involvement. We don't chant the Heart Sutra to understand it. We chant it to imbibe it.

In monasteries, every fourth and ninth day are free days. We still have zazen in the morning and evening, but the day is free to run errands, write letters, go for a hike or a swim, or whatever.

One of those mornings, I went in to see Suzuki. "What are you going to do today?" he asked. He glanced over at my shoes, which were by the door, placed neatly right next to his.

"Wash my clothes," I said.

He smiled. "Good."

We stay connected to the world through what we do, not what we think. It's important that we be fully engaged in our lives. The Heart Sutra is about intimacy. Three times I asked Suzuki about the Heart Sutra. Three times he immediately answered my question by demonstrating what the Heart Sutra means.

Today people frequently come into dokusan to talk about their ideas about Zen. I don't want to be rude, so I listen, but I'm not very interested in that. The bigger question is: What are you going to do, and how are you going to live? Life as a human being is short. What are you going to do with your time here?

When Ram Dass asked his guru Neem Karoli Baba, "How can I be enlightened?" Baba answered, "Love people, feed people, love people."

Later Ram Dass went back again and asked, "But what's the best path to awakening?" Baba said, "Feed people, love people, feed people."

So Ram Dass worked to help establish a community based on Baba's teachings in the United States. He tried and failed. Then he went back to Baba and asked, "What's the best technique for establishing community?" Baba said, "Love people, feed people, love people."

Dogen said, "To study Buddhism is to study the self." We just study the self, continuously, moment by moment. There's nothing more to do. We start this practice by studying the small self. Eventually, we meet our true boundaryless self. Love arises naturally from the ground of our being, which is the ground of *all* being.

"To study the self is to forget the self." When we penetrate the small self, we move beyond it. We begin to trust interconnectedness "the way a bird trusts the tree it builds its nest in." Shraddha (trust) is the realization that in an interdependent universe, all beings are completely nourished.

"To forget the self is to be intimate with all life." In Buddha's world, all life includes everything—from the cosmos to the marrow. From Orion, hero of the night sky, to a pair of disheveled shoes and everything in between: a little green sprout growing in cement, a cup of tea with a wise friend, your meditation cushion, persimmons, a cat tied to an altar, the bleating sound of goats, the loss of a loved one, a dream, a roadside shrine, discarded vegetables, prayer, karma, a magic melon—in Buddha's world, everything is our one interdependent body.

So let's take care of it, okay?

Acknowledgments

I met Suzuki Roshi just before I turned twenty-one, so this book was fifty years in the making. A lot of people contributed along the way. At the top of the list is my wife Linda, whom I met at San Francisco Zen Center in 1965. I thank you for your years of loving support. And my two children, Jed and Erin—I thank you for being who you are. I am a proud father (and grandfather)!

I can't possibly acknowledge all who contributed, directly and indirectly, but I know where to start: with my first teacher Suzuki Roshi, my second teacher, Katagiri Roshi, and my predecessor as guiding teacher at Minnesota Zen Meditation Center, Karen Sunna. I learned from them more than a lifetime of Zen teachings.

I thank Karl Weber for his insightful edits, and Dave O'Neal at Shambhala for his careful guidance through the entire process.

I appreciate the gentle advice, support, and encouragement that Guy Gibbon provided to Wanda Isle throughout the difficult process of compiling and editing this book. He was with her from the beginning, urging her onward, and in the end telling her when it was time to stop.

A heartfelt thank you to Norman Fischer—for his kind and generous comments in the foreword. And to Bussho Lahn, who Wanda could always count on to search out a quote or story among a decade worth of talks and notes. To Rosemary Taylor for reading through the first draft of the manuscript. And to Kim Johnson, who has been the silent, unacknowledged force holding Minnesota Zen Meditation Center together for the last thirteen years.

I'm happy for the opportunity to acknowledge David Chadwick for his dedication and meticulous recording of facts about Suzuki Roshi's teaching and life in his book *Crooked Cucumber* and on cuke.com. Thank you, David, for taking time out of your vacation to read the manuscript and offer insightful suggestions and gently point out inaccuracies in my memory.

Thanks to Bill Porter (aka Red Pine) for his endorsement of my work, and to Jack Kornfield, who has inspired me with his multitude of teaching tales, many of which I have repeated to my students.

Finally, to Wanda Isle. Wanda worked for more than three years, transcribing talks I had given over more than a decade, pulling out thematic material, developing a cohesive progression to teachings that were not given in any kind of progressive manner. I am very grateful to Wanda for her persistence, her artistry, and her careful attention to transferring my voice onto paper. Wanda, you are becoming an excellent Zen teacher in your own right!

Credits

Index

Hui Neng, 244–45
See also No Mirror
Hung Jen, 243–45

ill will, 165, 168–70, 171, 175, 186
impermanence, 7, 32, 135, 256–57,
262
swinging door metaphor about
selves, 31–33, 43, 124, 135
India
author's travels to, 103–4
Buddha's counterculture and,
255, 257–58, 259
caste system of, 255
during the time of the
Buddha, 255
Kabir, 229–30
interdependence
and emptiness, 156–57, 267
experience of oneness with the
universe, 51, 69, 146, 159,
237–38
Four Immeasurable
cornerstones of, 229–31, 236
reaffirmed in meditation, 243,
267, 276

Joplin, Janis, xii, 263–64

Kabir, 229–30
Kapleau, Philip, *The Three Pillars
of Zen*, 120
karma, 64, 158, 252
karmic consciousness, 251–52

Katagiri, Dainin
as abbot of Minnesota Zen
Center, 79, 109, 218
Each Moment is the Universe,
51, 52, 89, 242
Hokyoji established by, 79
and Tim Burkett, xii, 213
on transmission in Zen, 265–67
Katagiri Roshi. *See* Katagiri,
Dainin
Keller, Helen, 89
Kerouac, Jack, 259
koans. *See* Zen koans
Koestler, Arthur, 9, 20
Kornfield, Jack, 30, 169, 186

Laing, R.D., 77, 123
letting go, 178–80
Dogen on dropping away of
body and mind, 44, 251, 260
of effortless effort, 268
of fixed ideas, 38, 49
and restlessness and worry, 173
Loori, John Daido, 35
Lotus Sutra, 86
loving-kindness, 230–33, 235
LSD
"dry enlightenment" induced
by, 118–19
and Ram Dass, 137–38
and satori experiences, 8, 265

McLeod, Ken, 197
Maitreya Bodhisattva, 205–7, 211